Fodor's 94
New Zealand

Lathrop

W9-BYT-681

Reprinted from Fodor's *Australia & New Zealand '94*

Fodor's Travel Publications, Inc.
New York • Toronto • London • Sydney • Auckland

ISBN 0–679–02534–0

From *Return to Paradise*, by James Michener. Reprinted by permission of Random House, Inc., and the William Morris Agency, Inc., on behalf of the author. Copyright © 1951 by James A. Michener.

Fodor's New Zealand

Editor: Paula Rackow
Contributors: Bob Blake, Hannah Borgeson, Valerie Martone
Creative Director: Fabrizio La Rocca
Cartographer: David Lindroth
Illustrator: Karl Tanner
Cover Photograph: Andrea Pistolesi/Image Bank

Design: Vignelli Associates

About the Authors

Michael Gebicki is a Sydney-based freelance travel writer and photographer. He contributes regularly to *The Sydney Morning Herald*, *The Age*, and *Gourmet Traveller* magazine. **David McGonigal** is the author of more than 10 books about Australia, and his travel articles have appeared in publications around the world, including the *Los Angeles Times*.

Special Sales

Contents

Foreword

We wish to express our gratitude to those who helped in the preparation of this guide: to the personnel of the New Zealand Tourism Board, and in particular Mary Rose Trainor at the Sydney office and Graham Palmer at the Wellington head office; to Ken Boys and his staff at Qantas Airways; and to Heather Jeffery and her staff at Air New Zealand.

While every care has been taken to ensure the accuracy of the information in this guide, the passage of time will always bring change, and, consequently, the publisher cannot accept responsibility for errors that may occur.

All prices and opening times quoted here are based on information supplied to us at press time. Hours and admission fees may change, however, and the prudent traveler will avoid inconvenience by calling ahead.

Fodor's wants to hear about your travel experiences, both pleasant and unpleasant. When a hotel or restaurant fails to live up to its billing, let us know and we will investigate the complaint and revise our entries where the facts warrant it.

Send your letters to the editors of Fodor's Travel Publications, 201 East 50th Street, New York, NY 10022.

Highlights'94 and Fodor's Choice

Highlights '94

The number of international arrivals in New Zealand continues to increase in a world that is becoming more aware of the benefits of fresh air and sparkling water. Despite a low overall inflation rate, prices in the tourism industry—especially hotels and guided tours—have jumped by around 10%. However, the declining value of the New Zealand dollar means that a holiday in New Zealand is no more expensive this year.

As New Zealand's rural economy continues to slide, an increasing number of farmers are throwing open the farm gate to overnight visitors. For anyone who wants to experience the country as New Zealanders do, a farmstay is a great opportunity to get to know the land and its people. The regional tourist information offices have lists of the farmstays in their areas and sometimes make bookings on visitors' behalf.

New Zealand is soon to get its first casino. The $30 million **Christchurch Casino,** on Victoria Street opposite the Parkroyal Hotel, should bring new life to the heart of the garden city when it opens at the end of 1994. Meanwhile, the location of the Auckland's casino has yet to be finalized.

Fodor's Choice

No two people will agree on what makes a perfect vacation, but it's fun and helpful to know what others think. We hope you'll have the chance to experience some of Fodor's Choices yourself while visiting New Zealand. For detailed information about each entry, refer to the appropriate chapter in the guidebook.

Adventures

North Island	Black-water rafting, Waitomo Caves
	Rafting the Rangitaiki River, near Rotorua
South Island	Bungy jumping, near Queenstown
	Dart River Jet Boat Safari, Queenstown
	Glacier walking, Tasman, Fox, and Franz Josef Glaciers
	Kayaking in Abel Tasman National Park
	Walking the Routeburn Track, Fiordland National Park

City Dining

Auckland	The French Café (*Expensive*)
	Cin Cin on Quay (*Moderate*)
Christchurch	Espresso 124 (*Expensive*)
Dunedin	Palms Cafe (*Moderate*)
Wellington	Pierre's (*Very Expensive*)
	Bellissimo Trattoria Italiana (*Expensive*)
	Brasserie Flipp (*Expensive*)

City Lodging

Auckland	Hotel du Vin (*Very Expensive*)
	The Regent (*Very Expensive*)
	Devonport Villa (*Moderate*)
Christchurch	Parkroyal Christchurch (*Very Expensive*)
	Riverview Lodge (*Inexpensive*)
Napier	Mon Logis Guesthouse (*Moderate*)
Nelson	California Guest House (*Moderate*)
Wellington	Parkroyal Wellington (*Very Expensive*)

Sporting Lodges

North Island Huka Lodge, Lake Taupo (*Very Expensive*)

Puka Park Lodge, Coromandel Peninsula (*Expensive*)

South Island Lake Brunner Sporting Lodge, Kumara, near Greymouth (*Very Expensive*)

Nugget Point, Queenstown (*Very Expensive*)

National Park Attractions

North Island Lake Waikaremoana, Urewera National Park

Mount Ruapehu, Tongariro National Park

South Island Abel Tasman Track, Abel Tasman National Park

Fox and Franz Josef Glaciers, Westland National Park

The Milford Track, Fiordland National Park

Mitre Peak and Milford Sound, Fiordland National Park

Mount Cook and the Tasman Glacier, Mount Cook National Park

Pancake Rocks, Paparoa National Park

Special Moments

North Island Exploring the Coromandel Peninsula with Doug Johansen

First whiff of Rotorua

Listening to the Maori choir, St. Faith's Church, Rotorua

Strolling the Strand at sunset, Russell, Bay of Islands

South Island Cruising with the sperm whales off Kaikoura

Early morning flight over the Southern Alps, Mount Cook National Park

Kayaking with the dolphins off Abel Tasman National Park

Milford Sound in stormy weather

Sampling smoked snapper at Nature Smoke, Mapua

Sunset on Mount Cook from the Hermitage

Watching the seals, Lake Moeraki Wilderness Lodge

New Zealand

North Cape

Te Kao

Bay of Islands

Whangarei

Hauraki
Gulf

Great Barrier
Island

Te Kopuru

Whangarei

Coromandel
Peninsula

COROMANDEL
FOREST PARK

Cape
Runaway

Auckland

Whangamata

Waiuku

Tauranga

Bay of
Plenty

Port Waikato

Hamilton

Raglan

Rotorua

NORTH ISLAND

Tasman
Sea

North
Taranaki Bight

Lake
Taupo

Taupo

Cape Egmont

Hawke
Bay

Napier

Hastings

Wanganui

ABEL
TASMAN N. P.

Palmerston
North

Cape Farewell

TARARUA FOREST PARK

Upper
Hutt

Tasman
Bay

N.W. Nelson
Forest Park

Nelson

Lower Hutt

Blenheim

Cook Strait

Wellington

Cape Foulwind

Grey R.

Lake Sumner
Forest Park

Greymouth

Arthurs
Pass N. P.

Christchurch

WESTLAND
N. P.

Franz Josef

Banks Peninsula

Fox Glacier

MT. COOK
N. P.

Haast

Southern Alps

Haast River

Mt. Aspiring

Waitaki R.

SOUTH ISLAND

Lake Wanaka

Milford
Sound

Queenstown

Oamaru

SOUTH
PACIFIC OCEAN

Lake
Wakatipu

Lake
Te Anau

Te Anau

Lake
Manapouri

Dunedin

FIORDLAND
N. P.

Invercargill

KEY
—— Rail Lines

Foveaux Strait

N

Stewart
Island

0   200 miles

0   300 km

World Time Zones

Numbers below vertical bands relate each zone to Greenwich Mean Time (0 hrs.).
Local times frequently differ from these general indications,
as indicated by light-face numbers on map.

Algiers, **29**
Anchorage, **3**
Athens, **41**
Auckland, **1**
Baghdad, **46**
Bangkok, **50**
Beijing, **54**

Berlin, **34**
Bogotá, **19**
Budapest, **37**
Buenos Aires, **24**
Caracas, **22**
Chicago, **9**
Copenhagen, **33**
Dallas, **10**

Delhi, **48**
Denver, **8**
Djakarta, **53**
Dublin, **26**
Edmonton, **7**
Hong Kong, **56**
Honolulu, **2**

Istanbul, **40**
Jerusalem, **42**
Johannesburg, **44**
Lima, **20**
Lisbon, **28**
London (Greenwich), **27**
Los Angeles, **6**
Madrid, **38**
Manila, **57**

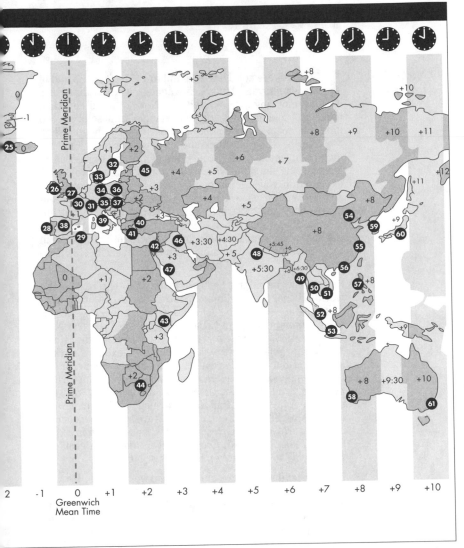

Introduction

By Michael Gebicki

I first laid eyes on New Zealand in 1967, near the end of an ocean voyage from Los Angeles to Australia. For a long morning, we skirted the New Zealand coastline north of Auckland, slipping past a land of impossibly green hills that seemed to be populated entirely by sheep. When the ship berthed in Auckland, I saw, parked along the quay, a museum-quality collection of vintage British automobiles, the newest of which was probably 15 years old. The explanation was simple enough: All cars were imported, and imports were taxed at an enormous rate. But to a teenager fresh from the U.S.A., it seemed as though we had entered a time warp. When we took a day tour into the hills, the bus driver kept stopping for chats with other drivers; in those days it seemed possible to know everyone in New Zealand.

Since then, Auckland has caught up with the rest of the world. Its cars, its cellular-phone-toting execs, its waterfront restaurants with sushi and French mineral water all exist, unmistakably, in the modern world. Yet rural New Zealand still belongs to a greener, cleaner, friendlier time. Nostalgia remains a strong suit in New Zealand's deck—second, of course, to the country's splendid scenery. If you travel in search of glamorous shopping, sophisticated nightlife, and gourmet pleasures, it's probably not the place for you. You can find these garnishes, in a minor way, in the cities, but New Zealand's cities are strictly sideshows on the world stage. Gracious, calm, and welcoming they may be, but Auckland, Christchurch, and Wellington are never going to be mistaken for Paris or New York.

New Zealand was a late arrival on the world scene. Its first settlers were Polynesians who reached its shores about AD 850, followed by a second wave of Polynesian migrants in the 14th century. These were not carefree, grass-skirted islanders living in a palmy utopia, but a fierce, martial people who made their homes in hilltop fortresses, from where they engaged in an almost continual state of warfare with neighboring tribes. It wasn't until the 1840s that European settlers, primarily from England, arrived in any numbers. Compared with such other immigrant societies as the United States and Australia, New Zealand is overwhelmingly British—in its love of gardens, its architecture, its political system, its food. The Maoris remain an assertive minority of 9%, a dignified, robust people whose art bears witness to a rich culture of legends and dreams. That culture comes dramatically to life in performances of traditional songs and dances, including the *haka*, or war dance, which was calculated to intimidate and demoralize the enemy; little wonder that the national rugby team performs a haka as a prelude to its games.

The New Zealand land mass is divided into two main islands. Most of the country's 3.36 million people live on the North Island, while the South Island has the lion's share of the national parks. (More than one-tenth of the country's total land area has been set aside as parks.) In a country about the size of Colorado—or just slightly larger than Great Britain—nature has assembled active volcanoes, subtropical rain forests, geysers, trout streams (some of the finest on earth), fiords, beaches, glaciers, and some two dozen peaks that soar to more than 3,000 meters (10,000 feet). The country has scenic spectaculars from top to bottom, but while the North Island often resembles a pristine golf course, the South Island is wild, majestic, and exhilarating.

Experiencing these wonders is painless. New Zealand has a well-developed infrastructure of hotels, motels, and tour operators—but the best the country has to offer can't be seen through the windows of a tour bus. A trip here is a hands-on experience: hike, boat, fish, hunt, cycle, raft, and breathe some of the freshest air on earth. And if these adventures sound a little too intrepid for you, the sheer beauty of the landscape and the clarity of the air will give you muscles you never knew you had.

1 Essential Information

Before You Go

*By Michael
Gebicki*

Government Tourist Offices

For information about travel to and within New Zealand, contact the nearest **New Zealand Tourism Board.**

In the U.S.: 501 Santa Monica Blvd., Los Angeles, CA 90401, tel. 800/388–5494.

In Canada: 888 Dunsmuir St., Suite 1200, Vancouver, BC V6C 3K4, tel. 800/388–5495.

In the U.K.: New Zealand House, Haymarket, London SW1 4TQ, tel. 71/973–0363.

In Australia: Downtown Duty Free House, 84 Pitt St., Sydney 2000, tel. 02/231–1322.

Tours and Packages

Should you buy your travel arrangements to New Zealand packaged or do it yourself? There are advantages either way. Buying packaged arrangements saves you money, particularly if you can find a program that includes exactly the features you want. You also get a pretty good idea of what your trip will cost from the outset. Generally, you have two options: fully escorted tours and independent packages. Escorted tours are most often via motorcoach, with a tour director in charge. They're ideal if you don't mind having limited free time and traveling with strangers. Your baggage is handled, your time rigorously scheduled, and most meals planned. Such tours are therefore the most hassle-free way to see a destination, as well as generally the least expensive. Independent packages allow plenty of flexibility. They generally include airline travel and hotels, with certain options available, such as sightseeing, car rental, and excursions. Such packages are usually more expensive than escorted tours, but your time is your own.

While you can book directly through tour operators, you will pay no more to go through a travel agent, who will be able to tell you about tours and packages from a number of operators. Whatever program you ultimately choose, be sure to find out exactly what is included: taxes, tips, transfers, meals, baggage handling, ground transportation, entertainment, excursions, sports or recreation (and rental equipment, if necessary). Ask about the level of hotel used, its location, the size of its rooms, the kind of bed, and its amenities, such as pool, room service, or programs for children, if they're important to you. Find out the operator's cancellation penalties. Nearly everyone charges them, and the only way to avoid them is to buy trip-cancellation insurance (*see* Trip Insurance, below). Also ask about the single supplement, a surcharge assessed to solo travelers. Some operators do not make you pay it if you agree to be matched up with a roommate of the same sex, even if one is not found by departure time. Remember that a program that has features you won't use may not be the most cost-wise choice for you.

Fully Escorted Tours Escorted tours are usually sold in three categories: deluxe, first-class, and tourist or budget class. The most important differences are the price, of course, and the level of accommodations. Some operators specialize in one category, while others offer a range.

Contact **Abercrombie & Kent** (1520 Kensingtion Rd., Oak Brook, IL 60521, tel. 708/954–2944 or 800/323–7308), **J & O Holidays** (3131 Camino del Rio N, Suite 1080, San Diego, CA 92108, tel. 619/282–3131 or 800/377–1080), **Olson Travelworld** (970 W. 190th St., Suite 425, Torrance, CA 90502, tel. 310/546–8400 or 800/421–2255), **Tauck Tours** (Box 5027, Westport, CT 06881, tel. 203/226–6911 or 800/468–2825), **Islands in the Sun** (760 W. 16th St., Suite L, Costa Mesa, CA 92627, tel. 714/645–8300 or 800/828–6877), and **Travcoa** (Box 2630, Newport Beach, CA 92658, tel. 714/476–2800 or 800/992–2004 in CA, 800/992–2003 in rest of U.S.) in the deluxe category; **Gadabout** (700 E. Tahquitz Canyon Way, Palm Springs, CA 92262, tel. 619/325–5556 or 800/952–5068), **Globus** (5301 S. Federal Circle, Littleton, CO 80123, tel. 800/221–0090), **Jetabout Quantas Vacations** (300 N. Continental Blvd., Suite 610, El Segundo, CA 90245, tel. 800/641–8772), and **Sunbeam Tours** (1631 W. Sunflower Ave., Suite C36, Santa Ana, CA 92704, tel. 714/434–1810 or 800/955–1818) in the first-class category; and Globus' sister company **Cosmos** (at the same number) in the tourist category.

Most itineraries are jam-packed with sightseeing, so you see a lot in a short amount of time (usually one place per day). To judge just how fast-paced the tour is, review the itinerary carefully. If you are in a different hotel each night, you will be getting up early each day to head out, travel to your next destination, do some sightseeing, have dinner, and go to bed; then you'll start all over again. If you want some free time, make sure it's mentioned in the tour brochure; if you want to be escorted to every meal, confirm that any tour you consider does that. Also, when comparing programs, be sure to find out if the motorcoach is air-conditioned and has a restroom on board. Make your selection based on price and stops on the itinerary.

Independent Packages Independent packages, which travel agents call FITs (for foreign independent travel), are offered by airlines, tour operators who may also do escorted programs, and any number of other companies from large, established firms to small, new entrepreneurs.

Contact **Abercrombie & Kent** (*see* above), **Austravel** (51 E. 42nd St., Suite 616, New York, NY 10017, tel. 212/972–6880 or 800/633–3404), **Globus** (*see* above), **Islands in the Sun** (*see* above), **J & O Holidays** (*see* above), **Olson Travelworld** (*see* above), **Sunbeam Tours** (*see* above), **Swain Australia Tours** (6 W. Lancaster Ave., Ardmore, PA 19003, tel. 800/227–9246), and **United Vacations** (tel. 800/351–4200). **SO/PAC** (tel. 800/551–2012) and **Guthreys Pacific** (tel. 800/227–5317) offer city packages.

Their programs come in a wide range of prices based on levels of luxury and options—in addition to hotel and airfare, sightseeing, car rental, transfers, admission to local attractions, and other extras. Note that when pricing different packages, it sometimes pays to purchase the same arrangements separately, as when a rock-bottom promotional airfare is being offered, for example. Again, base your choice on what's available at your budget for the destinations you want to visit.

Special-Interest Travel Special-interest programs may be fully escorted or independent. Some require a certain amount of expertise, but most are for the average traveler with an interest and are usually hosted by experts in the subject matter. When the program is escorted, it enjoys the advantages and disadvantages of all escorted programs; because your fellow travelers are apt to be passionate or knowledgeable about the subject, they can prove as enjoyable a part of your travel experience as the destination itself. The price range is wide, but the cost is usually higher—sometimes a lot higher—than for ordinary escorted tours and packages, because of the expert guiding and special activities.

Adventure **Adventure Center** (1311 63rd St., Suite 200, Emeryville, CA 94608, tel. 510/654–1879 or 800/227–8747), **Mountain Travel/Sobek** (6420 Fairmount Ave., El Cerrito, CA 94530, tel. 510/527–8100 or 800/227–2384), **Backroads Bicycle Touring** (1516 5th St., Berkeley, CA 91740, tel. 510/527–1555 or 800/245–3874), and **Nature Expeditions International** (474 Wilamette, Box 11496, Eugene, OR 97440, tel. 503/484–6529 or 800/869–0639) offer tours including bicycling, canoeing, fishing, river rafting, sea kayaking, skiing, trekking, and nature and wildlife expeditions.

Fishing **Rod & Reel Adventures** (3507 Tully Rd., Suite 5, Modesto, CA 95356, tel. 209/526–3007 or 800/423–9731) runs multi-day fishing trips.

Golf **ITC Golf Tours** (4134 Atlantic Ave., Suite 205, Long Beach, CA 90807, tel. 310/595–6905 or 800/257–4981) offers customized golf packages to New Zealand.

Wine Tours **World Travelers, Inc.** (6612 S.E. 24th St., Mercer Island, WA 98040, tel. 206/441–8682 or 800/426–3610) conducts week-long wine tours of New Zealand with stays in manor houses.

When to Go

New Zealand's climate varies from subtropical in the north to temperate in the south. Its seasons are the reverse of those in North America and Europe. Summers (December–March) are generally warm, with an average of seven to eight hours of sunshine per day throughout the country. Winters (June–September) are mild at lower altitudes on the North Island, but heavy snowfalls are common on the South Island, particularly on the peaks of the Southern Alps. Rain can pour at any time of the year. (Some areas on the west coast of the South Island receive an annual rainfall of more than 100 inches.)

The ideal months for comfortable travel are October–November and February–April, especially for anyone who wants to participate in adventure activities. Avoid the school holidays, when highways may be congested and accommodation is likely to be scarce and more expensive. The summer school holidays (the busiest) fall between mid-December and the end of January; other holiday periods are mid-May to the end of May, early July to mid-July, and late August to mid-September.

Climate The following are average daily maximum and minimum temperatures.

Auckland	**Jan.**	74F 61	23C 16	**May**	63F 52	17C 11	**Sept.**	61F 49	16C 9
	Feb.	74F 61	23C 16	**June**	58F 49	14C 9	**Oct.**	63F 52	17C 11
	Mar.	72F 59	22C 15	**July**	56F 47	13C 8	**Nov.**	67F 54	19C 12
	Apr.	67F 56	19C 13	**Aug.**	58F 47	14C 8	**Dec.**	70F 58	21C 14

Christchurch	**Jan.**	70F 54	21C 12	**May**	56F 40	13C 4	**Sept.**	58F 40	14C 4
	Feb.	70F 54	21C 12	**June**	52F 36	11C 2	**Oct.**	63F 45	17C 7
	Mar.	67F 50	19C 10	**July**	50F 36	10C 2	**Nov.**	67F 47	19C 8
	Apr.	63F 45	17C 7	**Aug.**	52F 36	11C 2	**Dec.**	70F 52	21C 11

Queenstown	**Jan.**	72F 49	22C 9	**May**	52F 36	11C 2	**Sept.**	56F 38	13C 3
	Feb.	70F 50	21C 10	**June**	47F 34	8C 1	**Oct.**	61F 41	16C 5
	Mar.	67F 47	19C 8	**July**	46F 34	8C 1	**Nov.**	65F 45	18C 7
	Apr.	61F 43	16C 6	**Aug.**	50F 34	10C 1	**Dec.**	70F 49	21C 9

For current weather information for cities in the United States and abroad, plus the local time and helpful travel tips, call the **Weather Channel Connection** (tel. 900/WEATHER; 95¢ per minute) from a touch-tone phone.

Festivals and Seasonal Events

Not surprisingly, sport features heavily in New Zealand's festival calendar. Horse and boat races, triathlons, and fishing competitions are far more prominent than celebrations of the arts. Just about every town holds a yearly agricultural and pastoral ("A&P") show, and these proud displays of local crafts, produce, livestock, and wood-chopping and sheep-shearing prowess provide a memorable look at rural New Zealand. An annual calendar of *New Zealand Special Events* is available from government tourist offices.

Jan. 1: New Year's Day is a nationwide holiday.
Feb. 1: for the **Auckland Anniversary Day Regatta,** Auckland's birthday party, the "City of Sails" takes to the water.
Feb. 6: Waitangi Day, New Zealand's national day, commemorates the signing of the Treaty of Waitangi between whites and Maoris in 1840. The focus of the nationwide celebration is, naturally enough, the town of Waitangi in the Bay of Islands.
Feb 12–13: Speights Coast to Coast is the ultimate iron-man challenge—a two-day, 238-kilometer marathon of cycling, running, and kayaking that spans the South Island from west to east. Information: Canterbury Information Centre, corner Worcester Street and Oxford Terrace, tel. 03/79–9629.
Feb. 25–Mar. 19: New Zealand International Festival of the Arts, a biennial event held in even-numbered years, is the country's

premier performing-arts festival, during which many international performers can be seen in Wellington. Information: Wellington City Information Centre, corner Wakefield and Victoria streets, tel. 04/499–4444.

Mar. 5–6: Golden Shears International Shearing Championship is a three-day event that pits men armed with shears against fleecy sheep in the town of Masterton, just north of Wellington. Information: Masterton Visitor Information Centre, 5 Dixon Street, tel. 059/8–7373.

Apr. 3–11: Bluff Oyster Festival celebrates the beginning of the oyster season at this tiny seaport on the southern tip of the South Island. Information: Invercargill Information Centre, 82 Dee Street, tel. 03/86–6091.

Apr. 1–4: the **Easter** holiday weekend lasts from Good Friday through Easter Monday.

Apr. 25: Anzac Day honors the soldiers who fought and died in World War I.

First Monday in June: the Queen's Birthday is celebrated nationwide.

Aug. 27–28: Women's FIS Ski Slalom is a two-day event on the slopes of Coronet Peak, near Queenstown. Information: Queenstown Information Centre, corner Shotover and Camp streets, Queenstown, tel. 03/442–8238.

Oct. 24: Labour Day is observed throughout the country.

Second Week in Nov.: Canterbury Agricultural and Pastoral Show spotlights the farmers and graziers of the rich countryside surrounding Christchurch. Information: Canterbury Information Centre, corner Worcester Street and Oxford Terrace, tel. 03/79–9629.

Dec. 25–26: on **Christmas Day** and **Boxing Day** the country virtually closes down.

What to Pack

Valuables, such as jewelry, should always be packed in your carry-on luggage. It is also important to pack prescription medicines, as well as any allergy medication you may need, in hand luggage.

Clothing Be prepared for a varied climate. Wet-weather gear and comfortable, sturdy shoes are essential. Dress is fairly casual in most cities, though top resorts and restaurants may require a jacket and tie. A light sweater or jacket will suffice for evenings in the autumn, but winter demands a heavier coat—a raincoat with a zip-out wool lining is ideal. Comfortable walking shoes are a must. You should have a pair of running shoes or the equivalent if you're planning to trek, and rubber-soled sandals or canvas shoes are needed for walking on reef coral.

Miscellaneous An extra pair of glasses, contact lenses, or prescription sunglasses is always a good idea. Stores carry the same cosmetic products as back home, so you don't need to carry extra supplies. If you have a health problem that may require you to purchase a prescription drug, take enough to last the durations of the trip. And don't forget to pack a list of the addresses of offices that supply refunds for lost or stolen traveler's checks.

Tea- and coffee-making facilities are supplied in almost every hotel and motel room, although decaffeinated coffee and sugar substitutes are rarely provided.

Electricity The electrical current in New Zealand is 230 volts, 50 cycles alternating current (AC); the United States runs on 110-volt, 60-cycle AC current. Unlike wall outlets in the United States, which accept plugs with two flat prongs, outlets in New Zealand take a slanted three-prong plug.

Adapters, Converters, Transformers To plug in U.S.-made appliances abroad, you'll need an adapter plug. To reduce the voltage entering the appliance from 220 to 110 volts, you'll also need a converter, unless it is a dual-voltage appliance, made for travel. There are converters for high-wattage appliances (such as hair dryers), low-wattage items (such as electric toothbrushes and razors), and combination models. Hotels sometimes have outlets marked "For Shavers Only" near the sink; these are 110-volt outlets for low-wattage appliances; don't use them for high-wattage appliances. However, some hotels have universal outlets for 240v or 110v electric razors. If you're traveling with a laptop computer, especially an older one, you may need a transformer—a type of converter used with electronic-circuitry products. Newer laptop computers are auto-sensing, operating equally well on 110 and 220 volts (so you need only the appropriate adapter plug). When in doubt, consult your appliance's owner's manual or the manufacturer. Or get a copy of the free brochure "Foreign Electricity Is No Deep Dark Secret," published by adapter-converter manufacturer Franzus (Murtha Industrial Park, Box 142, Beacon Falls, CT 06403, tel. 203/723–6664; send a stamped, self-addressed envelope when ordering).

Luggage *Regulations* Free baggage allowances on an airline depend on the airline, the route, and the class of your ticket. In general, on domestic flights and on international flights between the United States and foreign destinations, you are entitled to check two bags—neither exceeding 62 inches, or 158 centimeters (length + width + height), or weighing more than 70 pounds (32 kilograms). A third piece may be brought aboard as a carryon; its total dimensions are generally limited to less than 45 inches (114 centimeters), so it will fit easily under the seat in front of you or in the overhead compartment. There are variations, so ask in advance. The single rule, a Federal Aviation Administration safety regulation that pertains to carry-on baggage on U.S. airlines, requires only that carryons be properly stowed and allows the airline to limit allowances and tailor them to different aircraft and operational conditions. Charges for excess, oversize, or overweight pieces vary, so inquire before you pack.

If you are flying between two foreign destinations, note that baggage allowances may be determined not by the piece method but by the weight method, which generally allows 88 pounds (40 kilograms) of luggage in first class, 66 pounds (30 kilograms) in business class, and 44 pounds (20 kilograms) in economy. If your flight between two cities abroad *connects* with your transatlantic or transpacific flight, the piece method still applies. International passengers flying within Australia can check two pieces of luggage (you may be asked to show your international ticket); otherwise you are allowed up to 44 pounds of luggage in both countries.

Safeguarding Your Luggage Before leaving home, itemize your bags' contents and their worth; this list will help you estimate the extent of your loss if your bags go astray. To minimize that risk, tag them inside and out with your name, address, and phone number. (If you use your home address, cover it so that potential thieves can't see it.) At check-in, make sure that the tag attached by baggage handlers bears the correct three-letter code for your destination. If your bags do not arrive with you, or if you detect damage, do not leave the airport until you've filed a written report with the airline.

Taking Money Abroad

Traveler's Checks Although you will want plenty of cash when visiting small cities or rural areas, traveler's checks are usually preferable. The most widely recognized are **American Express, Barclay's, Thomas Cook,** and those issued by major commercial banks such as **Citibank** and **Bank of America.** American Express also issues *Traveler's Cheques for Two,* which can be signed and used by you or your traveling companion. Some checks are free; usually the issuing company or the bank at which you make your purchase charges 1% of the checks' face value as a fee. Be sure to buy a few checks in small denominations to cash toward the end of your trip, when you don't want to be left with more foreign currency than you can spend. Always record the numbers of checks as you spend them, and keep this list separate from the checks.

You can also buy traveler's checks in New Zealand dollars—a good idea if the American dollar is falling and you want to lock in the current rate.

Currency Banks and bank-operated exchange booths at airports and rail-
Exchange road stations are usually the best places to change money. Hotels, stores, and privately run exchange firms typically offer less favorable rates.

Before your trip, pay attention to how the dollar is doing vis-à-vis currency in New Zealand. If the dollar is losing strength, try to pay as many travel bills as possible in advance, especially the big ones. If it is getting stronger, pay for costly items overseas, and use your credit card whenever possible—you'll come out ahead, whether the exchange rate at which your purchase is calculated is the one in effect the day the vendor's bank abroad processes the charge, or the one prevailing on the day the charge company's service center processes it at home.

To avoid lines at airport currency-exchange booths, arrive in the foreign country with a small amount of the local currency already in your pocket—a so-called tip pack. **Thomas Cook Currency Services** (630 5th Ave., New York, NY 10111, tel. 212/ 757–6915) supplies foreign currency by mail.

Getting Money from Home

Cash Machines Automated-teller machines (ATMs) are proliferating; many are tied to international networks such as **Cirrus** and **Plus.** You can use your bank card at ATMs away from home to withdraw money from an account and get cash advances on a credit-card account (providing your card has been programmed with a personal identification number, or PIN). Check in advance on limits on withdrawals and cash advances within specified periods. Ask whether your bank-card or credit-card PIN number will need to be reprogrammed for use in the area you'll be visiting—a possibility if the number has more than four digits. Remember that you are charged interest from day you get the money from ATMs as well as from tellers. And note that, although transaction fees for ATM withdrawals abroad will probably be higher than fees for withdrawals at home, Cirrus and Plus exchange rates tend to be good. (At press time, Cirrus was expected to be operational in New Zealand by 1994).

Bank Transfers Just have your bank send money to another bank overseas. It's easiest to transfer money between like branches; otherwise, the process takes a couple days longer and costs more.

American Express Cardholder Services The company's **Express Cash** system lets you withdraw cash and/or traveler's checks from a worldwide network of 57,000 American Express dispensers and participating bank ATMs. You must *enroll first* (call 800/CASH–NOW for a form and allow two weeks for processing). Withdrawals are charged not to your card but to a designated bank account. You can withdraw up to $1,000 per seven-day period on the basic card, more if your card is gold or platinum. There is a 2% fee (minimum $2.50, maximum $10) for each cash transaction, and a 1% fee for traveler's checks (except for the platinum card), which are available only from American Express dispensers.

At AmEx offices, cardholders can also cash personal or counter checks for up to $1,000 in any seven-day period (21 days abroad); of this $200 can be in cash, more if available, with the balance paid in traveler's checks, for which all but platinum cardholders pay a 1% fee. Higher limits apply to the gold and platinum cards.

Wiring Money You don't have to be a cardholder to send or receive an **American Express MoneyGram** for up to $10,000. To send one, go to an American Express MoneyGram agent, pay up to $1,000 with a credit card and anything over that in cash, and phone a transaction reference number to your intended recipient, who needs only present identification and the reference number to the nearest MoneyGram agent to pick up the cash. There are MoneyGram agents in more than 60 countries (call 800/543-4080 for locations). Fees range from 5% to 10%, depending on the amount and how you pay. You can't use American Express, which is really a convenience card—only Discover, MasterCard, and Visa credit cards.

You can also use **Western Union.** To wire money, take either cash or a check to the nearest office. (Or you can call and use a credit card.) Fees are roughly 5%–10%. Delivery from the United States to New Zealand takes at least two business days. There are approximately 20,000 agents worldwide (call 800/325-6000 for locations).

Currency

New Zealand's unit of currency is the dollar, divided into 100 cents. Bills are in $100, $50, $10, and $5 denominations. Coins are $2, $1, 50¢, 20¢, 10¢, and 5¢. At press time, the rate of exchange was NZ$1.73 to the U.S. dollar, NZ$1.44 to the Canadian dollar, NZ$2.82 to the pound sterling, and NZ$1.30 to the Australian dollar. Prices quoted throughout are in New Zealand dollars.

What It Will Cost

For most travelers, New Zealand is not an expensive destination. The cost of meals, accommodation, and travel is slightly higher than in the United States but considerably less than in Western Europe. At about $1 per liter—equal to about US$2.20 per gallon—premium-grade gasoline is expensive by North American standards, but not by European ones.

Inflation, which reached a peak of almost 20% in the late 1980s, has now been reduced to less than 5%. Prices are expected to remain stable as the government pursues strict monetarist policies and continues to allow free market forces to determine costs.

Taxes A goods and services tax (GST) of 12.5% is levied throughout New Zealand. It's usually incorporated into the cost of an item, but in hotels and some restaurants it is added to the bill.

Visitors exiting the country must pay a departure tax of $20.

Sample Costs Cup of coffee: $2.50
Glass of beer in a bar: $2
Take-out ham sandwich or meat pie: $2.50
Hamburger in a café: $4
Room-service sandwich in a hotel: $12
A 2-kilometer (1¼-mile) taxi ride: $5

Passports and Visas

If your passport is lost or stolen abroad, report it immediately to the nearest embassy or consulate and to the local police. If you can provide the consulate with the information contained in the passport, they will usually be able to issue you a new passport. For this reason, it is a good idea to keep a copy of the data page of your passport in a separate place, or to leave the passport number, date, and place of issuance with a relative or friend at home.

U.S. Citizens All U.S. citizens, even infants, need a valid passport to enter New Zealand.

General Information You can pick up new and renewal application forms at any of the 13 U.S. Passport Agency offices and at some post offices and courthouses. Although passports are usually mailed within two weeks of your application's receipt, it's best to allow three weeks for delivery in low season, five weeks or more from April through summer. Call the Department of State Office of Passport Services' information line (1425 K St. NW, Washington, DC 20522, tel. 202/647–0518) for fees, documentation requirements, and other details.

Canadians All Canadians need a valid passport to enter New Zealand, but no visa is necessary for visits of less than three months. (Travelers may be asked to show a fully paid onward ticket.) Application forms are available at 23 regional passport offices as well as post offices and travel agencies. Whether applying for a first or subsequent passport, you must apply in person. Children under 16 may be included on a parent's passport but must have their own passport to travel alone. Passports are valid for five years and are usually mailed within two weeks of an application's receipt. For more information in English or French, call the passport office (tel. 514/283–2152).

U.K. Citizens Citizens of the United Kingdom need a valid passport to enter New Zealand, but provided your passport entitles you to permanent residence in the United Kingdom, you can remain in New Zealand for six months without a visa. Applications for new and renewal passports are available from main post offices as well as at the six passport offices, located in Belfast, Glasgow, Liverpool, London, Newport, and Peterborough. You may apply in person at all passport offices, or by mail to all except the London office. Children under 16 may travel on a parent's passport when accompanying the parent. All passports are valid for 10 years. Allow a month for processing.

Health Requirements No vaccinations are required for entry into New Zealand for visitors traveling directly from the United States, Canada, or the United Kingdom.

Customs and Duties

On Arrival New Zealand has stringent regulations governing the import of weapons, foodstuffs, and certain plant and animal material. Anti-drug laws are strict and penalties severe. In addition to personal effects, nonresidents over 17 years of age may bring in, duty-free, 200 cigarettes or 250 grams of tobacco or 50 cigars, 4½ liters of wine, one bottle containing not more than 1,125 milliliters of spirits or liqueur, and personal purchases and gifts up to the value of US $289 (NZ$500).

On Departure If you are bringing any foreign-made equipment with you from home, such as cameras, it's wise to carry the original receipt or register it with Customs before you leave (U.S. Customs Form 4457). Otherwise, you may end up paying duty on your return.

U.S. Customs Provided you've been out of the country for at least 48 hours and haven't already used the exemption, or any part of it, in the past 30 days, you may bring home $400 worth of foreign goods duty-free. So can each member of your family, regardless of age; and your exemptions may be pooled, so one of you can bring in more if another brings in less. A flat 10% duty applies to the next $1,000 of goods; above $1,400, the rate varies with the merchandise. (If the 48-hour or 30-day limits apply, your duty-free allowance drops to $25, which may not be pooled.) Please note that these are the *general* rules, applicable to most countries, including New Zealand.

Travelers 21 or older may bring back 1 liter of alcohol duty-free, provided the beverage laws of the state through which they reenter the United States allow it. In addition, 100 non-Cuban cigars and 200 cigarettes are allowed, regardless of your age. Antiques and works of art more than 100 years old are duty-free.

Gifts valued at less than $50 may be mailed duty-free to stateside friends and relatives, with a limit of one package per day per addressee (do not send alcohol or tobacco products, nor perfume valued at more than $5). These gifts do not count as part of your exemption, unless you bring them home with you. Mark the package "Unsolicited Gift" and include the nature of the gift and its retail value.

For a copy of "Know Before You Go," a free brochure detailing what you may and may not bring back to the United States, rates of duty, and other pointers, contact the **U.S. Customs Service** (Box 7407, Washington, DC 20044, tel. 202/927–6724).

Canadian Customs Once per calendar year, when you've been out of Canada for at least seven days, you may bring in $300 worth of goods duty-free. If you've been away less than seven days but more than 48 hours, the duty-free exemption drops to $100 but can be claimed any number of times (as can a $20 duty-free exemption for absences of 24 hours or more). You cannot combine the yearly and 48-hour exemptions, use the $300 exemption only partially (to save the balance for a later trip), or pool exemptions with family members. Goods claimed under the $300 exemption may follow you by mail; those claimed under the lesser exemptions must accompany you on your return.

Alcohol and tobacco products may be included in the yearly and 48-hour exemptions but not in the 24-hour exemption. If you meet the age requirements of the province through which you reenter Canada, you may bring in, duty-free, 1.14 liters (40 imperial ounces) of wine or liquor *or* two dozen 12-ounce cans or bottles of beer or ale. If you are 16 or older, you may bring in, duty-free, 200 cigarettes, 50 cigars or cigarillos, and 400 tobacco sticks or 400 grams of manufactured tobacco. Alcohol and tobacco must accompany you on your return.

Gifts may be mailed to friends in Canada duty-free. These do not count as part of your exemption. Each gift may be worth up to of $60—label the package "Unsolicited Gift—Value under $60." There are no limits on the number of gifts that may be sent per day or per addressee, but you can't mail alcohol or tobacco.

For more information, including details of duties on items that exceed your duty-free limit, ask the Revenue Canada Customs and Excise Department (Connaught Bldg., MacKenzie Ave., Ottawa, Ont., K1A 0L5, tel. 613/957–0275) for a copy of the free brochure "I Declare/Je Déclare."

U.K. Customs From countries outside the EC, such as New Zealand, you may import duty-free 200 cigarettes, 100 cigarillos, 50 cigars or 250 grams of tobacco; 1 liter of spirits or 2 liters of fortified or sparkling wine; 2 liters of still table wine; 60 millileters of perfume; 250 millileters of toilet water; plus £36 worth of other goods, including gifts and souvenirs.

For further information or a copy of "A Guide for Travellers," which details standard customs procedures as well as what you may bring into the United Kingdom from abroad, contact HM Customs and Excise (New King's Beam House, 22 Upper Ground, London SE1 9PJ, tel. 071/620–1313).

Traveling with Cameras, Camcorders, and Laptops

If your camera is new, or if you haven't used it for a while, shoot and develop a few rolls before leaving home. Pack some lens tissue and an extra battery for your built-in light meter, and invest in an inexpensive skylight filter, to both protect your lens and provide some definition in hazy shots.

Store film in a cool, dry place—never in the car's glove compartment or on the shelf under the rear window.

Films above ISO 400 are more sensitive to damage from airport security X-rays than others; very high speed films, ISO 1,000 and above, are exceedingly vulnerable. To protect your film, don't put it in checked luggage; carry it with you in a plastic bag and ask for a hand inspection. Such requests are honored at American airports, but up to the inspector abroad. Don't depend on a lead-lined bag to protect film in checked luggage—

the airline may very well turn up the dosage of radiation to see what you've got in there. Airport metal detectors do not harm film, although you'll set off the alarm if you walk through one with a roll in your pocket. Call the Kodak Information Center (tel. 800/242–2424) for details.

About Camcorders Before your trip, put new or long-unused camcorders through their paces, and practice panning and zooming. Invest in a sky-light filter to protect the lens, and check the lithium battery that lights up the LCD (liquid crystal display) modes. As for the rechargeable nickel-cadmium batteries that are the camera's power source, take along an extra pair, so while you're using your camcorder you'll have one battery ready and another recharging. Most newer camcorders are equipped with the battery (which generally slides or clicks onto the camera body) and, to recharge it, with what's known as a universal or world-wide AC adapter charger (or multivoltage converter) that can be used whether the voltage is 110 or 220. All that's needed is the appropriate plug.

About Videotape Unlike still-camera film, videotape is not damaged by X-rays. However, it may well be harmed by the magnetic field of a walk-through metal detector. Airport security personnel may want you to turn the camcorder on to prove that that's what it is, so make sure the battery is charged when you get to the airport. Note that although the United States, Canada, Japan, Korea, Taiwan, and other countries operate on the National Television System Committee video standard (NTSC), New Zealand uses PAL technology. So you will not be able to view your tapes through the local TV set or view movies bought there in your home VCR. Blank tapes bought in New Zealand can be used for NTSC camcorder taping, however—although you'll probably find they cost more in that country and wish you'd brought an adequate supply along.

About Laptops Security X-rays do not harm hard-disk or floppy-disk storage. Most airlines allow you to use your laptop aloft but request that you turn it off during takeoff and landing so as not to interfere with navigation equipment. Make sure the battery is charged when you arrive at the airport, because you may be asked to turn on the computer at security checkpoints to prove that it is what it appears to be. If you're a heavy computer user, consider traveling with a backup battery. For international travel, register your laptop with U.S. Customs as you leave the country, providing it's manufactured abroad (U.S.-origin items cannot be registered at U.S. Customs); when you do so, you'll get a certificate, good for as long as you own the item, containing your name and address, a description of the laptop, and its serial number, that will quash any questions that may arise on your return. If your laptop is U.S.-made, call the consulate of the country you'll be visiting to find out whether it should be registered with customs in that country upon arrival. Some travelers do this as a matter of course and ask customs officers to sign a document that specifies the total configuration of the system, computer and peripherals, and its value. In addition, before leaving home, find out about repair facilities at your destination, and don't forget any transformer or adapter plug you may need (*see* Electricity, above).

Language

The Maori language is still spoken by many New Zealanders of Polynesian descent, but English is the everyday language for all races. A number of Maori words have found their way into common usage, most noticeably in place-names, which often refer to peculiar features of the local geography or food supply. The Maori word for New Zealand, *Aotearoa*, means "land of the long white cloud." The South Island town of Kaikoura is famous for its crayfish—and the word means "to eat crayfish." *Whangapiro*, the Maori name for the Government Gardens in Rotorua, means "an evil-smelling place"; if you visit the town, you'll find out why. A Polynesian noun you'll sometimes come across in Maori churches is *tapu*—"sacred"—which has entered the English language as *taboo*. Another Maori word you will frequently encounter is *pakeha*, which means you, the non-Maori. The Maori greeting is *kia ora*, which can also mean "goodbye," "good health," or "good luck."

A Personal Kiwi-Yankee Dictionary, by Louis S. Leland, Jr., is an amusing and informative guide to New Zealand idioms.

Staying Healthy

Nutrition and general health standards in New Zealand are high, and it would be hard to find a more pristine natural environment. There are no venomous snakes, and the only poisonous spider, the katipo, is a rarity. One surprising health hazard is the water. While the country's alpine lakes might look like backdrops for mineral-water ads, some on the South Island harbor a tiny organism that can cause "duck itch," a temporary but intense skin irritation. The organism is found only on the shallow lake margins, so the chances of infection are greatly reduced if you stick to deeper water. Some streams are infected by giardia, a water-borne protozoal parasite that can cause gastrointestinal disorders, including acute diarrhea. Giardia is most likely to occur when streams pass through an area inhabited by mammals (such as cattle or possums). There is no risk of infection if you drink from streams above the tree line.

One New Zealander you will come to loathe is the tiny black sandfly, common to the western half of the South Island, which inflicts a painful bite that can itch for several days. Insect repellents are readily available throughout New Zealand.

If you have a health problem for which you might need to buy prescription drugs, have your doctor write a prescription using the drug's generic name (brand names can vary widely). Then get a local doctor to endorse the prescription, and a local pharmacist will fill it.

Finding a Doctor The International Association for Medical Assistance to Travelers (IAMAT, 417 Center St., Lewiston, NY 14092, tel. 716/754–4883; 40 Regal Rd., Guelph, Ont. N1K 1B5; in Europe: 57 Voirets, 1212 Grand-Lancy, Geneva, Switzerland; in Australia: 4 Bridge St., Sydney 2000, tel. 02/201–1014; in New Zealand: Box 5049, Christchurch 5) publishes a worldwide directory of English-speaking physicians whose qualifications meet IAMAT standards and who have agreed to treat members for a set fee. Membership is free.

Assistance Pretrip medical referrals, emergency evacuation or repatria-
Companies tion, 24-hour telephone hot lines for medical consultation, dispatch of medical personnel, relay of medical records, up-front
cash for emergencies, and other personal and legal assistance
are among the services provided by several membership organizations specializing in medical assistance to travelers.
Among them are **International SOS Assistance** (Box 11568,
Philadelphia, PA 19116, tel. 215/244–1500 or 800/523–8930; Box
466, Pl. Bonaventure, Montréal, Qué. H5A 1C1, tel. 514/874–
7674 or 800/363–0263), **Near Services** (450 Prairie Ave., Suite
101, Calumet City, IL 60409, tel. 708/868–6700 or 800/654–
6700), and **Travel Assistance International** (1133 15th St. NW,
Suite 400, Washington, DC 20005, tel. 202/331–1609 or 800/
821–2828), part of Europ Assistance Worldwide Services, Inc.
Because these companies will also sell you death-and-dismem-
berment, trip-cancellation, and other insurance coverage,
there is some overlap with the travel-insurance policies dis-
cussed below, which may include the services of an assistance
company among the insurance options or reimburse travelers
for such services without providing them.

Insurance

Every visitor to New Zealand is covered by the government's
Accident Compensation scheme. Under this scheme, anyone
who is injured in an accident is entitled to claim compensation,
irrespective of fault. Benefits include most medical and hospital expenses and lump-sum payments for physical disability,
but not loss of earnings outside New Zealand. (New Zealand
law prohibits any injured party from bringing legal action for
damages in New Zealand courts.)

For U.S. Residents Most tour operators, travel agents, and insurance agents sell
specialized health-and-accident, flight, trip-cancellation, and
luggage insurance as well as comprehensive policies with some
or all of these features. But before you make any purchase, review your existing health and homeowner policies to find out
whether they cover expenses incurred while travelling.

Health-and-Accident Supplemental health-and-accident insurance for travelers is
Insurance usually a part of comprehensive policies. Specific policy provisions vary, but they tend to address three general areas, beginning with reimbursement for medical expenses caused by
illness or an accident during a trip. Such policies may reimburse anywhere from $1,000 to $150,000 worth of medical expenses; dental benefits may also be included. A second common
feature is the personal-accident, or death-and-dismember-
ment, provision, which pays a lump sum to your beneficiaries if
your die or to you if you lose one or both limbs or your eyesight.
This is similar to the flight insurance described below, although
it is not necessarily limited to accidents involving airplanes or
even other "common carriers" (buses, trains, and ships) and
can be in effect 24 hours a day. The lump sum awarded can
range from $15,000 to $500,000. A third area generally addressed by these policies is medical assistance (referrals, evacuation, or repatriation and other services). Some policies
reimburse travelers for the cost of such services; others may
automatically enroll you as a member of a particular medical-
assistance company.

Flight Insurance This insurance, often bought as a last-minute impulse at the airport, pays a lump sum to a beneficiary when a plane crashes and the insured dies (and sometimes to a surviving passenger who loses eyesight or a limb); thus it supplements the airlines' own coverage as described in the limits-of-liability paragraphs on your ticket (up to $75,000 on international flights, $20,000 on domestic ones—and that is generally subject to litigation). Charging an airline ticket to a major credit card often automatically signs you up for flight insurance; in this case, the coverage may also embrace travel by bus, train, and ship.

Baggage Insurance In the event of loss, damage, or theft on international flights, airlines limit their liability to $20 per kilogram for checked baggage (roughly about $640 per 70-pound bag) and $400 per passenger for unchecked baggage. On domestic flights, the ceiling is $1,250 per passenger. Excess-valuation insurance can be bought directly from the airline at check-in but leaves your bags vulnerable on the ground.

Sources include **The Travelers Companies** (1 Tower Sq., Hartford, CT 06183, tel. 203/277–0111 or 800/243–3174) and **Wallach and Company, Inc.** (107 W. Federal St., Box 480, Middleburg, VA 22117, tel. 703/687–3166 or 800/237–6615), underwritten by Lloyds, London.

Trip Insurance There are two sides to this coin. **Trip-cancellation-and-interruption insurance** protects you in the event you are unable to undertake or finish your trip. **Default** or **bankruptcy insurance** protects you against a supplier's failure to deliver. Consider the former if your airline ticket, cruise, or package tour does not allow changes or cancellations. The amount of coverage to buy should equal the cost of your trip should you, a traveling companion, or a family member gets sick, forcing you to stay home, plus the nondiscounted one-way airline ticket you would need to buy if you had to return home early. Read the fine print carefully; pay attention to sections defining "family member" and "preexisting medical conditions." A characteristic quirk of default policies is that they often do not cover default by travel agencies or default by a tour operator, airline, or cruise line if you bought your tour and the coverage directly from the firm in question. To reduce your need for default insurance, give preference to tours packaged by members of the United States Tour Operators Association (USTOA), which maintains a fund to reimburse clients in the event of member defaults. Even better, pay for travel arrangements with a major credit card, so that you can refuse to pay the bill if services have not been rendered—and let the card company fight your battles.

Comprehensive Policies Companies supplying comprehensive policies with some or all of the above features include **Access America, Inc.,** underwritten by BCS Insurance Company (Box 11188, Richmond, VA 23230, tel. 800/284–8300); **Carefree Travel Insurance,** underwritten by The Hartford (Box 310, 120 Mineola Blvd., Mineola, NY 11501, tel. 516/294–0220 or 800/323–3149); **Tele-Trip** (Mutual of Omaha Plaza, Box 31762, Omaha, NE 68131; tel. 800/228–9792), a subsidiary of Mutual of Omaha; **The Travelers Companies** (1 Tower Sq., Hartford, CT 06183, tel. 203/277–0111 or 800/243–3174); **Travel Guard International,** underwritten by Transamerica Occidental Life Companies (1145 Clark St., Stevens Point, WI 54481, tel. 715/345–0505 or 800/782–5151); and **Wallach and Company, Inc.** (107 W. Federal St., Box 480,

Middleburg, VA 22117, tel. 703/687–3166 or 800/237–6615), underwritten by Lloyds, London. These companies may also offer the above types of insurance separately.

U.K. Residents Most tour operators, travel agents, and insurance agents sell specialized policies covering accident, medical expenses, personal liability, trip cancellation, and loss or theft of personal property. Some policies include coverage for delayed departure and legal expenses, winter-sports, accidents, or motoring abroad. You can also purchase an annual travel-insurance policy valid for every trip you make during the year in which it's purchased (usually only trips of less than 90 days). Before you leave, make sure you will be covered if you have a preexisting medical condition or are pregnant; your insurers may not pay for routine or continuing treatment, or may require a note from your doctor certifying your fitness to travel.

For advice by phone or a free booklet, "Holiday Insurance," that sets out what to expect from a holiday-insurance policy and gives price guidelines, contact the Association of British Insurers (51 Gresham St., London EC2V 7HQ, tel. 071/600–3333; 30 Gordon St., Glasgow G1 3PU, tel. 041/226–3905; Scottish Provincial Bldg., Donegall Sq. W, Belfast BT1 6JE, tel. 0232/249176; call for other locations).

Car Rentals

Despite the fact that New Zealanders drive on the left-hand side of the road, driving there is relatively easy. All the major car rental car companies are represented, including **Avis** (tel. 800/331–1212, 800/879–2847 in Canada); **Budget** (tel. 800/527–0700); **Dollar** (tel. 800/800–4000); **Hertz** (tel. 800/654–3131, 800/263–0600 in Canada); and **National InterRent** (tel. 800/227–7368). **Koala Tours** (tel. 800/535–0316) also handles car rentals, but these must be made through travel agents. Visitors are advised to make a reservation in advance.

Requirements Usually, you must be over 21 to rent a car (some rental companies require a driver to be 25) and some restrictions may apply to drivers over 60 years of age. Most companies will accept your current driver's license from home, but some may require an International Driver's Permit, available from the American Automobile Association (AAA) and the Canadian Automobile Association (CAA).

The cost (including compulsory insurance) for a small vehicle such as a Toyota Corolla is about $88 per day plus 28¢ per kilometer; for a Ford Fairmont, $105 per day plus 33¢ per kilometer. Local operators will rent to you for half that, but you have to return the car to the pick-up point, and the minimum hire period is usually four days.

The cost of a two-berth camper van varies from $100 to $185 per day, depending on the season; a six-berth camper runs $140 to $240 per day. The minimum hire period is usually six days. There are more than 400 motor camps, with communal bathroom and laundry facilities, grocery stores, and power sites, scattered the length and breadth of New Zealand; a van site at one of these goes for $6–$12 per night.

Extra Charges Picking up the car in one city or country and leaving it in another may entail drop-off charges or one-way service fees, which can be substantial. The cost of a collision or loss damage waiver (*see* below) can be high, also. Automatic transmissions and air-conditioning are not universally available abroad; ask for them when you book if you want them, and check the cost before you commit yourself to the rental.

Cutting Costs If you know you will want a car for more than a day or two, you can save by planning ahead. Major international companies have programs that discount their standard rates by 15%–30% if you make the reservation before departure (anywhere from two to 14 days), rent for a minimum number of days (typically three or four), and prepay the rental. Ask about these advance-purchase schemes when you call for information. More economical rentals are those that come as part of fly/drive or other packages, even those as bare-bones as the rental plus an airline ticket (*see* Packages for Independent Travelers, above).

Other sources of savings are the several companies that operate as wholesalers—companies that do not own their own fleets but rent in bulk from those that do and offer advantageous rates to their customers. Rentals through such companies must be arranged and paid for before you leave the United States. Among them are **Auto Europe** (Box 1097, Camden, ME 04843, tel. 207/236–8235 or 800/223–5555, 800/458–9503 in Canada), which rents cars in the United States, Europe, Australia, New Zealand, and other regions; and **Foremost Euro-Car** (5430 Van Nuys Blvd., Suite 306, Van Nuys, CA 91401, tel. 818/786–1960 or 800/272–3299), which rents in Europe as well as Australia and New Zealand. You won't see these wholesalers' deals advertised; they're even better in summer, when business travel is down. Always ask whether the prices are guaranteed in U.S. dollars or foreign currency and if unlimited mileage is available. Find out about any required deposits, cancellation penalties, and drop-off charges, and confirm the cost of the CDW.

One last tip: Remember to fill the tank just before you turn in the vehicle, to avoid being charged for refueling at what you'll swear is the most expensive pump in town.

Insurance and Collision Damage Waiver The standard rental contract includes liability coverage (for damage to public property, injury to pedestrians, etc.) and coverage for the car against fire, theft (not included in certain countries), and collision damage with a deductible—most commonly $2,000–$3,000, occasionally more. In the case of an accident, you are responsible for the deductible amount unless you've purchased the collision damage waiver (CDW), which costs an average $12 a day, although this varies depending on what you've rented, where, and from whom.

Because this adds up quickly, you may be inclined to say "no thanks"—and that's certainly your option, although the rental agent may not tell you so. Planning ahead will help you make the right decision. By all means, find out if your own insurance covers damage to a rental car while traveling (not simply a car to drive when yours is in for repairs). And check whether charging car rentals to any of your credit cards will get you a CDW at no charge. Note before you decline that deductibles are occasionally high enough that totaling a car would make you responsible for its full value.

Rail and Bus Passes

Travelers can purchase an **InterCity Travelpass** good for unlimited travel on trains, buses, and InterIsland ferries. The pass allows 8 days of travel within a 21-day period ($425), 15 days of travel within 36 days ($530), or 22 days of travel within 56 days ($650). Children aged 4 to 14 pay 67% of the adult fare. The **4 in 1 New Zealand Travelpass,** which is available for purchase outside New Zealand only, includes one flight sector on Ansett New Zealand between assigned city pairs. The flight may be at any time after the date of issue of the Travelpass and up to seven days after expiry of the Travelpass. The pass entitles the visitor to 8 days of travel in 21 days ($616), 15 days of travel in 36 days ($721), or 22 days of travel in 56 days ($841). Children aged 4 to 14 travel at 67% of the adult fare. An additional two flight sectors may be purchased at $191 per sector. For Youth Hostel Association members, the **InterCity Youth Hostel Travel Card** ($75 for 14 days, $99 for 28 days) gives a 50% discount on most train services, all InterCity coach services, and on the InterIsland ferries. Contact InterCity Reservations (tel. 09/358–4085 in Auckland, 03/379–9020 or 0800/802–802 in Christchurch, 04/498–3413 in Wellington) for ticket information.

Valid for travel in both Australia and New Zealand, the **Down Under Pass** is offered by Australian Coachlines and Mt. Cook Line. The passes range from nine to 45 days, to be used within prescribed time allotments that allow for a 10-day break in travel between the two countries. The passes are priced from $450 to $1,419.

Student and Youth Travel

In addition to the International Youth Hostels (*see* below), a network of low-cost, independent backpacker hostels operates in New Zealand. They can be found in nearly every city and tourist spot, and they offer clean, twin- and small-dormitory-style accommodations and self-catering kitchens, similar to those of the Youth Hostel Association (or YHA, the local version of IYIH), with no membership required. To find out about backpacker hostels in New Zealand, contact **Budget Backpackers Hostels NZ, Ltd.** (Rainbow Lodge, 99 Titiraupenga St., Taupo, tel. 074/8–5754 or Downtown Backpackers, 208 Kilgore St., Christchurch, tel. 03/366–9720).

Travel Agencies The foremost U.S. student travel agency is **Council Travel,** a subsidiary of the nonprofit Council on International Educational Exchange. It specializes in low-cost travel arrangements, is the exclusive U.S. agent for several discount cards, and, with its sister CIEE subsidiary, **Council Charter,** is a source of airfare bargains. The Council Charter brochure and CIEE's twice-yearly *Student Travels* magazine, which details its programs, are available at the Council Travel office at CIEE headquarters (205 E. 42nd Street, New York, NY 10017; tel. 212/661–1450) and at 37 branches in college towns nationwide (free in person, $1 by mail). The **Educational Travel Center** (ETC, 438 N. Francis St., Madison, WI 53703, tel. 608/256–5551) also offers low-cost rail passes, domestic and international airline tickets (mostly for flights departing from Chicago), and other budgetwise travel arrangements. Other travel agencies catering to students include **Travel Management International** (TMI, 18 Prescott St., Suite 4, Cambridge, MA 02138, tel. 617/661–

8187) and **Travel Cuts** (187 College St., Toronto, Ont. M5T 1P7, tel. 416/979–2406).

Discount Cards For discounts on transportation and on museum and attractions admissions, buy the **International Student Identity Card** (ISIC) if you're a bona fide student, or the **International Youth Card** (IYC) if you're under 26. In the United States the ISIC and IYC cards cost $15 each and include basic travel accident and sickness coverage. Apply to **CIEE** (*see* address above, tel. 212/661–1414; the application is in *Student Travels*). In Canada the cards are available for $15 each from **Travel Cuts** (*see* above). In the United Kingdom they cost £5 and £4 respectively at student unions and student travel companies, including Council Travel's London office (28A Poland St., London W1V 3DB, tel. 071/437–7767).

Hosteling An **International Youth Hostel Federation** (IYHF) membership card is the key to more than 5,300 hostel locations in 59 countries; the sex-segregated, dormitory-style sleeping quarters, including some for families, go for $7–$20 a night per person. Membership is available in the United States through **American Youth Hostels** (AYH, 733 15th St. NW, Washington, DC 20005, tel. 202/783–6161), the American link in the worldwide chain, and costs $25 for adults 18–54, $10 for those under 18, $15 for those 55 and over, and $35 for families. Volume 2 of the two-volume *Guide to Budget Accommodation*, which can be purchased from AYH and the other IYHF member organizations, lists hostels in Asia, Australia, and New Zealand as well as in Canada and the United States ($13.95 including postage). IYHF membership is available in Canada through the **Canadian Hostelling Association** (CHA, 1600 James Naismith Dr., Suite 608, Gloucester, Ont. K1B 5N4, tel. 613/748–5638) for $26.75, and in the United Kingdom through the **Youth Hostel Association of England and Wales** (Trevelyan House, 8 St. Stephen's Hill, St. Albans, Herts. AL1 2DY, tel. 0727/55215) for £9.

Traveling with Children

Publications *Family Travel Times*, published 10 times a year by **Travel With**
Newsletter **Your Children** (TWYCH, 45 W. 18th St., 7th Floor Tower, New York, NY 10011, tel. 212/206–0688; annual subscription $55), covers destinations, types of vacations, and modes of travel; an airline issue comes out every other year (the last one, February/March 1993, is sold to non-subscribers for $10). On Wednesday, the staff answers subscribers' questions on specific destinations.

Books *Great Vacations with Your Kids*, by Dorothy Jordan and Marjorie Cohen ($13; Penguin USA, 120 Woodbine St., Bergenfield, NJ 07621, tel. 800/253–6476), and *Traveling with Children—And Enjoying It*, by Arlene K. Butler ($11.95 plus $3 shipping per book; Globe Pequot Press, Box 833, Old Saybrook, CT 06475, tel. 800/243–0495 or 800/962–0973 in CT), help you plan your trip with children, from toddlers to teens.

Getting There All children, including infants, must have valid passports for foreign travel. Family passports are no longer issued.

Airfares On international flights, the fare for infants under two not occupying a seat is generally 10% of the accompanying adult's fare; children ages 2–11 usually pay half to two-thirds of the adult fare. On domestic flights, children under two not occupying a seat travel free, and older children currently travel on the "lowest applicable" adult fare.

Baggage In general, infants paying 10% of the adult fare are allowed one carry-on bag, not to exceed 70 pounds or 45 inches (length + width + height). The adult baggage allowance applies for children paying half or more of the adult fare. Check with the airline for particulars, especially regarding flights between two foreign destinations, where allowances for infants may be less generous than those above.

Safety Seats The FAA recommends the use of safety seats aloft and details approved models in the free leaflet **"Child/Infant Safety Seats Recommended for Use in Aircraft"** (available from the Federal Aviation Administration, APA–200, 800 Independence Ave. SW, Washington, DC 20591, tel. 202/267–3479). Airline policy varies. U.S. carriers must allow FAA-approved models, but because these seats are strapped into a regular passenger seat, they may require that parents buy a ticket even for an infant under two who would otherwise ride free. Foreign carriers may not allow infant seats, may charge the child's rather than the infant's fare for their use, or may require you to hold your baby during takeoff and landing, thus defeating the seat's purpose.

Facilities Aloft Airlines do provide other facilities and services for children, such as children's meals and freestanding bassinets (to those sitting in seats on the bulkhead, where there's enough legroom to accommodate them). Make your request when reserving. The annual February/March issue of *Family Travel Times* gives details of the children's services of dozens of airlines (*see* above). "Kids and Teens in Flight" (free from the U.S. Department of Transportation, tel. 202/366–2220) offers tips for children flying alone.

Regulations on infant air travel are in the process of changing. Until they are finalized, if you want to be sure that your infant is secure you must bring your own infant car seat and buy the child a separate ticket. Check with the airline in advance to make sure your seat meets the required standard. The booklet *Child/Infant Safety Seats Acceptable for Use in Aircraft* is available from the Federal Aviation Administration (APA–200, 800 Independence Ave. SW, Washington, DC 20591, tel. 202/ 267–3479). If you opt to hold your baby on your lap, do so with the infant outside the seat belt so he or she doesn't get crushed if there's a sudden stop. If possible, reserve a seat behind one of the plane's bulkheads, where there's usually more legroom and enough space to fit a bassinet (which is available from the airlines).

When reserving tickets, ask about special children's meals or snacks—most airlines offer them. The February 1990 and 1992 issues of *Family Travel Times* (*see* above) includes TWYCH's "Airline Guide," which contains a rundown of the children's services offered by 46 different airlines.

Dining New Zealanders are genuinely fond of and considerate toward children, and their own children are included in most of their parents' social activities. Children are welcome in all restaurants throughout the country. However, they are rarely seen in those restaurants that appear in Fodor's "Very Expensive" and "Expensive" price categories. These restaurants may not have high chairs, nor might they be prepared to make special children's meals. Major cities and important tourist centers have McDonald's and Kentucky Fried Chicken outlets.

Lodging In hotels in New Zealand, roll-away beds are usually free, and children under 12 sharing a hotel room with adults either stay free or receive a discount rate. Few hotels have separate facilities for children.

Home hosting provides an ideal opportunity for visitors to stay with a local family, either in town or on a working farm. For information on home and farm stays, *see* Lodging in Staying in New Zealand, below.

Family Adventure **Rascals in Paradise** (650 5th St., Suite 505, San Francisco, CA
Tours 94107, tel. 415/978–9800 or 800/872–7225) organizes innovative holidays in New Zealand, featuring swimming, snorkeling, horseback riding, and a host of other activities. Baby-sitters are provided for infants, and teacher-escorts organize activities to suit the interests of both parents and children. **Journeys** (4011 Jackson Rd., Ann Arbor, MI 48103, tel. 313/665–4407 or 800/225–8735) offers a series of 14-day "adventure expeditions" for parents and grandparents with children, to such diverse regions as the glaciers, seal colonies, and geothermal hot springs of New Zealand. Family group tours are arranged around holiday periods. **GrandTravel** (6900 Wisconsin Ave., Suite 706, Chevy Chase, MD 20815, tel. 301/986–0790 or 800/247–7651) offers international and domestic tours for grandparents traveling with their grandchildren. The catalogue, as charmingly written and illustrated as a children's book, positively invites armchair traveling with lap-sitters aboard.

Baby-sitting Most hotels and resorts have baby-sitters available through
Services the concierge or front desk, at a charge of around $8 to $10 an hour. Baby-sitting services are also listed in the yellow pages of city telephone directories.

Strollers and bassinets can be rented from the **Royal New Zealand Plunket Society** (472 George St., Dunedin North, tel. 03/477–0110). Most car-rental agencies provide "cocoons" for newborns as well as child safety seats.

Chemist's shops carry a wide range of baby products such as disposable diapers (ask for napkins or nappies), formula, and baby food. They are less expensive in supermarkets, which are scarce outside the major cities.

Hints for Travelers with Disabilities

New Zealand is at the forefront in providing facilities for the disabled. Contact the **Royal New Zealand Plunket Society** (472 George St., Dunedin North, tel. 03/477–0110).

Lodging The major hotel chains (such as Regent, Sheraton, InterContinental, Ramada, Hilton, Holiday Inn, and Hyatt) provide three or four rooms with disabled facilities in most of their properties. The **New Zealand Tourism Board** publishes *Access: A Guide for the Less Mobile Traveller*, listing accommodations, attractions, restaurants, and thermal pools with special facilities.

Getting Around On Air New Zealand, wheelchairs for in-flight mobility are
By Air standard equipment; seat-belt extensions, quadriplegic har-

nesses, and padded leg rests are also available. Ask for the company's brochure "Air Travel for People With Disabilities."

By Train Passengers on mainline passenger trains can request collapsible wheelchairs to negotiate the narrow interior corridors. However, compact toilet areas and platform access problems make long-distance train travel difficult.

By Taxi Companies in New Zealand have recently introduced vans equipped with hoists and floor clamps, but these should be booked several hours in advance if possible; contact the Plunket Society (*see* above) for more information.

Car Rental Only **Budget Rent-A-Car** (tel. 800/572–0700 in the U.S. and Canada) offers cars fitted with hand controls, but these are limited. **Hertz** (tel. 800/654–3131 in the U.S., 800/263–0600 in Canada) will fit hand-held controls onto standard cars by arrangement.

Organizations Several organizations provide travel information for people with disabilities, usually for a membership fee, and some publish newsletters and bulletins. Among them are the **Information Center for Individuals with Disabilities** (Fort Point Pl., 27-43 Wormwood St., Boston, MA 02210, tel. 617/727–5540 or 800/462–5015 in MA between 11 and 4, or leave message; TDD/TTY tel. 617/345–9743); **Mobility International USA** (Box 3551, Eugene, OR 97403, voice and TDD tel. 503/343–1284); the U.S. branch of an international organization based in Britain and present in 30 countries; **MossRehab Hospital Travel Information Service** (1200 W. Tabor Rd., Philadelphia, PA 19141, tel. 215/456–9603, TTD tel. 215/456–9602); The **Society for the Advancement of Travel for the Handicapped** (SATH, 347 5th Ave., Suite 610, New York, NY 10016, tel. 212/447–7284, fax 212/725–8253); the **Travel Industry and Disabled Exchange** (TIDE, 5435 Donna Ave., Tarzana, CA 91356, tel. 818/368–5648); and **Travelin' Talk** (Box 3534, Clarksville, TN 37043, tel. 615/552–6670).

Travel Agencies and Tour Operators **Directions Unlimited** (720 N. Bedford Rd., Bedford Hills, NY 10507, tel. 914/241–1700), a travel agency, has expertise in tours and cruises for the disabled. **Evergreen Travel Service** (4114 198th St. SW; Suite 13, Lynnwood, WA 98036, tel. 206/776–1184 or 800/435–2288) operates Wings on Wheels Tours for those in wheelchairs, White Cane Tours for the blind, and tours for the deaf and makes group and independent arrangements for travelers with any disability. **Flying Wheels Travel** (143 W. Bridge St., Box 382, Owatonna, MN 55060, tel. 800/535–6790 or 800/722–9351 in MN), a tour operator and travel agency, arranges international tours, cruises, and independent travel itineraries for people with mobility disabilities. **Nautilus,** at the same address as TIDE (*see* above), packages tours for the disabled internationally.

In the United Kingdom Main sources include the **Royal Association for Disability and Rehabilitation** (RADAR, 25 Mortimer St., London W1N 8AB, tel. 071/637–5400), which publishes travel information for the disabled in Britain, and **Mobility International** (228 Borough High St., London SE1 1JX, tel. 071/403–5688), the headquarters of an international membership organization that serves as a clearinghouse of travel information for people with disabilities.

Publications In addition to the fact sheets, newsletters, and books mentioned above are several free publications available from the Consumer Information Center (Pueblo, CO 81009): "New Horizons for the Air Traveler with a Disability," a U.S. Department of Transportation booklet describing changes resulting from the 1986 Air Carrier Access Act and those still to come from the 1990 Americans with Disabilities Act (include Department 608Y in the address), and the Airport Operators Council's *Access Travel: Airports* (Dept. 5804), which describes facilities and services for the disabled at more than 500 airports worldwide.

Twin Peaks Press (Box 129, Vancouver, WA 98666, tel. 206/694–2462 or 800/637–2256) publishes *The Directory of Travel Agencies for the Disabled* ($19.95), listing more than 370 agencies worldwide; *Travel for the Disabled* ($19.95), listing some 500 accessible places worldwide; *The Directory of Accessible Van Rentals* ($9.95), for campers and RV travelers worldwide; and *Wheelchair Vagabond* ($14.95), a collection of personal travel tips. Add $2 per book for shipping.

Hints for Older Travelers

In New Zealand, some senior-citizen discounts are available.

Organizations The **American Association of Retired Persons** (AARP, 601 E St. NW, Washington, DC 20049, tel. 202/434–2277) provides independent travelers with the Purchase Privilege Program, which offers discounts on hotels, car rentals, and sightseeing; and the AARP Motoring Plan, provided by Amoco, which furnishes domestic trip-routing information and emergency road-service aid for an annual fee of $39.95 per person or couple ($59.95 for a premium version). Travelers will need to check beforehand to see if a particular hotel participates in the AARP's Purchase Privilege Program; AARP provides information on participating hotels. AARP also arranges group tours, cruises, and apartment living through its AARP Travel Experience from American Express (400 Pinnacle Way, Suite 450, Norcross, GA 30071, tel. 800/927–0111; these can be booked through travel agents, except for the cruises, which must be booked directly (tel. 800/745–4567). AARP membership is open to those 50 or over; annual dues are $8 per person or couple.

Two other membership organizations offer discounts on lodgings, car rentals, and other travel products, along with such nontravel perks as magazines and newsletters. The **National Council of Senior Citizens** (1331 F St. NW, Washington, DC 20004, tel. 202/347–8800) is a nonprofit advocacy group with some 5,000 local clubs across the United States; membership costs $12 per person or couple annually. **Mature Outlook** (6001 N. Clark St., Chicago, IL 60660, tel. 800/336–6330), a Sears Roebuck & Co. subsidiary with 800,000 members, charges $9.95 for an annual membership.

Note: When using any senior-citizen identification card for reduced hotel rates, mention it when booking, not when checking out. At restaurants, show your card before you're seated; discounts may be limited to certain menus, days, or hours. If you are renting a car, ask about promotional rates that might improve on your senior-citizen discount.

Educational Travel **Elderhostel** (75 Federal St., 3rd floor, Boston, MA 02110, tel. 617/426–7788) is a nonprofit organization that has inexpensive study programs for people 60 and older since 1975. Programs take place at more than 1,800 educational institutions in the United States, Canada, and 45 countries overseas, and courses cover everything from marine science to Greek myths and cowboy poetry. Participants generally attend lectures in the morning and spend the afternoon sightseeing or on field trips; they live in dorms on the host campuses. Fees for programs in the United States and Canada, which usually last one week, run about $300, not including transportation.

Interhostel (University of New Hampshire, 6 Garrison Ave., Durham, NH 03824, tel. 800/733–9753), a slightly younger enterprise than Elderhostel, caters to a slightly younger clientele—that is, 50 and over—and runs programs overseas in some 25 countries. But the idea is similar: Lectures and field trips mix with sightseeing, and participants stay in dormitories at cooperating educational institutions or in modest hotels. Programs are usually two weeks in length and cost $1,500–$2,100, not including airfare from the United States.

Tour Operators **Saga International Holidays** (222 Berkeley St., Boston, MA 02116, tel. 800/343–0273), which specializes in group travel for people over 60, offers a selection of variously priced tours and cruises covering five continents. If you want to take your grandchildren, look into Grand Travel (*see* Traveling with Children, above).

Further Reading

History *The Oxford Illustrated History of New Zealand,* edited by Keith Sinclair, provides a comprehensive but highly readable account of the country's social, political, cultural, and economic evolution from the earliest days of settlement to 1989. *The Colonial New Zealand Wars,* by Tim Ryan and Bill Parham, is a vivid history of the Maori-British battles. Lavishly illustrated with photographs of colonial infantry and drawings of Maori hill forts, flags, and weapons, the book makes far more compelling reading than the dry military history suggested by the title. J. C. Beaglehole's *The Discovery of New Zealand* is an authoritative and scholarly analysis of the voyages of discovery, from the first Polynesians to the Europeans of the late 18th century.

Fiction New Zealand's best-known novelist is Katherine Mansfield (1888–1923), whose early stories were set in and around the city of Wellington, her birthplace. The most celebrated work of fiction to come from New Zealand in recent years is Keri Hulme's *The Bone People,* winner of the Booker McConnell Prize in 1985. Set on the isolated west coast of the South Island, this challenging, vital novel weaves Polynesian myth with Christian symbolism and the powerful sense of place that characterizes modern Maori writing. Another important contemporary writer is Janet Frame, who made an impact on the literary scene with the publication of *The Carpathians* in 1985.

Specialized Guidebooks Strictly for wine buffs, *The Wines and Vineyards of New Zealand,* by Michael Cooper, is an exhaustive evaluation in words and pictures of every vineyard in the country. For travelers who plan to make hiking a major component of their vacations,

Tramping in New Zealand, published by Lonely Planet, is an invaluable guide.

Illustrated Books *Salute to New Zealand*, edited by Sandra Coney, is a coffeetable book that intersperses lavish photographs with chapters by some of the country's finest contemporary writers. *Wild New Zealand*, published by Reader's Digest, is a pictorial account of the country's landscape, flora, and fauna, supplemented by an informative text with such a wealth of detail that it turns the sensory experience of the landscape into a cerebral one.

Arriving and Departing

From North America by Plane

Flights are either nonstop, direct, or connecting. A **nonstop** flight requires no change of plane and makes no stops. A **direct** flight stops at least once and can involve a change of plane, although the flight number remains the same; if the first leg is late, the second waits. This is not the case with a **connecting** flight, which involves a different plane and a different flight number.

Airlines and Airports Currently, the following airlines serve New Zealand from the United States and Canada: Australia's national airline, **Qantas** (tel. 800/227–4500 in the U.S. and Canada); **Air New Zealand** (tel. 800/262–1234 the U.S., 800/663–5494 in Canada); **Continental** (tel. 800/231–0856 in the U.S. and Canada); **United** (tel. 800/538–2929 in the U.S., 800/241–6522 in Canada); and **Canadian Air International** (tel. 800/665–1177 in Canada, 800/426–7000 in the U.S.).

Flights leave from Los Angeles, San Francisco, Dallas-Fort Worth, Honolulu, New York, Toronto, and Vancouver. Air New Zealand is the only carrier with direct flights from North America to Christchurch as well as Auckland.

Flying Times Flying time from New York to Auckland (via Los Angeles) is about 19 hours; from Los Angeles or San Francisco to Auckland (nonstop), about 13 hours. These are all actual air hours and do not include ground time.

Cutting Flight Costs The Sunday travel section of most newspapers is a good source of deals. When booking, particularly through an unfamiliar company, call the Better Business Bureau to find out whether any complaints have been registered against the company, pay with a credit card if you can, and consider trip-cancellation and default insurance (*see* Insurance, above).

Promotional Airfares Most scheduled airlines offer three classes of service: first class, business class, and economy or coach. To ride in the first-class or business-class sections, you pay a first-class or business-class fare. To ride in the economy or coach section—the remainder of the plane—you pay a confusing variety of fares. Most expensive is full-fare economy or unrestricted coach, which can be bought one-way or round-trip and can be changed and turned in for a refund.

All the less expensive fares, called promotional or discount fares, are round-trip and involve restrictions. The exact nature of the restrictions depends on the airline, the route, and the season and on whether travel is domestic or international, but you must usually buy the ticket—commonly called an APEX (advance purchase excursion) when it's for international travel—in advance (seven, 14, or 21 days are usual). You must also respect certain minimum- and maximum-stay requirements (for instance, over a Saturday night or at least seven and no more than 30, 45, or 90 days), and you must be willing to pay penalties for changes. Airlines generally allow some changes for a fee. But the cheaper the fare, the more likely the ticket is nonrefundable; it would take a death in the family for the airline to give you any of your money back if you had to cancel. The cheapest fares are also subject to availability; because only a certain percentage of the plane's total seats will be sold at that price, they may go quickly.

Consolidators Consolidators or bulk-fare operators—also known as bucket shops—buy blocks of seats on scheduled flights that airlines anticipate they won't be able to sell. They pay wholesale prices, add a markup, and resell the seats to travel agents or directly to the public at prices that still undercut the airline's promotional or discount fares. You pay more than on a charter but ordinarily less than for an APEX ticket, and, even when there is not much of a price difference, the ticket usually comes without the advance-purchase restriction. Moreover, although tickets are marked nonrefundable so you can't turn them in to the airline for a full-fare refund, some consolidators sometimes give you your money back. Carefully read the fine print detailing penalties for changes and cancellations. If you doubt the reliability of a company, call the airline once you've made your booking and confirm that you do, indeed, have a reservation on the flight.

The biggest U.S. consolidator, C.L. Thomson Express, sells only to travel agents. Well-established consolidators selling to the public include **UniTravel** (Box 12485, St. Louis, MO 63132, tel. 314/569–0900 or 800/325–2222); **Council Charter** (205 E. 42nd St., New York, NY 10017, tel. 212/661–0311 or 800/800–8222), a division of the Council on International Educational Exchange and a longtime charter operator now functioning more as a consolidator; and **Travac** (989 6th Ave., New York, NY 10018, tel. 212/563–3303 or 800/872–8800), also a former charterer.

Charter Flights Charters usually have the lowest fares and the most restrictions. Departures are limited and seldom on time, and you can lose all or most of your money if you cancel. (Generally, the closer to departure you cancel, the more you lose, although sometimes you will be charged only a small fee if you supply a substitute passenger.) The charterer, on the other hand, may legally cancel the flight for any reason up to 10 days before departure; within 10 days of departure, the flight may be canceled only if it becomes physically impossible to operate it. The charterer may also revise the itinerary or increase the price after you have bought the ticket, but if the new arrangement constitutes a "major change," you have the right to a refund. Before buying a charter ticket, read the fine print for the company's refund policy and details on major changes. Money for charter flights is usually to be paid into a bank escrow account, the name of which should be on the contract. If you don't pay by credit card, make your check payable to the escrow account (unless you're dealing with a travel agent, in which case, his or her check should be payable to the escrow account). The Department of Transportation's Consumer Affairs Office (I-25, Washington, DC 20590, tel. 202/366–2220) can answer questions on charters and send you its "Plane Talk: Public Charter Flights" information sheet.

Charter operators may offer flights alone or with ground arrangements that constitute a charter package. Well-established charter operators include **Council Charter** (205 E. 42nd St., New York, NY 10017, tel. 212/661–0311 or 800/800–8222), now largely a consolidator, despite its name, and **Travel Charter** (1120 E. Long Lake Rd., Troy, MI 48098, tel. 313/528–3570 or 800/521–5267), with Midwestern departures. **DER Tours** (Box 1606, Des Plains, IL 60017, tel. 800/782–2424), a charterer and consolidator, sells through travel agents.

Discount Travel Clubs Travel clubs offer their members unsold space on airplanes, cruise ships, and package tours at nearly the last minute and at well below the original cost. Suppliers thus receive some revenue for their "leftovers," and members get a bargain. Membership generally includes a regular bulletin or access to a toll-free telephone hot line giving details of available trips departing anywhere from three or four days to several months in the future. Packages tend to be more common than flights alone, so if airfares are your only interest, read the literature before joining. Reductions on hotels are also available. Clubs include Discount Travel International (114 Forrest Ave., Suite 203, Narberth, PA 19072, tel. 215/668–7184; $45 annually, single or family), Moment's Notice (425 Madison Ave., New York, NY 10017, tel. 212/486–0503; $45 annually, single or family), Travelers Advantage (CUC Travel Service, 49 Music Sq. W, Nashville, TN 37203, tel. 800/548–1116; $49 annually, single or family), and Worldwide Discount Travel Club (1674 Meridian Ave., Miami Beach, FL 33139, tel. 305/534–2082; $50 annually for family, $40 single).

Enjoying the Flight Fly at night if you're able to sleep on a plane. Because the air aloft is dry, drink plenty of beverages while on board; remember that drinking alcohol contributes to jet lag, as do heavy meals. Sleepers usually prefer window seats to curl up against; restless passengers ask to be on the aisle. Bulkhead seats, in the front row of each cabin, have more legroom, but since there's no seat ahead, trays attach awkwardly to the arms of your seat, and you must stow all possessions overhead. Bulkhead seats are usually reserved for the disabled, the elderly, and people traveling with babies.

Smoking Since February 1990, smoking has been banned on all domestic flights of less than six hours duration; the ban also applies to domestic segments of international flights aboard U.S. and foreign carriers. On U.S. carriers flying to New Zealand and other destinations abroad, a seat in a no-smoking section must be provided for every passenger who requests one, and the section must be enlarged to accommodate such passengers if necessary as long as they have complied with the airline's deadline for check-in and seat assignment. If smoking bothers you, request a seat far from the smoking section.

Foreign airlines are exempt from these rules but do provide no-smoking sections, and some nations, including Canada as of July 1, 1993, have gone as far as to ban smoking on all domestic flights; other countries may ban smoking on flights of less than a specified duration. The International Civil Aviation Organization has set July 1, 1996, as the date to ban smoking aboard airlines worldwide, but the body has no power to enforce its decisions.

From the United Kingdom by Plane

British Airways, Cathay Pacific, Japan Airlines (JAL), Qantas, and **Singapore Airlines** (tel. 081/747–0007) operate between London and Auckland via Asia. **Air New Zealand, Continental** (tel. 02/937–76464), and **United** (tel. 081/990–9900) operate between London and Auckland via the United States. The flying time from London to Auckland is about 24 hours via either route.

Cutting Flight Costs A round-trip ticket from London to Auckland can cost more than £3,000. Fortunately, a number of specialist travel companies, such as **Trailfinders** (tel. 071/938–3366) and **Travel Cuts** (tel. 071/255–2082), offer significant reductions on scheduled fares, though little or nothing in the way of frills. Book several months in advance, especially for peak periods. Check the advertisements in *Time Out* magazine for further information.

Staying in New Zealand

Geography

New Zealand consists of three main islands: North Island (44,197 square miles), South Island (58,170 square miles), and Stewart Island (676 square miles). If it were stretched out along the west coast of the United States, the country would extend from Los Angeles to Seattle. No point is more than 70 miles from the sea, and owing to the hilly nature of the country, rivers tend to be short, swift, and broad. More than 70% of the total population of 3.36 million lives on the North Island, where industry and government are concentrated. The South Island is dominated by the Southern Alps, a spine of mountains running almost two-thirds the length of the island close to the west coast.

Getting Around

By Plane The major domestic airlines are **Air New Zealand** (tel. 09/379–3000) and **Ansett New Zealand** (tel. 09/302–2146). Both compete on intercity trunk routes, while a third carrier, **Mount Cook Airline** (tel. toll-free 0800/800–737) services the country's resort areas. Economy-price air travel is expensive compared with the cost of bus or train travel; however, multi-trip tickets offer a substantial saving. Ansett's **Down Under Discount Deals** are valid for flights within New Zealand and afford up to 60% savings with a minimum purchase of two sectors and include the option of discounted travel between Australia and New Zealand on Qantas. Air New Zealand has a **New Zealand Pass** entitling you to fly four sectors (i.e., point-to-point flights) for $523; a six-sector pass is $732. Either is valid for 60 days and must be purchased prior to your arrival. You can fly one sector on Ansett New Zealand between designated city pairs as part of the **4 in 1 InterCity New Zealand Travelpass** (*see* Rail Passes, above) and can add up to two sectors for an additional fare. Air

New Zealand and Mount Cook offer similar discount tickets, available through travel agents.

Smoking Smoking is not allowed on any flight within New Zealand.

By Train New Zealand's railroad system operates under the **InterCity** (tel. 09/358–4085) banner. Trains usually cost the same as buses and are marginally quicker, but they run far less frequently. The country's most notable rail journey is the **TranzAlpine Express,** a scenic spectacular across the mountainous spine of the South Island between Greymouth and Christchurch (*see* Arriving and Departing by Train for Marlborough, Nelson, and the West Coast in Chapter 5).

By Bus New Zealand is served by an extensive bus network, and for many travelers, buses offer the optimal combination of cost and convenience. The main bus line is **InterCity** (tel. 09/358–4085), which also operates the railroad system. The other major operator on the North Island is **Newmans** (tel. 09/309–9738), and on the South Island **Mount Cook Landline** (tel. 03/379–0690 in Christchurch or toll-free 0800/800–737). The **InterCity Travelpass** allows unlimited travel on all InterCity buses and trains and on the InterIslander ferries that link the North and South Islands (*see* Rail and Bus Passes, *above*).

By Car A valid American, Canadian, or British license allows you to drive in New Zealand, and nothing beats the freedom and mobility of a car for exploring. Even for those nervous about traveling on the "wrong" side of the road, driving here is relatively easy. Roads are well maintained and generally uncrowded, though signposting, even on major highways, is often poor. The speed limit is 100 kilometers per hour (62 mph) on the open road and 50 kph (31 mph) in towns and cities. A circular sign with the letters "LSZ" (Limited Speed Zone) means there is no speed limit—speed should be governed by prevailing road conditions.

If you drive in rural New Zealand, you will encounter one-lane bridges. These must be crossed with caution. A yellow sign on the left will warn that you are approaching a one-lane bridge, and another sign will tell you whether you have the right-of-way. A rectangular blue sign means you have the right-of-way; a circular sign with a red border means you must pull over to the left and wait to cross until oncoming traffic has passed. Even when you have the right-of-way, slow down and take care. Some one-lane bridges on the South Island are used by trains as well as cars; trains always have the right-of-way.

Telephones

Most pay phones now accept **PhoneCards** rather than coins. These plastic cards, available in denominations of $5, $10, $20, or $50, are sold at shops displaying the green PhoneCard symbol. To use a PhoneCard, lift the receiver, put the card in the slot in the front of the phone, and dial. The cost of the call is automatically deducted from your card; the display on the telephone tells you how much credit you have left at the end of the call.

Local Calls A local call from a public phone costs 20¢ per minute.

International Calls International calls may be dialed direct. The country codes are listed at the front of the telephone book. For international directory assistance, dial 0172. For the international operator, dial 0170. A convenient way to call home from New Zealand is with the **Home Country Direct Service.** By calling one of these toll-free numbers, you are connected with an operator in your home country, who will place either a collect or credit-card call for you. The Home Country Direct numbers are: USA (AT&T), tel. 000–911; (MCI) tel. 000–912, (Sprint) tel. 000–999; UK, tel. 000–944; Canada, tel. 000–919; Australia, tel. 000–961.

Mail

Postage Rates Post offices are open weekdays 9–5. The cost of mailing a letter within New Zealand is 45¢ standard post, 80¢ fast post. Sending a standard-size letter by air mail costs $1.50 to North America, $1.80 to Europe, and $1 to Australia. Aerogrammes and postcards are $1 to any overseas destination.

Receiving Mail Mail will be held for collection for one month at the central post office in any town or city if it is addressed to you "c/o Poste Restante, CPO," followed by the name of the town. This service is free.

Tipping

Tipping is not widely practiced in New Zealand. Only in the better city restaurants will you be expected to show your appreciation for good service with a 10% tip.

Opening and Closing Times

Banks are open weekdays 9–4:30, but trading in foreign currencies ceases at 3. Shops are generally open Monday–Thursday 9–5:30, Friday 9–9, and Saturday 9–noon.

Shopping

New Zealand produces several unique souvenirs, but don't expect to find many bargains. Sheepskins and quality woolens are widely available. Bowls hewn from native timbers and polished to a lustrous finish are distinctive souvenirs, but a fine example will cost several hundred dollars. Greenstone, a type of jade once prized by the Maoris, is now used for ornaments and jewelry—especially the figurine known as a *tiki*, which is often worn as a pendant. The two major areas for crafts are the Coromandel Peninsula, close to Auckland, and the environs of Nelson, at the northern tip of the South Island. The Parnell area of Auckland and the Galleria in Christchurch Arts Centre are the places to shop for souvenirs. In Nelson, Craft Habitat brings together some of the finest local arts and crafts under one roof.

Sports and the Outdoors

Bicycling Despite its precipitous topography, New Zealand offers superb biking. A temperate climate, excellent roads with relatively little traffic, and scenic variety make cycling a delight for anyone who is reasonably fit and has the time to travel slowly. The most common problem for cyclists is buckled wheel rims: Narrow, lightweight alloy rims won't stand up long to the rigors of the road. A wide-rimmed hybrid or a mountain bike with road tires is a better bet for extensive touring.

If two-wheel touring sounds appealing but pedaling a heavily laden bicycle doesn't, consider a guided cycle tour. The tours last from 2 to 18 days; bikes are supplied, and your gear is loaded on a bus or trailer that follows the riders. (You have the option of busing in the "sag wagon" when your legs give out.) Contact **New Zealand Pedaltours** (Box 49-039, Auckland, tel. 09/302–0968) or **Unravel Tours** (Square Edge Building, Palmerston North, tel. 06/356–5500).

Boating and Sailing
The country's premier cruising regions are the Bay of Islands and Marlborough Sounds, near the northern tips of the North and South Islands respectively. Both areas offer sheltered waters, marvelous scenery, and secluded beaches. Of the two, the Bay of Islands enjoys warmer summer temperatures, while Marlborough Sounds has a wild, untamed quality. Both are well supplied with operators offering either bare-boat or skippered charters, and a range of vessels from small motor cruisers to sleek Beneteau yachts. For more information, contact **Rainbow Yacht Charters** (Box 8327, Symonds St., Auckland, tel. 09/78–0719) or **Charterlink** (Box 246, Picton, tel. 03/573–6591).

Fishing
Considering that they were introduced from California little more than a hundred years ago, the explosion in New Zealand's **trout** population has been phenomenal. The average summer rainbow trout taken from Lake Tarawera, near Rotorua, weighs 5 pounds, and 8-to-10-pound fish are not unusual. In the lakes of the North Island, fingerlings often reach a weight of 4 pounds nine months after they are released. Trout do not reach maturity until they grow to 14 inches, and in fact all trout below that length must be returned to the water.

Trout fishing has a distinctly different flavor on the two islands. In the Rotorua-Taupo region of the North Island, the main quarry is rainbow trout, which are usually taken from the lakes with a wet fly or spinners. Trolling is also popular and productive. On the South Island, where brown trout predominate, the streams offer outstanding dry-fly fishing. It's best in the Nelson region and in the Southern Lakes district, at the top and bottom end of the South Island respectively. On both islands, anglers who can afford to indulge their passion are well catered to. Several specialist lodges provide guides and transport to wilderness streams that are sometimes accessible only by helicopter. The trout season lasts from October through April in most areas, though Lakes Taupo and Rotorua are open all year.

Salmon are found in the rivers that drain the eastern slopes of the Southern Alps, especially those that reach the sea between Christchurch and Dunedin. Anglers are usually transported by jetboat up these shallow rivers to the pools where the salmon rest on their spawning run. The salmon season, which runs from October to April, is at its peak from January to March.

Fishing licenses are available from fishing-tackle and sports shops on a daily, weekly, monthly, or seasonal basis. The cost ranges from $10.50 for a single day to $53 for the season, and each is valid for the entire country, with the exception of Lake Taupo, for which a separate license is required. For anyone who plans to fish extensively, the best buy is a tourist fishing license—available from Visitor Information Centres in all the major cities—which, for $56.26, permits fishing anywhere in New Zealand for one month.

The seas off the east coast of the North Island are among the world's finest **big-game fishing** waters. The quarry is mako, hammerhead, tiger shark, and marlin—especially striped marlin, which average around 250 pounds. For light tackle fishing, bonito and skipjack tuna and kahawai (sea trout) offer excellent sport. Many anglers maintain that kahawai are better fighters, pound for pound, than freshwater trout. The bases for big-game fishing are the towns of Pahia and Russell, which have a number of established charter operators. The season runs from January to April, although smaller game fishing is good all year. No fishing license is required for big-game fishing.

Wherever they fish, and whatever they fish for, anglers will profit immensely from the services of a local guide. On Lake Taupo or Rotorua, a boat with a guide plus all equipment will cost around $130 for two hours. On the South Island, a top fishing guide who can supply all equipment and a four-wheel drive vehicle will charge about $400 per day for two people. In the Bay of Islands region, an evening fishing trip aboard a small boat can cost as little as $35. For a big-game fishing boat, expect to pay between $600 and $1,000 per day.

For more information and brochures on fishing in New Zealand, contact **Simon Dickie Adventures** (Box 682, Taupo, tel. 07/378–9680); **Lake Brunner Lodge** (Mitchells, RD1 Kumara 7871, Westlands, tel. 03/738–0163); or **Bay of Islands Sportfishing Ltd.** (Box 48, Russell, tel. 09/403–7008).

Hunting New Zealand offers superb hunting. Faced with an abundance of food and a complete lack of predators, wild animals such as the deer that were introduced last century have multiplied to such numbers that they're considered pests, and an open season applies to many species. Sika stag are found in the beech forests of the North Island, and red stag are common to the forests of both islands. Higher altitudes of the Southern Alps are inhabited by the prized tahr and chamois.

Hunters can choose between "fair chase" hunts, for which they pay a minimum daily fee for a minimum number of days, and "ranch" hunts, in which the owner controls the game and the fee is charged per trophy. Ammunition is widely available for all common calibers. If you plan to bring a firearm into the country, you must present it on arrival to the police, who will issue you a license. March and April are the prime months for hunting most deer, May and June for tahr and chamois.

Except for national parks, forest parks, scenic reserves, and conservation areas, no hunting permit is necessary for deer; however, special conditions apply in some areas. When required, a permit can be obtained from Department of Conservation offices and from the visitor centers located in all national parks. A hunting guide is essential, not only for success but also for safety. For more information, contact **New Zealand Hunting and Fishing Consultants** (210–212 Lake Terr., Taupo. tel. 07/378–7070); **Mid Southern Tracks** (Box 2, Lake Tekapo, tel. 03/680–6774); or **Wildsouth** (Box 199, Mosgiel, tel. 03/489–7322).

Golf Golf is played all year; winter is the major season. Most of New Zealand's 400 courses welcome visitors. Greens fees range from $5 at country courses to $40 at the exclusive city courses. Many have clubs for hire, and the better urban courses offer resident professionals and golf carts for hire. For more information, contact the Executive Director, **NZ Golf Association,** Box 11–842, Wellington.

Hiking If you want to see the very best the country has to offer, put on a pair of walking boots and head for the hills. Range upon range of mountains; deep, ice-carved valleys; wilderness areas that have never been farmed, logged, or grazed; and a first-class network of marked trails and tramping huts are just some of the reasons that hiking is a national addiction.

The traditional way to hike in New Zealand is freedom walking. Freedom walkers carry their own provisions, sleeping bags, food, and cooking gear, and sleep in basic huts. A more refined alternative—usually available only on the more popular trails—is the guided walk, on which you trek with just a light day pack, guides do the cooking, and you sleep in heated lodges. If you prefer your wilderness served with hot showers and an eiderdown on your bed, the guided walk is for you.

There are almost 900 **back country huts** in New Zealand; they provide basic shelter but few frills. Huts are usually placed about four hours apart, although in isolated areas it can take a full day to get from one hut to the next. They are graded 1 to 4, and the cost varies from nothing to $14 per person per night. Category 1 huts (the $14 ones) have cooking equipment and fuel, bunks or sleeping platforms with mattresses, toilets, washing facilities, and a supply of water. At the other end of the scale, Category 4 huts (the free ones) are simple shelters without bunks or other facilities. Payment is by coupons, available in books from Department of Conservation offices. If you plan to make extensive use of huts, an annual pass giving access to all Category 2 and 3 huts for one year is available for $58.

The most popular walks are located in the Southern Alps, where the postcard views of mountains, wild rivers, mossy beech forests, and fjords issue a challenge to the legs that is hard to resist. The trekking season in the mountains usually lasts from October to mid-April. The best-known of all New Zealand's trails is the **Milford Track,** a four-day walk through breathtaking scenery to the edge of Milford Sound. Its main drawback is its popularity. This is the only track in New Zealand on which numbers are controlled: You are required to obtain a permit and to begin walking on the day specified (to ensure that the overnight huts along the track don't become impossibly crowded). If you plan to walk the Milford in December or January, book at least six months in advance; at other times, three months is usually sufficient. (If you arrive without a booking, there are sometimes last-minute cancellations, and parties of one or two can often be accommodated.) The Milford Track is closed from the end of April to early September. Bookings, either as a freedom walker or on a guided walk, can be made by contacting the THC Milford Track Office, THC Te Anau Resort Hotel, Box 185, Te Anau, tel. 03/249–7411.

While the Milford gets the lion's share of publicity, many other walks offer a similar—some would say better—combination of scenery and exercise. The **Routeburn Track** is a three-day walk that rises through beech forests, traverses a mountain face across a high pass, and descends through a glacial valley. The

Kepler and the **Hollyford** are both exceptional, and the **Abel Tasman,** at the northern end of the South Island, is a spectacular three-to-four-day coastal track that can be walked year-round.

Clothing and footwear are major considerations. Even at the height of summer the weather can change quickly, and hikers must be prepared—especially for the rainstorms that regularly drench the Southern Alps. (The Milford Sound region, with its average annual rainfall of 160 inches, is one of the wettest places on earth.) The most cost-effective rain gear you can buy is the U.S. Army poncho. For more information, contact Routeburn Walk Ltd. (Box 185, Te Anau, tel. 03/249–7411) or Abel Tasman National Park Enterprises (Old Cedarman House, Main Rd., Riwaka, Motueka RD3, tel. 03/528–7801).

Skiing New Zealand has 27 peaks that top the 10,000-foot mark, and the June–October ski season is the reason many skiers head "down under" when the snow melts in the northern hemisphere. On the South Island, the site of most of the country's 13 commercial skifields, the outstanding areas are **Treble Cone and Cardrona,** served by the town of Wanaka, and **Coronet Peak and the Remarkables,** close to Queenstown. The North Island has only two commercial skifields, **Whakapapa and Turoa,** both near Lake Taupo on the slopes of Mount Ruapehu. Lift prices average about $40 per day.

What the New Zealand skifields lack is sophistication. By international standards they are comparatively small, and the slopes lack the extensive interlocking lift systems that are a feature of European skiing. There is no such thing as snowfield accommodation: Skiers must stay in one of the nearby subalpine towns.

Heliskiing is very popular. Harris Mountains Heliski, the second largest heliski operation in the world, gives access from the town of Wanaka to more than 200 runs on more than 100 peaks accessible to skiers by no other means. The ultimate heliski adventure is the 13-kilometer (8½-mile) run down the Tasman Glacier, available from Glentanner Park, near Mount Cook Village.

Beaches

The list of great New Zealand beaches is almost endless. There are no private beaches, no risks from pollution; the greatest danger is sunburn. Most New Zealanders prefer the beaches along the east coast of the North Island, where the combination of gentle seas and balmy summers is a powerful attraction in the January holidays. During the summer months, popular beaches close to the cities and in major holiday areas are patrolled by lifeguards. Swim with caution on unpatrolled beaches.

Dining

Auckland, Wellington, and Christchurch offer cosmopolitan dining, but, apart from a few expensive sporting lodges, most country cooking still gets its recipes from the meat-and-two-veg school of English cuisine. The country's greatest culinary asset is its raw materials. The lamb and the New Zealand crayfish, often known as spiny or rock lobster, are delicious, and the succulent, white-shelled Bluff oysters, available from March to about July, are rated highly by gourmets. Watch for orange roughy, a delicate white-fleshed fish that is at its best with a light sauce. Venison is widely available.

A New Zealand specialty is the *hangi*, the Maori feast of steamed meat and vegetables. Several hotels in Rotorua offer a hangi, usually combined with an evening of Maori song and dance. (These days it's unlikely that the food will be cooked by steaming it in the traditional hot earth oven.)

The difference in price between a reasonable meal and a very good one is often not great. A three-course meal for two at an average restaurant will cost at least $50, while a meal for two at a top restaurant, such as Auckland's French Café, will cost less than $80. For cheap lunches, the standard take-aways are meat pies and fish and chips. Most country pubs serve inexpensive cooked lunches and sometimes a selection of salads. In season, stock up on fruit from the roadside stalls scattered throughout the country's fruitgrowing areas.

New Zealand wines can be excellent, but there are few bargains. Hawke's Bay and Marlborough are the premier winegrowing regions. Some restaurants are not licensed to serve alcohol, but diners are welcome to bring their own; check when reserving a table.

Lodging

The New Zealand Tourism Board publishes an annual *Where to Stay* directory listing more 1,000 properties.

Motels Motels are by far the most common accommodations, and most offer comfortable rooms for $60–$90 per night. Some motels have two-bedroom suites for families. All motel rooms come equipped with tea- and coffee-making facilities, many have toasters or electric frying pans, and full kitchen facilities are not uncommon.

Home and Farm Stays If you want more than just a bed for the night, farm stays and home stays are a great way to get to know the land and its people. Farm-stay guests can generally expect to share meals with the family and share in the farmwork if they feel inclined. For two people, the average cost is $90–$150 per night, including all meals. Home stays, the urban equivalent of farm stays, are less expensive. For a list, contact **New Zealand Farm Holidays Ltd.** (Box 256, Silverdale, Auckland, tel. 09/307–2024) or **Homestay Ltd. Farmstay Ltd.** (Box 25–115, Auckland, tel. 09/55–5980).

Tourist Cabins and Flats The least expensive accommodations are the tourist cabins and flats in most of New Zealand's 400 motor camps. Tourist cabins offer basic accommodation and shared cooking, laundry, and bathroom facilities. Bedding and towels are not provided. A notch higher up the comfort scale, tourist flats usually provide bedding, fully equipped kitchens, and private bathrooms. Overnight tariffs run about $6–$20 for cabins and $25–$70 for flats.

Sporting Lodges At the other end of the price scale, a number of luxury sporting lodges offer the best of country life plus fine dining and superb accommodation. Fishing is a specialty at most, but there is usually a range of outdoor activities for nonanglers. Tariffs run about $350–$700 per day for two people; meals are generally included.

Credit Cards

The following credit card abbreviations are used: AE, American Express; DC, Diner's Club; MC, MasterCard; V, Visa.

Great Itineraries

Highlights of the North and South Islands

New Zealand is an experience to be savored, not rushed, but if a one-week visit is all you can manage, this itinerary will introduce you to the main attractions of both islands.

Length 7 days

The Main Route **Day 1:** Arrive in Auckland and explore the city. Take an evening ferry ride across the harbor to Devonport.
Day 2: Travel to the Waitomo Caves; tour the Glow-worm Cave and hike the Waitomo Walkway, then continue to Rotorua.
Day 3: Take the Waimangu Round Trip day tour, finish off with a soak in the Polynesian Pools, then take in a Maori hangi.
Day 4: Catch the morning flight to Mount Cook. Hike along the Hooker Valley and watch the sun set over the Southern Alps.
Day 5: Take an early-morning scenic flight around the Southern Alps with a glacier landing; then travel to Queenstown. Explore Arrowtown.
Day 6: Join a day tour to Milford Sound with a midday cruise, returning to Queenstown in the evening.
Day 7: Fly to Christchurch and explore the city center. Spend your last afternoon shopping for souvenirs in the Galleria.

Experiencing New Zealand

For anyone who wants to hike, canoe, fish, and explore some of the less well-known attractions, 10 days on each island is a practical minimum. This tour includes the main cities as well as the country's natural splendors, with emphasis on wildlife.

Length 20 days

The Main Route **Day 1:** Arrive in and explore Auckland. Take an evening ferry to Devonport and dine on the waterfront.
Day 2: Travel north to the Bay of Islands. Explore the Treaty House, and cross by ferry to spend the night in Russell.
Day 3: Explore Russell and take a catamaran trip out to Cape Brett, followed by an evening fishing trip.
Day 4: Travel to the Coromandel Peninsula via Auckland.
Day 5: Explore the seascapes and wilderness of the Coromandel Peninsula, preferably on a half-day tour with Doug Johansen. Travel to Rotorua in the late afternoon.
Day 6: Take the Waimangu Round Trip day tour. End with a mineral bath, and spend the evening at a Maori hangi.
Day 7: Travel to Taupo and view the thermal infernos along the way. Spend the evening on a sightseeing cruise of the lake, or trawling in champion trout territory.
Day 8: Travel to Napier and explore the city's art deco architecture and the surrounding wineries.
Day 9: Travel to Wellington and explore the national capital.

Day 10: Cross to the South Island by ferry, then travel to Nelson along the edge of the Marlborough Sounds.

Day 11: Join a one-day guided cruise along the coastline of the Abel Tasman National Park, with a flight back at the end.

Day 12: Travel to the west coast glacier country and spend the night at Franz Josef.

Day 13: Take an early scenic flight across the glaciers and Mount Cook, the highest peak in the country, or join a glacier-walking party. Travel on to Lake Moeraki Lodge and spend the evening canoeing on the lake.

Day 14: Join a beach tour from Lake Moeraki Lodge to see the penguins and seals; travel to Queenstown in the afternoon.

Day 15: Explore Queenstown and Arrowtown, go bungy jumping or trail riding, or take the Dart River jetboat safari.

Day 16: Join a one-day tour to Milford Sound, traveling through the spectacular wilderness of Fiordland National Park, followed by a cruise on the sound.

Day 17: Drive to Dunedin and visit the royal albatross colony at Taiaroa Head.

Day 18: Travel to Christchurch and spend the afternoon on a walking tour of the city.

Day 19: Travel to Kaikoura and join a whale-watching expedition. Return to Christchurch in the evening.

Day 20: Explore Akaroa and return to Christchurch for souvenir and duty-free shopping.

South Island Adventure Tour

This action-packed tour takes place against some of the finest natural backdrops in the country. It begins with a biking tour across the Southern Alps to the rugged west coast, travels south to Fiordland National Park for a hike on the Milford Track, and ends with a kayaking and camping trip along the edge of Abel Tasman National Park. While this might sound demanding, both the biking and the Milford Track are guided tours requiring only a moderate level of fitness.

Length 21 days

The Main Route **Day 1:** Arrive at Christchurch. Take a walking tour of the city and stock up on any necessary provisions.

Day 2–10: Join a nine-day Pedaltours Southern Comfort cycling tour, traveling to Queenstown via Arthur's Pass and the west coast glaciers. This tour concludes with a scenic flight to Milford Sound and a cruise.

Day 11: Travel to Te Anau and spend the afternoon preparing for the Milford Track, "the finest walk in the world."

Days 12–15: Walk the Milford Track.

Day 16: Return to Queenstown and spend the rest of the day exploring the surroundings—or bungy jumping, jet boating, or trying any of the other heart-stopping thrills in the area.

Day 17: Take the early-morning flight to Mount Cook. Walk the Hooker Valley and watch the sun set.

Day 18: Fly to Nelson and spend the night in the town.

Days 19–21: Travel to Marahau, hire a kayak, and spend two days along the coastline of the Abel Tasman National Park.

2 Portraits of New Zealand

New Zealand at a Glance: A Chronology

c. AD 750 The first Polynesians arrive, settling mainly in the South Island, where the moa, a flightless bird and an important food source, is concentrated.

950 Kupe, the Polynesian voyager, names the country Aotearoa, "land of the long white cloud." He returns to his native Hawaiki, believed to be present-day French Polynesia.

1300s A population explosion in Hawaiki triggers a wave of immigrants who quickly displace the archaic moa hunters.

1642 Abel Tasman of the Dutch East India Company becomes the first European to sight the land—he names his discovery Nieuw Zeeland. But after several of his crew are killed by Maoris, he sails away without landing.

1769 Captain James Cook becomes the first European to set foot on New Zealand. He takes possession in the name of the British crown.

1790s Sealers, whalers, and timber cutters arrive, plundering the natural wealth and introducing the Maoris to the musket, liquor, and influenza.

1814 The Reverend Samuel Marsden establishes the first mission station, but 11 years will pass before the first convert is made.

1832 James Busby is appointed British Resident, charged with protecting the Maori people and fostering British trade.

1840 Captain William Hobson, representing the crown, and Maori chiefs sign the Treaty of Waitangi. In return for the peaceful possession of their land and the rights and privileges of British citizens, the chiefs recognize British sovereignty.

1840–1841 The New Zealand Company, an association of British entrepreneurs, establishes settlements at Wanganui, New Plymouth, Nelson, and Wellington.

1852 The British parliament passes the New Zealand Constitution Act, establishing limited self-government.

1861 Gold is discovered in the river valleys of central Otago, west of Dunedin.

1860–1872 Maori grievances over loss of land trigger the Land Wars of the North Island. The Maoris win some notable victories, but lack of unity ensures their ultimate defeat. Vast tracts of ancestral land are confiscated from rebel tribes.

1882 The first refrigerated cargo is dispatched to England, giving the country a new source of prosperity—the sheep. A century later, there will be 20 sheep for every New Zealander.

1893 Under the Liberal government, New Zealand becomes the first country to give women the vote.

1914 New Zealand enters World War I.

1931 The Hawke's Bay earthquake kills 258 and levels the city of Napier.

1939 New Zealand enters World War II.

1950 New Zealand troops sail for Korea.

1965 Despite public disquiet, troops are sent to Vietnam.

1973 Britain joins the European Economic Community, and the loss of this traditional export market is reflected in a crippling balance-of-payments deficit two years later.

1981 Violent antigovernment demonstrations erupt during a tour by a South African rugby team.

1985 The Greenpeace ship *Rainbow Warrior* is sunk by a mine in Auckland Harbour and a crewman is killed. Two of the French secret service agents responsible are arrested, jailed, and, shortly afterward, transferred to French custody—from which they are soon released.

Sir Paul Reeves is sworn in as the first Maori Governor-General. The newly elected Labour government of David Lange begins a process of drastic economic reform that includes dismembering the traditional welfare state. The resulting social unrest worsens when unemployment tops 10%.

Relations with the United States sour when the government bans visits by ships carrying nuclear weapons. The U.S. government responds by ejecting New Zealand from the ANZUS alliance.

1989 David Lange resigns as prime minister.

1990 The National Party replaces the Labour Party in government.

From *Return to Paradise*

By James A. Michener

New Zealand is probably the most beautiful country on earth. The official school history says that when Richard John Sedon, the great Prime Minister, died, "he passed on to a better place even than God's Own Country."

The New Zealander finds it difficult to believe that there could be a better land than his, either on earth or in heaven. He is always ready to boast of four national distinctions. "We have a land of unmatched beauty. (True) We have demonstrated that two races of different color can inhabit one land in peace and honor. (True) We showed the world how to pass social legislation for the good of all. (True) And today we enjoy the highest standard of living known by any nation. (False)"

As regards the first claim, the natural beauty of New Zealand is difficult to believe. Its two islands, no larger than Colorado, combine all types of alluring scenery, all kinds of climates. Consider what you could see in one day's travel.

At the northern tip of North Island you find a dazzling tropical beach sixty miles long. (New Zealanders call it Ninety Mile Beach.) It ends in a cluster of handsome islands around which sport immense marlin and swordfish. Farther south are prehistoric sub-tropical forests with towering kauri pines that took 1500 years to mature. In the center of North Island is a brooding desert surmounted by three majestic volcanoes, one or the other of which seems always to be active, spouting lava ash by day and beacon fires at night. At Rotorua the wonders of Yellowstone Park are challenged, for here geysers play, mud pools bubble and hot waters tumble down over colored terraces.

On the west coast you will see Mount Egmont, rising in beauty, the perfect snow-capped cone of a dead volcano, cloud wreathed and pointed like Fujiyama. But in New Zealand you always say, "Fujiyama looks a lot like Mount Egmont."

Now you leave the North Island and fly south across Cook Strait, where vast mountains sank into the sea until only their tips remained aloft. Here earth and ocean mingle in astonishing beauty, varied, twisted, glowing in the sunlight.

Ahead lies South Island, where the real beauty of New Zealand is found. Here Mount Cook rises more than 12,000 feet, perpetually glaciated, with huge fingers of ice reaching almost into the sea. Nearby are the Southern Alps, immense rows of jagged peaks beneath which nestle dozens of wonderful lakes, each serving as a mirror for some great range of mountains.

On the coast, near the glaciers, you find dramatic evidence of New Zealand's turbulent geological history. During millions of years this land rose and fell repeatedly. When it lay under the sea, sand covered it. When it was thrust upward, limestone deposits collected. Finally the resulting rocks were forced high into the air, where howling winds eroded the sandstone layers and left tall rounded pillars of limestone wafers piled one upon the other, appropriately called The Pancakes. And then, since New Zealand scenery is completely prodigal in its wonders, the hungry Tasman Sea ate huge caverns beneath The Pancakes into which tides roar, bursting upward through crevices and shooting thin strands of spray high into the air.

Farther south lies Milford Sound, first and finest of the fjords. Cutting deep inland, it is enclosed by brooding and majestic peaks. High waterfalls plunge from mountain plateaus directly into its waters, and jagged bays probe into dark forests. At the head of one such indentation Sutherland Falls leaps nearly 2,000 feet down into a solemn glen, one of the superb waterfalls of the world. Almost inaccessible, it is reached by means of a difficult trail labeled on maps "The World's Finest Walk." Along ten casual miles I counted forty sheer granite cliffs, each at least 800 feet high, three of them dropping precipitously for more than a thousand feet. I also saw at least 200 waterfalls, some of them hundreds of feet high. One unnamed one—there are so many wonders in this part of New Zealand that they are not even recorded—fell 300 feet and then leaped backward, borne aloft on surging currents of air. Another zigzagged eight times to get down a cliff face. A third fell some hundred feet, then dashed upon a huge projecting boulder which split the fall and threw each half high into the air, so that the falling plumes looked like two Grecian horses plunging into battle. At no point in the ten miles did I fail to see at least three waterfalls. Frequently more than ten were visible. And this was in the dry season!

In the same ten miles there were other spectacular phenomena so far unnamed: a cataract that has gnawed its way sixty feet through solid rock, leaving at the land's surface a gorge only 36 inches across; a tiny lake of perfect ultramarine; a balanced boulder bigger than a cathedral; a walled valley hidden in circles of granite cliff. And often above me flamed that most brilliant tree, the pohutukawa, at the end of whose branches grow massive clusters of scarlet flowers, so that sometimes the forest seemed to be on fire.

On even the best maps the land south of Milford Sound is marked UNEXPLORED. New Zealand has dozens of fjords still to be opened to travel. It has hundreds of natural wonders still to be discovered. One who knows the region said,

"For the rest of this century my country could open up each year some new spectacle that would astonish the eye."

Proof of this came dramatically in 1949. New Zealand is geologically a recent land and has few animals that resemble those found elsewhere. It does, however, have some that are unique. Among those still living is the kiwi, a long-billed, flightless bird that has become the national symbol. (New Zealand fighting men are Kiwis.) Now almost extinct, the kiwi is famous for two qualities: it feeds by stomping its feet over worm holes to imitate rain, thus luring the hors d'oeuvre into position; and it lays an egg of ridiculous size. If a hen were to do comparatively as well, chicken eggs would be 14 inches long and would weigh three pounds each!

The most famous of New Zealand's extinct creatures was the moa, a gigantic bird that towered above the heads of men who liked its rich meat so much they exterminated it about 150 years ago. (There's a great fight on about this, some scholars maintaining that moas were never seen after 1350.) Another of the extinct birds was the notornis, a beautiful turkey-like creature with blue-green feathers and a brilliant red toucan-like bill. The last one was seen in 1898, a previous specimen having been eaten by ship-wrecked sailors some years before.

Then in 1949 some explorers in the wild southern valleys came upon a family of notornis that had miraculously survived. Cautious investigators probed the area and discovered perhaps fifty of the handsome fowl. A surge of excitement swept across the scientific world and other expeditions were hastily outfitted. Warned the Government: "It is ridiculous to call these excursions moa hunts. No moa could possibly be alive in New Zealand." But the scientists point out that there used to be a dwarf moa and in most bars you can get even money that sooner or later a moa is going to turn up in those southern valleys marked UNEXPLORED.

3 Auckland and the North

By Michael Gebicki

Auckland, with a population of more than 800,000, is the largest city in New Zealand and the country's major gateway. It's the only city in the nation large enough to have a traffic problem (though one most international cities would envy), and your first impressions will probably be of calm, cleanliness, and a fertility that extends into the heart of the city. The drive from the airport will take you past the tall cones of extinct volcanoes, where grass as green and smooth as a billiards table is cropped by four-footed lawnmowers known as sheep.

Chances are that along the way you'll pass knots of cyclists and joggers. Aucklanders, like all New Zealanders, are addicted to the outdoors. There are some 70,000 powerboats and sailing craft in the Greater Auckland area—about one for every four households. Within an hour's drive of the city center are 102 beaches. Yet the city has not been kind to its greatest asset, Waitemata Harbour—a Maori name meaning "Sea of Sparkling Waters." Where there should be harborfront parks edged with palm trees and gardens, there are dockyards and warehouses instead.

Auckland is not an easy city to explore: It sprawls across its isthmus, with the Pacific Ocean on one side and the Tasman Sea on the other. If you arrive at the end of a long flight and time is limited, the best introduction to the city is the commuter ferry that crosses the harbor to Devonport, where you can soak up the atmosphere in a leisurely stroll.

Beyond Auckland, the Bay of Islands, to the north, is an area that's both beautiful and—as the place where modern New Zealand came into being with the signing of the Treaty of Waitangi in 1840—historic. Finally, off in a different direction, we outline a drive around the rugged and exhilarating Coramandel Peninsula.

Auckland

Important Addresses and Numbers

Tourist Information

Auckland Visitor Information Centre. *Aotea Sq., Queen and Myers Sts., tel. 09/366–6888. Open Mon.–Wed. and Fri. 8:30–5:30, Tues. 9:30–5:30, weekends 9–4.*

Published every Thursday, *Auckland Tourist Times* is a free newspaper with the latest information on tours, exhibitions, and shopping. The paper is available from hotels and from the Visitor Information Centre.

Consulates

U.S. Consulate. *General Assurance Bldg., Shortland and O'Connell Sts., tel. 09/303-2724. Open weekdays 8-4:30.*

British Consulate. *Fay Richwhite Bldg., 151 Queen St., tel. 09/303-2971. Open weekdays 9:30–12:20.*

Canadian Consulate. *Princes Court, 2 Princes St., tel. 09/309–8516. Open weekdays 8:30–4:30.*

Australian Consulate. *Union House, 32–38 Quay St., tel. 09/303-2429. Open weekdays 8:30–4:45.*

Emergencies

Dial 111 for **fire, police,** or **ambulance** services.

Hospital Emergency Rooms

Auckland Hospital. *Park Rd., Grafton City, tel. 09/379–7440. Open daily 24 hrs.*

Doctors **Auckland Accident and Emergency Clinic.** *122 Remuera Rd., tel. 09/524–5943 or 09/524–7906. Open daily 24 hrs.*

Dentists For emergency dental services, telephone **St John's Ambulance** and ask for the nearest dentist on duty. *Tel. 09/579–9099. Open daily 24 hrs.*

Where to Change Money The Bank of New Zealand branch inside the international terminal of Auckland International Airport is open for all arriving and departing flights. There are several currency-exchange agencies at the lower end of Queen Street, between Victoria and Customs streets, offering the same rate as the banks (weekdays 9–5, Sat. 9–1; closed Sun.). Foreign currency may also be exchanged daily 8–4 at the cashier's office above Celebrity Walk, at the Drake Street entrance of Victoria Park Market (tel. 09/309–6911).

Late-night Pharmacy **The Late-night Pharmacy.** *60 Broadway, tel. 09/520–6634. Open weekdays 5:30 PM–7 AM, weekends 9 AM–7 AM.*

Travel Agencies **American Express Travel Service.** *95 Queen St., tel. 09/379–8243.*

Thomas Cook. *10–12 Commerce St., tel. 09/379–3924.*

Arriving and Departing by Plane

Airport **Auckland International Airport** lies 21 kilometers (13 miles) southwest of the city center. The nearby **Visitor Information Centre** provides free maps and brochures as well as a booking service for tours and accommodation (open 5 AM–2 AM). Avis, Budget, and Hertz have offices inside the international terminal. A blue-and-white **Interterminal Bus** (cost: $2) links the international and domestic terminals, with frequent departures in each direction 6 AM–10 PM. Alternatively, the walk between the two terminals takes about 10 minutes along the signposted walkway. Luggage for flights aboard the two major domestic airlines, Air New Zealand and Ansett New Zealand, can be checked in at the international terminal.

Airlines Major international carriers serving Auckland include **American Airlines** (tel. 09/309–9159), **British Airways** (tel. 09/367–7500), **Canadian Airlines International** (tel. 09/309–0735), **Continental Airlines** (tel. 09/379–5680), **Qantas Airways** (tel. 09/379–0306), and **United Airlines** (tel. 09/379–3800).

Domestic carriers with services to Auckland are **Air New Zealand** (tel. 09/379–3000), **Air Nelson** (tel. 09/379–3510), **Ansett New Zealand** (tel. 09/302–2146), and **Mount Cook Airlines** (tel. 09/309–5395).

Between the Airport and City Center The journey between the airport and the city center takes about 30 minutes.

By Bus **Johnston's Shuttle Express** (tel. 09/256–0333) operates a minibus service between the airport and any address in the city center. The cost is $12 for a single traveler, $9 per person for two traveling together. The service meets all incoming flights.

The **Airporter Bus Service** leaves the international terminal every 30 minutes between 6:30 AM and 8 PM. The fixed route between the airport and the Downtown Airline Terminal, on the corner of Quay Street and Albert Road, includes a stop at the railway station and, on request, at any bus stop along the way. Returning from the city, the bus leaves the Downtown Airline Terminal at 30-minute intervals between 6:45 AM and 8:45 PM. *Cost: $9 adults, $3 children 5–14.*

By Taxi The fare to the city is between $30 and $35.

By Limousine **Gateway Limousines and Tours** (tel. 09/528–9198) operates Ford LTD limousines between the airport and the city. The cost is approximately $60.

Arriving and Departing by Car, Train, and Bus

By Car By the standards of most cities, Auckland's traffic is light, parking space is inexpensive and readily available, and motorways pass close to the heart of the city. On the other hand, unless your accommodation is some distance from the city, there's no real advantage in having a car of your own.

By Train The terminal for all InterCity train services is **Auckland Central Railway Station** (tel. 09/358–4085) on Beach Road, about 1 mile east of the city center. A booking office is located inside the Auckland Visitor Information Centre at 299 Queen Street.

By Bus The terminal for **InterCity Coaches** (tel. 09/358–4085) is the Auckland Central Railway Station (*see* above). **Newmans Coaches** (tel. 09/309–9738) arrive and depart from the Downtown Airline Terminal, on the corner of Quay and Albert streets.

Getting Around

By Bus Auckland's public bus system, the **Yellow Bus Company,** operates Monday–Saturday 6 AM–11:30 PM, Sunday 9 AM–5 PM. The main terminal for public buses is the **Municipal Transport Station,** between Commerce Street and Britomart Place near the Central Post Office. The bus network is divided into zones; fares are calculated according the number of zones traveled. For travel within the inner city, the fare is 40¢ for adults, 20¢ for children 5–15. **BusAbout passes,** which allow unlimited travel on all buses after 9 AM daily, are available from bus drivers for $8 adults, $4 children. For timetables, bus routes, fares, and lost property, stop by the **Bus Place,** on the corner of Hobson and Victoria streets (weekdays 8:15–5), or call **Buz A Bus** (tel. 09/366–6400, Mon.–Sat. 7–7).

By Taxi Taxis can be hailed in the street but are more readily available from the cab ranks located throughout the city. Auckland taxis operate on a two-tier tariff system—a green rate, weekdays 6 AM–10 PM, and a red rate at all other times. The red tariff is about 25¢ per kilometer higher than the green rate. Most taxis will accept American Express, Diners, MasterCard, or Visa cards. **Alert Taxis** (tel. 09/309–2000), **Auckland Cooperative Taxi Service** (tel. 09/300–3000), and **Eastern Taxis** (tel. 09/527–7077) are reliable operators with radio-controlled fleets.

Guided Tours

Orientation The most economical introduction to Auckland is the **United Airlines Explorer Bus.** The blue-and-red double-decker bus travels in a circuit, stopping at seven of the city's major attractions; passengers can leave at any stop and reboard any following Explorer bus. The buses depart the Downtown Airline

Terminal every hour between 10 and 4 daily; tickets are available from the driver. *Fares: $10 adults, $5 children 5–15.*

Scenic Tours (tel. 09/634–0189) operates a three-hour *City Sights* guided bus tour, which takes in the main attractions in the city and Parnell and the view from the lookout on Mount Eden. Tours leave at 9:30 and 2, and tickets are $32 adults, $16 children 5–14, $5 children 2–4. The **Grey Line** (tel. 09/377–0904) operates a Morning Highlights tour, which includes admission to Kelly Tarlton's Underwater World (*see* What to See and Do with Children, below). This tour departs daily from the Downtown Airline Terminal on Quay Street at 9:15 and costs $35 adults, $17.50 children 5–14.

Special-Interest Tours   The **Antipodean Explorer** (tel. 09/521–9150) offers a minibus tour of the wineries of West Auckland, and a sampling of wines made from kiwi fruit as well as grapes. The six-hour trip includes a drive through the rain forest of the Waitakere Ranges west of Auckland. It costs $55 and departs daily at 9:30 from the Downtown Airline Terminal.

Boat Tours   Various companies offer cruises of Waitemata Harbor; one of the best and least expensive is the **Devonport commuter ferry.** The ferry terminal is located on the harbor side of the Ferry Building on Quay Street, near the corner of Albert Street. Ferries depart 6:15 to 10 on Sunday, till 11 Monday–Thursday, till midnight Friday and Saturday. *Round-trip tickets: $6 adults, $3 children 5–15.*

The **Pride of Auckland Company** (tel. 09/373–4557) operates lunch and dinner sailing cruises on the inner harbor, departing at 12:30 and 6 from the wharf opposite the Downtown Airline Terminal on the corner of Quay and Albert streets. *Tickets: $44 lunch, $73 dinner.*

Fullers Cruise Centre (tel. 09/377–1771) offers a variety of cruises of the harbor and to the islands of the Hauraki Gulf. The 90-minute coffee cruise ($18 adults, $8 children 4–14) departs daily at 2:30. The Supercat cruise ($50 adults, $25 children) to Great Barrier Island, the most distant of the Hauraki Gulf Islands, is a popular day trip for Aucklanders. The cruise departs Tuesday, Thursday, and weekends at 9.

Exploring Auckland

Numbers in the margin correspond to points of interest on the Auckland map.

❶ This walk begins at the **Civic Theatre** on the corner of Queen and Wellesley streets, one block down Queen Street from the Visitor Information Centre. This extravagant art nouveau movie theater was the talk of the town when it opened in 1929, but just nine months later the owner, Thomas O'Brien, went bust and fled, taking with him the week's revenues and an usherette. During World War II a cabaret show in the basement was popular with Allied servicemen in transit to the battlefields of the Pacific. One of the entertainers, Freda Stark, is said to have appeared regularly wearing nothing more than a coat of gold paint.

❷ Walk up Wellesley Street toward the white building with the clock on top. This is the **Auckland City Art Gallery,** which houses the country's finest collection of contemporary art as

Auckland

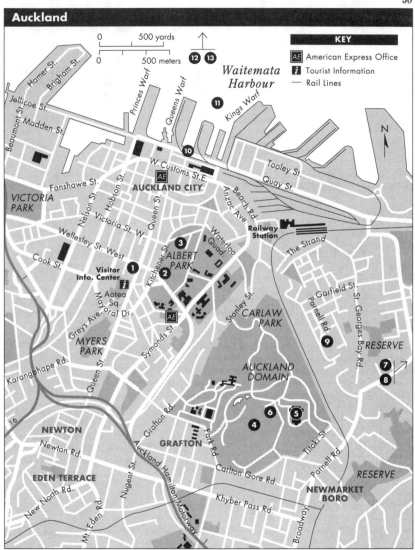

0   500 yards

0   500 meters

KEY

AE American Express Office

ℹ Tourist Information

— Rail Lines

Waitemata Harbour

VICTORIA PARK

Fanshawe St.

Hamer St.

Brigham St.

Jellicoe St.

Beaumont St.

Madden St.

Princes Warf

Queens Warf

Kings Warf

Tooley St.

Quay St.

W.Customs St.E.

AUCKLAND CITY

Nelson St.

Hobson St.

Victoria St. W.

Queen St.

Wellesley St. West

Cook St.

Visitor Info. Center

Aotea Sq.

Greys Ave.

Mayoral Dr.

MYERS PARK

Karangahape Rd.

Queen St.

Symonds St.

Kitchener St.

ALBERT PARK

Waterloo Quad.

Beach Rd.

Anzac Ave.

Railway Station

The Strand

Garfield St.

St. Georges Bay Rd.

Stanley St.

CARLAW PARK

Parnell Rd.

RESERVE

AUCKLAND DOMAIN

Grafton Rd.

Park Rd.

GRAFTON

Auckland Hamilton Motorway

Newton Rd.

NEWTON

Mt. Eden Rd.

New North Rd.

EDEN TERRACE

Nugent St.

Carlton Gore Rd.

Titoki St.

Parnell Rd.

Khyber Pass Rd.

Broadway

NEWMARKET BORO

RESERVE

N

Index

well as paintings of New Zealand dating back to the time of Captain Cook. Watch for works by Frances Hodgkins, New Zealand's best-known artist. *Corner Kitchener and Wellesley St. East, tel. 09/379-2020. Admission free. Open 10-4:30.*

③ Turn into Kitchener Street, walk past the fountain, and climb the stone stairs on the right. At the top is **Albert Park,** 15 acres of formal gardens, fountains, and statue-studded lawns. The park is built on the site of a garrison that was intended to protect the settlement from the neighboring Maori tribes. There are still remnants of its stone walls (with rifle slits) behind the university buildings on the eastern side of the park.

④ Leave the park and cross onto Alfred Street. Continue downhill and at the bottom cross Stanley Street and take the red path that climbs into the **Auckland Domain.** This rolling, 340-acre park is a favorite leisure space for Aucklanders. The hillside you are climbing is the side of an extinct volcano, Pukekawa, and the track is part of the Coast to Coast Walkway, a 13-kilometer (8-mile) track that spans the isthmus between the Pacific Ocean on the east and the Tasman Sea on the west.

⑤ At the top of the path, off to the left, is the sprawling gray **War Memorial Museum.** The museum is known especially for its Maori artifacts, the largest and finest collection of its kind. The portraits of Maori chiefs by C. F. Goldie are splendid character studies of a fiercely martial people. Other collections in the museum are dedicated to natural history, geology, military history, and a reconstructed streetscape of early Auckland. *Auckland Domain, tel. 09/309-0443. Admission free. Open daily 10-5.*

⑥ Leave the museum by the front door, pausing for a fine view of Waitemata Harbour with Rangitoto Island to the right. Turn left and walk down toward the twin domed buildings. These are the greenhouses of the **Wintergardens,** housing an exotic collection of tropical plants and palms. The wisteria-covered loggia surrounding the sunken courtyard is a shady spot for a rest on a warm day. *Auckland Domain. Admission free. Open daily 10-4.*

⑦ Return to the museum, walk past the entrance and on to the back of the building, and follow the road down the hill past the Parnell Lawn Tennis Club. Continue as this road becomes Maunsell Road, turn left into Parnell Road, and turn right at Ayr Street. Behind a white picket fence on the left is **Ewelme Cottage,** built by the Reverend Vicesimus Lush and inhabited by his descendants for more than a century. The house is constructed of kauri, a resilient timber highly prized by the Maoris for their war canoes. With the arrival of Europeans, kauri became the basic building material for the new settlement, and the kauri forests were rapidly depleted. All kauris are now protected by law, but only a few majestic examples of mature ones remain in the forests. Ewelme Cottage contains much of the original furniture and personal effects of the Lush family. *14 Ayr St., tel. 09/379-0202. Admission: $2 adults, 50¢ children 5-15. Open daily 10:30-noon and 1-4:30.*

⑧ Return to Parnell Road and turn right. The splendid white church on the right is the Anglican **Cathedral Church of St Mary,** built in 1886 and regarded as one of the world's finest examples of a Gothic wooden church. This is one of a number of churches built by Bishop Selwyn, an early Anglican missionary bishop. The craftsmanship inside the church is remarkable, but just as remarkable is the story of the church's relocation. St Mary's originally stood on the other side of Parnell Road, but in 1982 the entire structure was jacked up, placed on a bed of steel girders, put on rollers, and hauled across to the other side. Photographs inside show the progress of the work. The church now forms part of the Cathedral of the Holy Trinity. *Parnell Rd. and St. Stephen's Ave. Open daily 8–6.*

Just below the intersection of St Stephens Road, the streetscape suddenly changes character. This is the beginning of **Parnell Village,** an avenue of pretty Victorian timber villas that have been transformed into antiques shops, designer boutiques, street cafés, and restaurants. Parnell Village is the creation of Les Harvey, who saw the potential of the quaint but rundown shops and houses and almost single-handedly snatched them from the jaws of the developers' bulldozers by buying them, renovating them, and leasing them out. Harvey's vision has paid handsome dividends, and today this village of trim pink-and-white timber facades is a delightful part of the city. At night its restaurants, pubs, and discos attract Auckland's smart set. Parnell is also one of the few places in Auckland where the shops are open Sunday.

Time Out At the heart of Parnell Village, **Konditorei Boss** is a pleasant and inexpensive sidewalk café selling open sandwiches, soups, salads, and a wicked but irresistible collection of cakes. There is no table service; walk inside and make your selection from the counter. *305 Parnell Rd., Parnell, tel. 09/377–8953. Open daily 8–5.*

Find the United Airlines Explorer Bus stop, about 50 yards above Konditorei Boss, and take the next bus to the Downtown Airline Terminal ($1 adults, 50¢ children 5–15). Explorer buses depart this stop at 10:45 and then at one-hour intervals until 4:45.

At the terminal, cross Quay Street to the imposing **Ferry Building** and purchase a ferry ticket for Devonport ($6 adults, $3 children 5–15 round-trip). Ferries leave for Devonport weekdays on the hour between 10 and 3, and at half-hour intervals during the morning and evening commuter periods; on Saturday they leave on the hour from 7 AM until midnight, on Sunday until 10.

The 20-minute ride to Devonport across **Waitemata Harbour** provides one of the finest views of Auckland. The first harbor ferry service began with whaleboats in 1854. Later in the century the Devonport Steam Ferry Co. began operations, and ferries scuttled back and forth across the harbor until the Harbour Bridge opened in 1959. The bridge now carries the bulk of the commuter traffic, but the ferry still has a small, devoted clientele.

From the Devonport wharf, cross Marine Square and walk along **Victoria Road.** Devonport, the first settlement on the north side of the harbor, was originally known as Flagstaff, after the signal station on the summit of Mount Victoria. Later the area drew some of the city's wealthiest traders, who built their homes where they could watch their sailing ships arriving with cargoes from Europe. These days the village of Devonport has a relaxed, seaside atmosphere, despite its proximity to the city.

Walk away from the harbor along Victoria Street, past the shops and cafés that line this pleasant avenue. At the end of the street, bear right into Kerr Street and turn left to climb **Mount Victoria.** Don't be put off by the name—this is more molehill than mountain. Long before the era of European settlement, this ancient volcano was the site of a Maori *pa*, a fortified village of the local Kawerau tribe. On the northern and eastern flanks of the hill you can still see traces of the terraces that palisades of sharpened stakes once protected.

Return to the ferry terminal via Victoria Road. On weekdays, ferries leave for the city every hour on the half hour between 9:30 and 2:30, and every half hour during the morning and evening commuter periods. On weekends, ferries leave Devonport at 6:30 AM, then every hour on the half hour until 9:30 PM. The last boat leaves Devonport at 11:30 PM Monday–Thursday and Saturday, 12:15 on Friday, and 9:30 PM on Sunday.

Auckland for Free

On weekdays during the spring and summer months, **Aotea Square** becomes the venue for a series of free outdoor performances by groups ranging from classical string quartets to jazz artists to Pacific Islander dance companies. The one-hour performances generally begin at 12:30. For recorded "what's on" information, phone the **Aotea Centre Hotline** (tel. 09/309–2678). *BNZ Foyer, Aotea Square, Queen St. near Myers St.*

What to See and Do with Children

Kelly Tarlton's Underwater World. The creation of New Zealand's most celebrated undersea explorer and treasure hunter, this harborside marine park offers a fish-eye view of the sea without getting wet. The main attraction is a submerged transparent tunnel, 120 yards long, where a slowmoving walkway makes a circuit while moray eels and lobsters peer from rock caverns and sharks and stingrays glide overhead. *Orakei Wharf, 23 Tamaki Dr., tel. 09/528–0603. Admission: $10 adults, $5 children 4–12. Open daily 9 AM–9 PM.*

Museum of Transport and Technology. This fascinating collection of aircraft, telephones, cameras, locomotives, steam engines, and farming equipment is a tribute to Kiwi ingenuity. One of the most intriguing exhibits is the remains of an aircraft built by Robert Pearse, who made a successful powered flight barely three months after the Wright brothers first took to the skies. The flight ended inauspiciously when his plane crashed into a hedge, but Pearse, considered a wild eccentric by his farming neighbors, is recognized today as a mechanical genius. *Great North Rd., Western Springs, tel. 09/846–0199. Admission: $8.50 adults, $4.50 children 5–15. Open weekdays 9–5, weekends 10–5.*

Off the Beaten Track

On Friday and Saturday after 7 PM, the regular Devonport ferry is replaced by the **MV** *Kestrel,* a turn-of-the-century ferry restored to its brassy splendor and fitted out with a bar and a jazz band ($6 adults, $3 children 5–15). For a night to remember, leave the ferry at Devonport, stop off for a drink at the Esplanade Hotel across from the ferry terminal, and have dinner at one of the many restaurants along Victoria Road.

Shopping

Shopping Districts Auckland's main shopping precinct for clothes, outdoor gear, duty-free goods, greenstone jewelry, and souvenirs is **Queen Street. Ponsonby,** about 1½ kilometers (1 mile) west of the city center, is known for its antiques shops and fashion boutiques.

Department Stores **Smith and Caughey Ltd.** is Auckland's only department store. *253–261 Queen St., tel. 09/377–4770. Open Mon.–Thurs. 9–5, Fri. 9–9, Sat. 9–1.*

Street Markets **Victoria Park Market** is Auckland's main bazaar—2½ acres of clothing, footwear, sportswear, furniture, souvenirs, and crafts at knock-down prices. It's housed in the city's former garbage incinerator. The International Foodhall has a range of inexpensive dishes from Thai to Texan. Corner Victoria and Wellesley Sts., tel. 09/309–6911. Open Mon.–Sat. 9–7, Sun. 10–7.

Specialty Stores **Whitcoulls** is a general bookshop with a good selection of New
Books Zealand titles. *186 Queen St., tel. 09/77–8329. Open Mon.– Thurs. 9–5:30, Fri. 9–9, Sat. 9–noon.*

Clothes **Action Downunder** is part of a nationwide chain of stores selling high-quality outdoor clothing for men and women. *75 Queen St., tel. 09/309–0241. Open Mon.–Thurs. 9–5:30, Fri. 9–9, Sat. 9–noon.*
Wool 'n' Threads has a quality selection of knitted woolen garments and woven hangings. *Shop 7, Ferry Bldg., 99 Quay St., City, tel. 09/309–5864. Open daily 9–6.*

Sports and Hiking **Kathmandu** sells quality New Zealand–made clothing and equipment for the outdoor enthusiast. *12 O'Connell St., tel. 09/ 358–2554. Open Mon.–Thurs. 9–5:30, Fri. 9–9., Sat. 9–2, Sun. 10–2.*
Infomaps, published by the Department of Survey and Land Information, are essential equipment for wilderness walkers. The complete range is available from the department's office. *6th floor, AA Centre, corner Albert and Victoria Sts., tel. 09/ 377–1899. Open weekdays 8–4.*

Souvenirs **He Kohinga** specializes in high-quality Maori art, including carved greenstone and wooden bowls and flutes made from native totara. *259 Parnell Rd., tel. 09/366–4585. Open Mon.–Sat. 9–5:30, Sun. 11–4.*
Wild Places sells posters, T-shirts, books, and cards on the themes of whales, rain forests, and native birds. All proceeds go to conservation projects in New Zealand and the Pacific. *28 Lorne St., City, tel. 09/358–0795. Open Mon.–Thurs. 9–5:30, Fri. 9–9, Sat. 9–noon.*

Sports and the Outdoors

Biking Auckland is a pleasant and relaxed city for two-wheeled exploring, especially around its waterfront. **Penny Farthing Cycle Shop** hires out mountain bikes for $25 per day or $100 per week. *Corner Symonds St. and Khyber Pass Rd., tel. 09/379–2524. Open Sept.–Apr., Mon.–Thurs. 8:30–5:30, Fri. 8:30–9, week-*

ends *9:30–3; May–Aug., Mon.–Thurs. 8:30–5:30, Fri. 8:30–9,
Sat. 9:30–3.*

Golf **Chamberlain Park Golf Course** is an 18-hole public course in a
parkland setting a five-minute drive from the city. Clubs and
golf carts can be hired from the club shop. *Linwood Ave., Western Springs, tel. 09/846–6758.*

Titirangi Golf Course, a 15-minute drive south of the city, is one
of the country's finest 18-hole courses. Nonmembers are welcome to play provided they contact the professional in advance
and show evidence of membership at an overseas golf club.
Clubs and golf carts can be hired; the greens fee is $50. *Links
Rd., New Lynn, tel. 09/827–5749.*

Jogging Auckland's favorite running track is **Tamaki Drive,** a 10-
kilometer (6-mile) route that heads east from the city along the
southern shoreline of Waitemata Harbour and ends at St.
Heliers Bay. Close to the city, the **Auckland Domain** (*see* Exploring Auckland, above) is popular with executive lunchtime
joggers.

Tennis **Auckland Tennis Inc.** offers a choice of 12 hard courts, either
indoors or outdoors, a half mile east of the city center. *48 Stanley St., City, tel. 09/373–3623. Cost: $18 per hour outdoors, $13
per hour indoors. Open weekdays 8 AM–10:30 PM, weekends 8–8.*

Swimming **The Tepid Baths,** located near the heart of Auckland, has a
large indoor swimming pool, a spa pool, saunas, and a steam
room. *102 Customs St. West, tel. 09/379–4794. Admission:
$5.50 adults, $3 children under 15; swimming pool only, $3.50
adults, $1.50 children under 15. Open weekdays 6 AM–10 PM,
weekends 7–7.*

Spectator Sports **Eden Park** is the city's major stadium for sporting events. For
information on current events, *Just the Ticket* is a quarterly
guide available from the Visitor Information Centre. Tickets
can be booked through Bass New Zealand (tel. 09/307–5000).

Beaches

Auckland's beaches are commonly categorized by area—East,
West, or North. The ones closest to the city are the east coast
beaches along Tamaki Drive, which are well protected and safe
for children. **Judge's Bay** and **Mission Bay** are particularly recommended for their settings. The best swimming is at high
tide. The west coast beaches are popular in the summer, but
the sea is often rough, and sudden rips and holes can trap the
unwary. The most popular of these is **Piha,** some 40 kilometers
(25 miles) from Auckland, which has pounding surf as well as a
sheltered lagoon dominated by the reclining mass of Lion Rock.
Whatipu, south of Piha, is a broad sweep of sand offering safe
bathing behind the sand bar that guards Manukau Harbour;
while **Bethells,** to the north, is exposed and often subject to
heavy surf. Across Waitemata Harbour from the city, a chain of
magnificent beaches stretches north as far as the Whanga-
paraoa Peninsula, 40 kilometers (25 miles) from Auckland. In
the Hauraki Gulf, the island of **Waiheke** is ringed by a number
of splendid small beaches.

Dining

Highly recommended restaurants are indicated by a star ★.

Category	Cost*
Very Expensive	over $40
Expensive	$30–$40
Moderate	$20–$30
Inexpensive	under $20

*per person, excluding drinks, service, and general sales tax
(12½%)*

Very Expensive **Varick's.** Set in an atmospheric old brick building in a harborside suburb, this modern, stylish restaurant has made its reputation on the strength of its original cuisine. Venison carpaccio with pickled cucumber salad, and grilled goat cheese with an eggplant, tomato, and basil salad are two of the first-course choices on a varied and imaginative menu. Main courses include duck breast with liver and port, and salmon with pine and hazelnut vinaigrette. The restaurant is the home of a much copied dessert known as Death by Chocolate, which is worth saving yourself for. Varick's attracts a sophisticated, dressy clientele. *70 Jervois Rd., Herne Bay, tel. 09/376–2049. Reservations recommended. Dress: casual. AE, DC, MC, V. No lunch Mon., Tues., Sat. Closed Sun.*

Expensive **The French Café.** Despite its gilt-edged reputation and a long
★ list of awards, prices at this smart city-fringe restaurant are not astronomical. The tapas platter—artichoke and potato frittata, hummus "crouton" with capers and sundried tomatoes, marinated olives, venison, and deep-fried anchovies—is superb, while main courses such as braised lamb shanks in an herb and sherry sauce, and a chargrilled eye fillet served with zucchini *rösti*, are simple but masterful. The restaurant has a brasserie-style dining room looking out onto the street and a more formal restaurant at the rear. On warm evenings you can sit in the courtyard. *210B Symonds St., tel. 09/77–1911. Reservations recommended. Jacket required. AE, DC, MC, V. No lunch Sat. Closed Sun., Mon.*

Harbourside Restaurant. Overlooking the water from the upper level of the restored ferry building, this modern, airy restaurant is the place to sample New Zealand seafood in style, although the service sometimes falters on busy nights. Some of the finest New Zealand fish, including orange roughy, salmon, and snapper, feature on the menu, often chargrilled and served with a light sauce. Lobster fresh from the tank is a house specialty and the reason the restaurant is a favorite with Japanese tourists. Non–fish eaters have their choice of venison, lamb, and poultry. On warm nights, book ahead and request a table outside on the deck. *Auckland Ferry Bldg, 99 Quay St., tel. 09/ 307–0556. Reservations recommended. Dress: casual. AE, DC, MC, V.*

Moderate **Cin Cin on Quay.** This stylish waterfront brasserie is no place
★ for a quiet night out, but the varied menu, brisk service, and lively atmosphere make this one of the most popular eateries in town. Some of the first courses—chargrilled assorted fresh seafood with cos lettuce, olive pâté, parmesan vinaigrette, and new season potatoes—are meals in themselves. The apple and pecan cake with sorbet is delicious. The atmosphere is a combination of art deco and disco: terrazzo floors, chrome, and loud music. Pizzas from the wood-fired oven are good value, and the

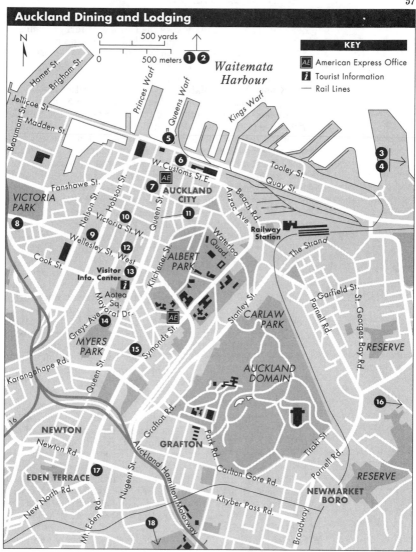

Auckland Dining and Lodging

Dining
BNZ Tower Food Hall, **3**
Cin Cin on Quay, **5**
Five under Five, **15**
The French Café, **17**
Harbourside Restaurant, **5**
Hard to Find Mexican Café, **11**

Mai Thai, **10**
Rick's Café Americain, **8**
Something Fishy, **1**
Varick's, **3**

Lodging
Albion Hotel, **9**
Ascott Parnell, **16**
Centra, **12**
Devonport Villa, **2**
Florida Motel, **4**
Hotel du Vin, **18**
Pan Pacific, **14**
Parkroyal, **6**
The Regent, **7**

wine list has more than 100 entries, most of them from New Zealand. The site right next to the Devonport ferry terminal is a bonus for anyone with time to kill before the next ferry. *Auckland Ferry Bldg., 99 Quay St., tel. 09/307-6966. Reservations advised. Dress: casual. AE, DC, MC, V. No breakfast weekdays.*

Five Under Five. Situated opposite the Sheraton Hotel, this breezy, attractive café offers better value than Number Five, its dressed-up big brother on the floor above. The simpler dishes are often outstanding, although the sauces occasionally enter the realm of fantasy. First courses include avocado with warm smoked chicken and tomato, while the mains feature such robust dishes as lamb shanks flavored with fresh tomato chili and *gremolada* (lemon rind, garlic, and parsley). Lunches are an especially good value, and they attract a steady clientele of office workers. The restaurant is open until midnight, which makes it a good choice for supper after performances at the nearby Aotea Centre. The Sunday brunch is very popular, and jazz combos perform on Sunday afternoons. *5 City Rd., City, tel. 09/373-2843. Reservations not required. Dress: casual. AE, DC, MC, V.*

Mai Thai. This is one of the few Auckland restaurants serving authentic Asian cooking. Try the spicy seafood salad in lemon sauce; the chicken breast sautéed with cashew nuts, dried toasted chili, and onion; or the king prawns with garlic and pepper topped with fresh coriander. Sauces are fiery but can be toned down on request. This inner-city restaurant has been dressed up with painted paper umbrellas, and the service borders on slavish. Classical Thai dancers perform on Friday nights. *57B Victoria St. West, tel. 09/303-2550. Reservations advised on weekends. Dress: casual. AE, DC, MC, V. BYOB. No lunch Sat. Closed Sun.*

Rick's Café Americain. Owned by an American named Rick, this casual bistro in the Victoria Park Markets is aimed at a young market, but the chrome-and-neon decor, spirited service, reasonable prices, and subdued rock and funky jazz give it a wide appeal. Burgers, spare ribs, steaks, and pasta are staples on the menu, but there are several exotic surprises, such as tandoori lamb satay, wild mushroom ragout, and a Caribbean goat curry. Rick's is open daily for breakfast. In Parnell, **Rick's Blue Falcon** has an identical menu. *Victoria Park Market, tel. 09/309-9074. No reservations. Dress: casual. AE, DC, MC, V. Rick's Blue Falcon: 27 Falcon St., Parnell, tel. 09/309-0854.*

★ **Something Fishy.** The seafood dishes at this lively and good-value restaurant, on the north side of the harbor in Devonport, have been drawn from a range of culinary styles to suit all tastes. The menu lists fish-and-chips, calamari with a spicy tomato and garlic dressing, crab meat and prawns in won ton wrappers, and mussels in the half shell. The fresh snapper in lemon and butter is simple and sublime. Something Fishy is especially recommended on Friday and Saturday evenings in tandem with the jazz cruise aboard the *Kestrel* (*see* Off the Beaten Track, above). *71 Victoria Rd., Devonport, tel. 09/445-4263. Reservations recommended. Dress: informal. AE, DC, MC, V. BYOB. No lunch. Closed Mon., Tues.*

Inexpensive **BNZ Tower Food Hall.** If you're looking for a quick, inexpensive lunch in the city center, do what the office workers of Auckland do and head for the basement level of this Queen Street office tower. Inside you'll find a range of exotic take-aways from Italy, China, and Turkey, as well as fish-and-chips, salads, meat pies, and sandwiches. *BNZ Tower, Queen St. near Wellesley St. No dinner. Closed weekends.*

Hard to Find Mexican Café. Practically impossible to find is more like it, but persist and you'll be rewarded with a memorable Mexican meal. Tucked away at the end of an arcade, this brightly decorated restaurant serves tortillas, enchiladas, and all the other Mexican favorites, accompanied by the obligatory beans, peppers, and onions and spiced with fire. *Canterbury Arcade, 47 High St., tel. 09/373-4681. No reservations. Dress: casual but neat. MC, V. BYOB. No lunch weekends.*

Lodging

Highly recommended lodgings are indicated by a star ★.

Category	Cost*
Very Expensive	over $200
Expensive	$125–$200
Moderate	$80–$125
Inexpensive	under $80

*All prices are for a standard double room, excluding general sales tax (12½%).

Very Expensive
★ **Hotel du Vin.** There can be no finer introduction to New Zealand than to head south from the Auckland International Airport to this smart, luxurious hotel, set on the floor of a valley and surrounded by native forests and the grapevines of the de Redcliffe Estate. Standard rooms are palatial. The decor is crisp and modern, and the central restaurant and reception areas glow with honey-colored wood and rough stone fireplaces. The restaurant has an excellent reputation, though prices are high. The hotel is 40 miles from Auckland, a 45-minute drive from both Auckland airport and the city via the motorway. *Lyons Rd., Mangatawhiri Valley, tel. 09/233-6314, fax 09/233-6215. 46 rooms with bath. Facilities: bar, restaurant, heated indoor pool, spa, gym, tennis courts, bicycles, winery. AE, DC, MC, V.*

Pan Pacific. When this atrium-style hotel opened early in 1990, it became the most glamorous member of the city's five-star elite. Guest rooms are spacious and elegantly furnished, and the bathrooms are particularly well equipped. The best views are from the rooms that overlook the parklands and the harbor to the east. Polished granite and warm, earthy tones have been used liberally throughout the hotel. A favorite with business travelers, it is located close to the Aotea Centre and the business and shopping districts. *Mayoral Dr., tel. 09/366-3000, fax 09/366-0121. 286 rooms with bath. Facilities: 2 bars, 2 restaurants, 24-hr coffee shop, tennis court. AE, DC, MC, V.*

Parkroyal. This was Auckland's premier hotel for almost two decades after it was built in the late '60s, but its age is difficult to ignore. The hotel is scrupulously maintained and constantly upgraded, but no amount of tender loving care can overcome the slightly cramped rooms and, by today's standards, limited natural lighting. On the positive side, it has a comforting clublike atmosphere, and its location at the lower end of Queen Street, close to the ferry terminal, is one of the best of any city hotel. *8 Customs St., tel. 09/377–8920, fax 09/307–3739. 188 rooms with bath. Facilities: 4 bars, 2 restaurants. AE, DC, MC, V.*

★ **The Regent.** This mid-city hotel brought a dash of style to Auckland when it opened in the mid-'80s, and despite some energetic competitors, its service, sophistication, and attention to detail keep it on top. Standard rooms are large and furnished extensively with natural fabrics and native timbers. The marble bathrooms are luxuriously appointed. The best rooms are on the harbor side—the higher the better. *Albert St., tel. 09/ 309–8888, fax 09/379–6445. 332 rooms with bath. Facilities: bar, 3 restaurants, heated outdoor pool. AE, DC, MC, V.*

Expensive **Centra.** Rooms at this city landmark are equal to those in just about any of Auckland's leading hotels, but cutting down on the facilities and the glossy public areas has made the price substantially lower. Rooms have a standard, functional layout, and each has its own iron and ironing board. Accommodation begins on the 16th floor, and every room has a view. The suites on the 28th floor have great views and bigger bathrooms for just a slightly higher price. The hotel, which opened in 1991, is aimed primarily at the business traveler. Service is keen and professional. *128 Albert St., tel. 09/302–1111, fax 09/302–3111. 252 rooms with bath. Facilities: bar, restaurant, gym. AE, DC, MC, V.*

Moderate **Ascott Parnell.** Accommodations and facilities in this sprawling guest house are comfortable and functional, but space and character have been sacrificed to provide rooms with *en suite* facilities or private bathrooms at a reasonable price. The room with the attached sunroom at the back of the house is small but pleasant. The house stands on a leafy back street, within easy walking distance of the shops and nightlife of Parnell Village. Smoking is not permitted inside, and children ages 2–8 are not accommodated. *36 St Stephens Ave., Parnell, tel. 09/309–9012, fax 09/309–3729. 9 rooms with bath. Tariff includes full breakfast. AE, MC, V.*

★ **Devonport Villa.** Tucked away in a historic waterfront suburb, this exquisite timber guest house combines tranquil, historic surroundings and fresh sea air—with the city just a boat ride away. The middle room, "Sarah," is large and very comfortable. The house is extensively furnished with New Zealand antiques and decorated in period style. The breakfasts are prepared to order by the American owner. Cheltenham Beach, which offers safe swimming, is a one-minute walk away. The house is a 10-minute walk from the ferry terminal, but the owner will collect arriving guests. In terms of facilities, charm, location, and value for money, this is the finest accommodation of its type in Auckland. *21 Cheltenham Rd., Devonport, tel. 09/ 445–2529. 4 rooms, 2 with bath. Tariff includes full breakfast. Facilities: outdoor freshwater pool, courtyard, guest lounge. AE, V.*

Florida Motel. Located in a harborside suburb a 15-minute drive east of the city center (and close to a major bus route into the city), this motel offers exceptional value. Rooms come in three versions: studios or one- or two-bedroom units. The units have a lounge room separate from the bedroom, and the two-bedroom units are particularly good for families. All rooms have separate, fully equipped kitchens and a few extra touches of luxury, such as wall-mounted hair dryers, plunger-type coffee makers, and ironing boards with irons. The motel is immaculately maintained and extremely popular, and rooms must be booked several months in advance. *11 Speight Rd., Kohimarama, tel. 09/521–4660, fax 09/521–4662. 8 rooms with bath. AE, DC, MC, V.*

Inexpensive **Albion Hotel.** If you're looking for comfortable, modern accommodation in the heart of the city and outstanding value, look no further. The rooms are modest in size and offer no views, but all are neat and well kept. The best room in the house, the Hobson Suite, is equipped with a waterbed and Jacuzzi and costs only slightly more than the standard rooms. Despite the busy corner location, the area is quiet after 6 PM. Rooms on the lower floor may be affected by noise from the pub on the ground floor, which is especially popular on Friday nights. The Aotea Centre and the shops of Queen Street are only two blocks away. *Corner Hobson and Wellesley Sts., tel. 09/379–4900, fax 09/379–4901. 20 rooms with bath. Facilities: pub, brasserie. AE, DC, MC, V.*

The Arts

For a current listing of plays, opera, dance, and musical events in Auckland, a brochure called *Just the Ticket* is available from the Visitor Information Centre and the Aotea Centre. For current films, check the entertainment pages of the daily newspapers. Auckland's main venue for music and the performing arts is the **Aotea Centre** (at Aotea Square, near the corner of Queen and Myers streets), which hosts performances of music and drama throughout the year. For general inquiries there is an Information Desk (tel. 09/307–5050) in the Owens Foyer, level 2 of the complex. For recorded information on current events at the Aotea Centre, phone 09/309–2678. For bookings, phone **Bass New Zealand** (tel. 09/307–5000). Bass is the central booking agency for all theater, music, and dance, as well as for major sporting events.

Theater **The Mercury Theatre,** the country's largest professional company, gives regular performances of the latest hits in its 700-seat auditorium. The theater has two bars and a café, open before and after all shows. *9 France St., Newton, tel. 09/303–3869. Shows Mon.–Sat.*

Music The **Auckland Philharmonia Orchestra** performs regularly at the Aotea Centre (*see* above). The **New Zealand Symphony Orchestra** performs at the Town Hall and at the Aotea Centre.

Opera Dame Kiri Te Kanawa often performs at the Aotea Centre on return visits to her homeland, but tickets are usually sold out months in advance.

Nightlife

After sunset, the liveliest area of the city is Parnell, which has several restaurants, bars, and nightclubs.

Bars and Lounges **Cactus Jacks** is a mid-city bar that would like to believe it's somewhere deep in the heart of Texas. If you're looking for a convivial bar with a Tex-Mex menu and an impressive lineup of tequilas, this is the place. *Finance Plaza, 96 Albert St., City, tel. 09/302–0942. Open Mon.–Sat. 11 AM–1 AM.*
The Safari Bar, on the top floor of the Exchange Hotel, is a lively and attractive place that attracts a young, well-heeled crowd, especially on Friday and Saturday nights. On the floor

below, the **Long Room** is a more subdued cocktail bar. Drinks are expensive. *99 Parnell Rd., Parnell, tel. 373–2531. Open Mon.–Sat 11 AM–midnight.*

The Shakespeare Tavern is an atmospheric and popular pub in the middle of the city. The Shakespeare makes and serves its own beers, which go by such colorful names as Willpower Stout and Falstaff's Real Ale. There are several bars inside and live rock or jazz most evenings. *Corner Albert and Wyndham Sts., tel. 09/373–5396. Open Mon.–Sat. 11–11.*

The Civic, at the heart of the city center, looks unremarkable from street level, but the **London Bar** on the floor above has a vast selection of beers and jazz every night from Wednesday to Saturday. *1 Wellesley St., City, tel. 09/373–3684. Open Mon.– Sat. 11 AM–midnight.*

Nightclubs **Club Parnell** is a long-standing favorite with Auckland's sophisticates, and you'll have to dress up to get through the door. On most evenings the club offers live jazz as well as disco music. *7 Windsor St., Parnell, tel. 09/379–4341. Admission: $6–$10. Open Wed.–Sat. 9 PM–3 AM.*

The Oak and Whale, easily recognized at night by the flares that blaze out in the front, is the place where Auckland's smart set comes to see and be singed. Friday and Saturday nights are very popular—go before 8 or be prepared to queue. *269 Parnell Rd., tel. 09/309–4124. Open Tues.–Sat. 5 PM–3 AM.*

Rick's Blue Falcon is Auckland's version of the Hard Rock Café: a voguish interior decorated with car parts, rainbow-colored cocktails, and a steak and burger menu. Here, as elsewhere, this well-tested recipe attracts a varied clientele. Prices are moderate. The Attic Bar has live jazz or restrained rock every night. *27 Falcon St., Parnell, tel. 09/309–0854. Open daily midday–midnight.*

Discos **Don't Tell Mama's,** popularly abbreviated to **DTM,** is the hottest dance club in town. The decor is high-tech and black, the crowd is young and avant-garde, and the house music is medium-loud. The cavernous two-level complex includes several bars, a restaurant, and the biggest dance floor in the country. Drinks are moderately priced. *340 Karangahape Rd., City, tel. 09/379–0320. Admission: $5–$10. Open Wed.–Sun. 10 PM– 5 AM.*

Northland and the Bay of Islands

Beyond Auckland, the North Island stretches a long arm into the South Pacific. This is Northland, an undulating region of farms, forests, and marvelous beaches. The main attraction here is the Bay of Islands, an island-studded seascape with a mild, subtropical climate, and one of the finest game-fishing waters in the country—witness its record catches of marlin and mako shark. Big-game fishing is expensive, but many small fishing boats will take you out for an evening of trawling for as little as $35.

It was on the Bay of Islands that the first European settlement was established, and here that New Zealand became a nation with the signing of the Treaty of Waitangi in 1840. The main town is Paihia, a strip of motels and restaurants along the waterfront. If you plan to spend more than a day in the area, the town of Russell, just a short ferry trip away, makes a more atmospheric and attractive base.

Important Addresses and Numbers

Tourist Information **Bay of Islands Visitor Information Centre.** *Maritime Reserve, Paihia, tel. 09/402–7426. Open Nov.–Mar., daily 7:30–7:30; Apr.–Oct., daily 8–5.*

Emergencies Dial 111 for **fire, police,** or **ambulance** services.

Arriving and Departing

By Car The main route from Auckland is Highway 1. Leave the city by the Harbour Bridge and follow the signs to Whangarei. Driving time for the 250-kilometer (150-mile) journey to Paihia is about four hours.

By Bus **Northliner Express** (tel. 09/307–5873), **InterCity** (tel. 09/358–4085), and **Newmans** (tel. 09/309–9738) operate several daily bus services between Auckland and Paihia.

Guided Tours

Orientation **Fullers Northland** operates a full-day tour from Paihia to Cape Reinga, close to the northern tip of New Zealand. The trip includes lunch and a spectacular dash along the water's edge at Ninety Mile Beach. *Maritime Bldg., Paihia, tel. 09/402–7421. Tickets: $75 adults, $42 children 4–14. Tours depart 7:30 AM.*

Russell Mini Tours offers a one-hour guided tour of the historic sights of Russell. Tours depart from the Fullers office, opposite the wharf. *Box 70, Russell, tel. 09/403–7891. Tickets: $8 adults, $4 children 5–15. Tours at 11, 1, 2, 3:30.*

Boat Tours **Fullers Northland** (*see* above) operates several cruises in the Bay of Islands, departing from both Paihia and Russell. The most popular is the half-day catamaran cruise to Cape Brett, at the eastern extremity of the bay. The Cream Trip is a six-hour cruise that stops in at many of the bay islands. *Tickets: Cape Brett, $45 adults, $22 children 4–14; Cream Trip, $49 adults, $24 children. Cape Brett Cruise departs Paihia daily 9 AM and 1:30 PM; Cream Trip departs Paihia 10 AM, daily Oct.–May; Mon., Wed., Thurs., Sat. 10 June–Sept.*

Exploring Northland

This tour begins at Auckland, traveling north to the Bay of Islands via Highway 1 and returning along the western side of the peninsula. The return route, Highway 12, adds almost two hours to the driving time, but the tranquil landscape makes an attractive alternative to Highway 1, which is particularly busy during the December–January holiday period.

Numbers in the margin correspond to points of interest on the Northland and the Bay of Islands map.

North of Waitemata Harbour, Highway 1 quickly leaves the city and the suburbs behind and weaves into rolling green hills around the town of **Albany.** In December, the pohutukawa trees along the roadside celebrate the arrival of Christmas by erupting in a blaze of scarlet blossoms, and hence their other name—the New Zealand Christmas tree. To the Maoris, the flowers had another meaning: the beginning of the shellfish season. The spiky-leaved plants that grow in clumps by the roadside are the New Zealand flax. The fibers of this plant, the raw material for linen, were woven into clothing by the Maoris. The huge tree ferns—common throughout the forests of North Island, where they can grow as high as 10 meters—are known locally as "pungas."

At the town of **Warkworth,** 69 kilometers (43 miles) from Auckland, turn right into McKinney Road, right again into Thompson Road, and then follow the signs to the **Warkworth Museum.** The main attraction here is the two giant kauri trees in the car park. The larger one, the **McKinney Kauri,** measures almost 25 feet around its base, yet this 800-year-old colossus is a mere adolescent by kauri standards. Kauri trees, once prolific in this part of the North Island, were highly prized by Maori canoe builders, since a canoe capable of carrying a hundred warriors could be made from a single trunk. Unfortunately these same characteristics—strength, size, and durability—made kauri timber ideal for ships, furniture, and housing, and the kauri forests were rapidly depleted by the early European settlers. Today the trees are protected by law, and many infant kauris are again appearing in the forests of the North Island, although their growth rate is painfully slow. The museum itself contains a collection of Maori artifacts and farming and domestic implements from the pioneering days of the Warkworth district. *Parry Kauri Park, Warkworth, tel. 09/425-7093. Admission: $2 adults, 50¢ children 5-15. Open Dec.-Feb., daily 9:30-4; Mar.-Nov., daily 10-3:30.*

When you get to the town of **Whangarei,** cross the river and look for a sign on your left to **Clapham's Clock Museum.** Just about every conceivable method of telling time is represented in this collection of more than 1,400 clocks, from primitive water clocks to ships' chronometers to ornate masterworks from Paris and Vienna. Some of the most intriguing specimens were made by the late Mr. Clapham himself, including a World War II air force clock that automatically changed the position of aircraft over a map. Ironically, the one thing you won't find here is the correct time. If all the bells, chimes, gongs, and cuckoos went off together the noise would be deafening, so all the clocks are set to different times. *Water St., Cafler Park, Whangarei, tel. 09/438-3993. Admission: $3.50 adults, $1.50 children 5-15. Open daily 10-4.*

Paihia, the main holiday base for the Bay of Islands, is an unremarkable stretch of motels at odds with the quiet beauty of the island-studded seascape and the rounded green hills that form a backdrop to the town, yet nearby is one of the country's most important historic sites. It was near here that the Treaty of Waitangi, the founding document for modern New Zealand, was signed.

At the northern end of town, on the far side of the Waitangi River, a side road turns right toward the **Waitangi National Reserve.** Inside the visitor center, a 23-minute video, which screens every hour on the hour, sketches the events that led to the Treaty of Waitangi. The center also houses a display of Maori artifacts and weapons, including a musket that belonged to Hone Heke Pokai, the first Maori chief to sign the treaty. Af-

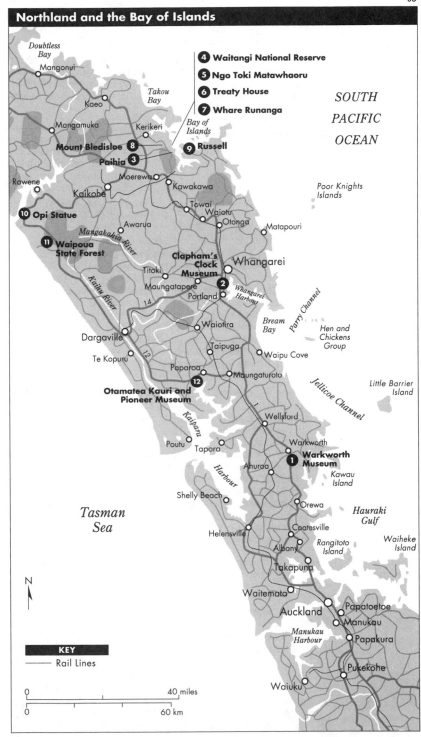

Northland and the Bay of Islands

4 Waitangi National Reserve
5 Ngo Toki Matawhaoru
6 Treaty House
7 Whare Runanga

SOUTH
PACIFIC
OCEAN

Doubtless
Bay

Mangonui

Kaeo

Takou
Bay

Mangamuka

Kerikeri

Bay of
Islands

Mount Bledisloe 8

9 Russell

Paihia 3

Rawene

Moerewa

Poor Knights
Islands

Kaikohe

Kawakawa

10 Opi Statue

Towai
Waiotu

Awarua

Otonga

Matapouri

Mangakahia River

11 Waipoua
State Forest

Clapham's
Clock
Museum

Whangarei

Kaihu River

Titoki

Maungatapere

2

Whangarei
Harbour

Portland

14

Bream
Bay

Parry Channel

Hen and
Chickens
Group

Dargaville

Waiotira

Te Kopuru

12

Taipuga

Waipu Cove

Jellicoe Channel

Little Barrier
Island

Paparoa

12

Maungaturoto

Otamatea Kauri and
Pioneer Museum

Kaipara

Wellsford

Warkworth

1 Warkworth
Museum

Kawau
Island

Poutu

Tapora

Ahuroa

Harbour

Shelly Beach

Orewa

Hauraki
Gulf

Tasman
Sea

Helensville

Coatesville

Albany

Rangitoto
Island

Waiheke
Island

Takapuna

Waitemata

Auckland

Papatoetoe

Manukau

Manukau
Harbour

Papakura

N

Pukekohe

KEY
—— Rail Lines

Waiuku

0   40 miles
0   60 km

ter his initial display of enthusiasm for British rule, Hone Heke was quickly disillusioned, and less than five years later he attacked the British in their stronghold at Russell.

⑤ From the visitor center, follow the short track through the forest to **Nga Toki Matawhaoru,** a Maori war canoe. This huge kauri canoe, capable of carrying 150 warriors, is named after the vessel in which Kupe, the Polynesian navigator, is said to have discovered New Zealand.

⑥ Follow the shoreline track and then cross the vast lawn to the **Treaty House,** a five-minute stroll from the war canoe. There can have been few more modest beginnings on the road to nationhood than this simple white timber cottage, which has a remarkable air of dignity despite its scale. The interior is fascinating, especially at the back, where exposed walls give an insight into the difficulties that the early administrators faced—such as an acute shortage of bricks (since an insufficient number had been shipped out from New South Wales) with which to finish the walls.

The Treaty House was prefabricated in New South Wales for the British Resident, James Busby, who arrived in New Zealand in 1832. Busby had been appointed to protect British commerce and put an end to the brutalities of the whaling captains against the Maoris, but Busby lacked either the judicial authority or the force of arms necessary to impose peace. On one occasion, unable to resolve a dispute between Maori tribes, Busby was forced to shelter the wounded of one side in his house. While tattooed head hunters screamed war chants outside the windows, one of the warriors sheltered Busby's infant daughter, Sarah, in his cape.

The real significance of the Treaty House lies in the events that took place here on February 6, 1840, the day that the **Treaty of Waitangi** was signed by Maori chiefs and a representative of the British crown. Under the treaty, the chiefs agreed to accept the authority of the crown; in return, the British recognized the Maoris as the legitimate landowners and granted them all the rights and privileges of British subjects. The treaty also confirmed the status of New Zealand as a British colony, forestalling French overtures in the area, and legitimized—at least according to European law—the transfer of land from Maori to European hands. In recent years the Maoris have used the treaty successfully to reclaim land that, they maintain, was misappropriated by white settlers.

The Treaty House has not always received the care its significance merits. When Lord Bledisloe bought the house and presented it to the nation in 1932, it was being used as a shelter for sheep.

⑦ On the northern boundary of Waitangi National Reserve is **Whare Runanga,** a Maori meeting house with an elaborately carved interior. Inside, an audio show offers a brief outline of traditional Maori society. *Waitangi Rd., Waitangi, tel. 09/402–7437. Admission: $5 adults, children under 15 free. Open daily 9–5.*

⑧ Three kilometers (2 miles) from the Treaty House, on the other side of the Waitangi Golf Course, there is a small parking area on the right of Waitangi Road. Stop here and take the short track, which rises above a pine forest to the summit of **Mount**

Bledisloe and a splendid view across Paihia and the Bay of Islands. The handsome ceramic marker at the top showing the distances to major world cities was made by Doulton in London and presented by Lord Bledisloe in 1934 during his term as governor-general of New Zealand.

The second town in the Bay of Islands, at the tip of a peninsula opposite Paihia, is **Russell.** You can drive, but the quickest and most convenient route is by ferry. Three passenger ferries make the crossing between Paihia and Russell, with departures at least every 30 minutes in each direction from 7:30 AM to 11 PM. The one-way adult fare is $2.50–$3.50, half that for children 5–14. The car ferry is at Opua, about 5 kilometers (3 miles) south of Paihia. This ferry operates from 6:40 AM to 8:50 PM (9:50 PM Friday), with departures at approximately 20-minute intervals from either shore. The last ferry leaves from Russell at 8:50 (9:50 Friday), from Opua at 9 (10 Friday). The one-way fare is $6 for the car and driver plus $1 for each passenger.

Hard as it is to believe these days, sleepy little Russell was once dubbed the Hellhole of the Pacific. Early last century (when it was still known by its Maori name, Kororareka) it was a swashbuckling frontier town, a haven for sealers and for whalers who found one of the richest whaling grounds on earth along the east coast of New Zealand. The tales of debauchery were probably exaggerated, but the British administrators in New South Wales (as Australia was known at the time) were sufficiently concerned to dispatch a British Resident in 1832 to impose law and order. After the Treaty of Waitangi, Russell was the national capital, until in 1844 the Maori chief Hone Heke attacked the British garrison and most of the town burned to the ground. Hone Heke was finally defeated in 1846, but Russell never recovered its former prominence, and the seat of government was shifted first to Auckland, then to Wellington. Today Russell is a delightful town of timber houses and big trees that swoon low over the seafront, framing the yachts and the big-game fishing boats in the harbor. The atmosphere can best be absorbed in a stroll along the Strand, the path along the waterfront.

At the southern end of the Strand is **Pompallier House,** named after the first Catholic bishop of the South Pacific. Marist missionaries built the original structure out of rammed earth (mud mixed with dung or straw—a technique known as *pise* in their native France), since they lacked the funds to buy timber. For several years the priests and brothers operated a press here, printing Bibles in the Maori language. The original building forms the core of the elegant timber house that now stands on the site. The house is presently closed to the public for restoration. *The Strand, Russell, tel. 09/3–7861.*

Set back slightly from the waterfront some 50 yards to the north is the **Captain Cook Memorial Museum,** which houses a collection of Maori tools and weapons and some fine portraits. The pride of its display is a ⅕-scale replica of Captain Cook's ship, HMS *Endeavour,* which entered the bay in 1769. *York St., Russell, tel. 09/403–7701. Admission: $2 adults, 50¢ children 5–15. Open daily 10–5.*

A block farther back from the harbor is **Christ Church,** the oldest church in the country. One of the donors to its erection in 1835 was Charles Darwin, at that time a wealthy but unknown young man making his way around the globe on board HMS

Beagle. Behind the white picket fence that borders the church-yard, the gravestones tell a fascinating and gruesome story of life in the early days of the colony. Several graves belong to sailors from HMS *Hazard* who were killed in this churchyard by Hone Heke's warriors in 1845. Another headstone marks the grave of a Nantucket sailor from the whaler *Mohawk.* As you walk around the church, look for the musket holes made when Hone Heke besieged the church. The interior is simple and charming; the embroidered cushions on the pews are examples of a folk-art tradition that is still very much alive. *Church and Robertson Sts., Russell. Open daily 8–5.*

To return to Auckland via the west coast road, turn south toward the town of Kawakawa, then right onto Highway 1, and after about 16 kilometers (10 miles), take Highway 12 left toward Kaikohe. This road winds into steep green hills before wandering down toward a broad sea inlet, Hokianga Harbour. In the town of **Opononi,** near the mouth of the harbor, a statue ⑩ in front of the pub commemorates a tame dolphin, **Opi,** that came to play with swimmers in the mid-1950s, putting the town on the national map for the first and only time in its history.

⑪ South of Opononi is the **Waipoua State Forest,** the largest remnant of the kauri forests that once covered this part of the country. A short path leads from the parking area through the forest to **Tane Mahuta,** "Lord of the Forest," standing nearly 173 feet high and measuring 43 feet around its base. The largest tree in New Zealand, it's said to be 1,200 years old.

⑫ The **Otamatea Kauri and Pioneer Museum** is one of the most intriguing museums in the country. Its vast collection of artifacts, tools, photographs, documents, and memorabilia tells the story of the pioneers who settled this part of the country in the second half of the 19th century—a story that is interwoven with the kauri forests. Here you'll find superb examples of kauri craftsmanship and furniture, a complete kauri house, and an early example of an American-built Caterpillar bulldozer, which was used to drag logs from the forest. One of the most fascinating displays is the room of kauri gum, the transparent lumps of resin that form when the sticky sap of the kauri tree hardens. This gum, which was used to make varnish, can be polished to a warm, lustrous finish that looks remarkably like amber—right down to the insects that are sometimes trapped and preserved inside. At one time collecting this gum was an important rural industry. Many of the gum diggers, as they were known, came from Dalmatia, part of present-day Croatia. *Matakohe, tel. 09/431–7417. Admission: $4 adults, $1.50 children 5–15. Open daily 9–5.*

Twenty kilometers (12½ miles) beyond the museum, Highway 12 joins Highway 1 for the final leg of the return journey to Auckland.

What to See and Do with Children

High and dry on the banks of the Waitangi River, the *Tui* is a historic kauri sailing vessel that was built to carry sugar to a refinery in Auckland. Below decks is an exhibition of artifacts recovered from shipwrecks by the famous New Zealand salvage diver Kelly Tarlton. In addition to the brass telescopes, sextants, and diving helmets that can be tried on for size, there is an exquisite collection of jewelry that belonged to Isidore Jonah Rothschild (of the famous banking family), which was lost when the SS *Tasmania* sank in 1897. Rothschild was on a sales trip to New Zealand at the time. *Waitangi Bridge, Paihia, tel. 09/402–7018. Admission: $4 adults, $2 children under 12. Open daily 10–5.*

Sports and the Outdoors

Boating   **Marine Rentals** (tel. 09/402–8105), on the waterfront at Paihia, offers catamarans, jet skis, kayaks, and aqua bikes for hire. In the same location, **Charter Pier Paihia** (tel. 09/402–7127) has 16-foot powerboats suitable for fishing and diving for up to six people, available by the hour or the day. For experienced sailors, **Great Escape Yacht Rentals** (Box 345, Kerikeri, tel. 025/97–0135) charters 16-foot trailer sailers that are light, responsive, and easy for two people to handle.

Diving   The Bay of Islands offers some of the finest scuba diving in the country, particularly around Cape Brett, where the marine life includes moray eels, stingrays, and grouper. Water temperature at the surface varies from 62°F in July to 71°F in January. From September to November, underwater visibility is often affected by a plankton bloom. **Paihia Dive Hire and Charter** (Box 210, Paihia, tel. 09/402–7551) offers complete equipment hire and regular boat trips for accredited divers.

Fishing   The Bay of Islands is one of the world's premier game-fishing grounds for marlin and several species of shark. Operators in the area include **Dudley Smith** (Box 203, Russell, tel. 09/403–7200); **Nighthawk** (tel. 09/407–8999); and **NZ Billfish Charters** (Box 416, Paihia, tel. 09/402–8380). A far less expensive alternative is to fish for snapper, kingfish, and John Dory in the inshore waters of the bay. Among several boat operators in Russell and Paihia who offer a half day of fishing, including bait and rods, for about $35 per person are **Skipper Jim** (tel. 09/402–7355) and **MV** *Arline* (tel. 09/402–8511).

Dining

During the January summer-vacation period, dinner reservations are essential at all restaurants in the area. Price categories are the same as in the Auckland Dining section, above. Highly recommended restaurants are indicated by a star ★.

Expensive   **The Gables.** This trim little cottage restaurant on the waterfront at Russell is one of the more sophisticated in the Bay of Islands. First courses include smoked salmon and spinach mousse with an orange sauce, and mussels steamed in wine and herbs with French bread. The pan-fried snapper fillets with balsamic vinegar and the chargrilled fillet of lamb with a ginger and honey sauce are recommended. The lunch menu is limited but less expensive. *The Strand, Russell, tel. 09/403–7618. Reservations advised. Dress: casual. MC, V. No lunch weekdays except during summer. Closed Mon.*

Moderate   **Bay of Islands Swordfish Club.** Overlooking Kororareka Bay in a pretty cream-and-white timber building, the restaurant of the Swordfish Club is dedicated to fish and fish people, from the decor to the menu to the conversation. First courses are a salad of mussels or fresh oysters; entrées include fresh scallops and asparagus with oyster sauce. Request a table at the window, and begin the evening with a drink in the friendly bar upstairs—where, in the summer holiday period, you may have to wait for a table anyway. Officially visitors must be signed in by a member of the club, but provided you look sober, neat, and capable of enthusing over marlin fishing, the barman will request a club member to countersign the visitors book for you (after which it would be diplomatic to stand the member to a drink). *The Strand, Russell, tel. 09/403-7652. No reservations. Dress: casual. AE, MC, V. No lunch.*

Cafe Over the Bay. This breezy, bistro-style restaurant has an unambitious menu with an Italian accent, but the fish is excellent. First courses include wok-fried venison, seafood chowder, and sweet and sour fish. Mains are tortellini with a wine and cream sauce, and fish with a tomato and herb sauce. All the fish dishes are made with the delicate, white-fleshed orange roughy. *Waterfront, Paihia, tel. 09/402-8147. No reservations. Dress: casual but neat. DC, MC, V.*

The Quarterdeck. The specialty of this seafront restaurant is fish al fresco—crayfish, lobster, flounder, scallops, and snapper, and chips and salads—and while the prices are rather steep for less than glamorous dining, the outdoor tables overlooking the lively harbor are a pleasant spot on a warm evening. The restaurant is popular with families. *The Strand, Russell, tel. 09/403-7761. No reservations. Dress: informal. BYOB. AE, DC, MC, V. No lunch weekdays except summer.*

Lodging

Price categories for hotels are the same as in the Auckland Lodging section, above. Highly recommended lodgings are indicated by a star ★.

Very Expensive **Kimberley Lodge.** The most luxurious accommodation in the
★ Bay of Islands, this splendid white timber mansion occupies a commanding position overlooking Russell and Kororareka Bay. The house has been designed with big windows and sunny verandas to take maximum advantage of its location. Below, terraced gardens fall away down a steep hillside to the sea. The house is opulently furnished in contemporary style, and the en suite bathrooms are equipped to five-star standards. Only one bedroom at the rear of the house—Pompallier—lacks impressive views. The best room in the house is the Kimberley Suite, which costs more than the standard suites. Dinner is available by arrangement. *Pitt St., Russell, tel. 09/403-7090, fax 09/403-7239. 4 rooms with bath. Facilities: outdoor heated pool. Tariff includes breakfast. No smoking indoors. AE, DC, MC, V.*

Moderate **Austria Motel.** The large, double-bedded rooms at this motel are typical of motel accommodation in the area—clean and moderately comfortable. Each has a kitchenette. The motel also offers a family unit on the ground level of the two-story accommodation wing. The shops and waterfront at Paihia are a two-minute walk away. *36 Selwyn Rd., Paihia, tel. 09/402-7480. 7 rooms with bath. Facilities: spa. AE, DC, MC, V.*

Duke of Marlborough Hotel. This historic hotel is a favorite with the yachting fraternity, for whom ready access to the harbor and the bar downstairs are the most important considerations. Rooms are clean and tidy enough, and all have en suite facilities, but they offer no memorable character despite the hotel's long and colorful history. The front rooms with harbor views are the most expensive but also the ones most likely to be affected by noise from the spirited crowd in the bar, especially on weekends. *The Waterfront, Russell, tel. 09/403-7829, fax 09/403-7760. 29 rooms with bath. Facilities: restaurant, bar. DC, MC, V.*

Waitangi Resort Hotel. The biggest hotel north of Auckland and a favorite with coach tour groups, this complex sprawls along a peninsula within walking distance of the Treaty House. Standard rooms, which are often booked by coach parties, show signs of long and heavy use, but many "premium" rooms were renovated in 1991 and offer more stylish accommodation. *Waitangi Rd., Paihia, tel. 09/402-7411, fax 09/402-8200. 138 rooms with bath. Facilities: outdoor pool, guest laundry, 3 restaurants, 2 bars. AE, DC, MC, V.*

Inexpensive **Russell Lodge.** Surrounded by quiet gardens two streets back from the waterfront, this lodge—owned and operated by the Salvation Army—offers neat, clean rooms in several configurations. It's an especially good value for budget travelers and families. The family units have a separate bedroom with two single beds, and either a double or a single bed in the main room. The largest room is Unit 15, a two-bedroom flat with a kitchen, which will sleep six. Backpacker-style accommodation is also available in rooms for four; towels and sheets are not provided in these rooms but may be hired. All rooms have en suite bathrooms, and five have kitchen facilities. *Chapel and Beresford Sts., Russell, tel. 09/403-7640, fax 09/403-7641. 24 rooms with bath. Facilities: outdoor pool, guest laundry. AE, MC, V.*

The Coromandel Peninsula

New Zealand has countless pockets of beauty that are not included in the standard tourist itineraries. One of the most accessible is the Coromandel Peninsula, which juts out like a hitchhiker's thumb east of Auckland. The center of the peninsula is dominated by a craggy spine of volcanic peaks that rise sharply to a height of almost 900 meters (3,000 feet). The west coast is sheltered, while on the unprotected east coast the Pacific Ocean has gnawed a succession of beaches and inlets separated by rearing headlands. From the town of Thames, the gateway to the region, Highway 25 makes a circuit of the lower two-thirds of the peninsula—an exhilarating drive with the sea on one side and big forested peaks on the other. The journey will add a day (at the very least) to your New Zealand itinerary, but it would be hard to find a finer introduction to the country.

Important Addresses and Numbers

Tourist Information **Coromandel Visitor Information Centre.** *Kapanga Rd., Coromandel, tel. 07/866-8958. Open weekdays 10-3.*

Thames Visitor Information Centre. *405 Queen St., Thames, tel. 07/866-7284. Open weekdays 9-5, weekends 10-3.*

Emergenices Dial 111 for **fire**, **police**, or **ambulance** services.

Arriving and Departing

By Car From Auckland, take the Southern Motorway, following the signs to Hamilton. Just past the end of the motorway, turn left onto Highway 2 and follow the signs to Thames. Allow 90 minutes for the 118-kilometer (73-mile) journey.

By Bus   **Peninsula Buses** and **Murphy Buses** link Whitianga, Thames, and Auckland daily. Bookings can be made through InterCity (tel. 09/358–4085).

Guided Tours

Doug Johansen's full- and half-day tours are a fascinating—and often hilarious—look at a majestic part of the country that he has known and loved since birth. Glowworm caves, abandoned gold mines, flora and fauna, thermal springs, and odd bits of history and bush lore are all covered in the tour, which will provide some of the most evocative memories of your visit to New Zealand. But be warned: Doug Johansen is an incurable practical joker. *Box 76, Pauanui Beach, tel. 07/864–8859. Tickets: $75 full day, $45 half day.*

Aotearoa Adventures operates hiking, rafting, diving, and four-wheel-drive tours of the peninsula. Tours operate from Aotearoa Lodge, on the east coast of the peninsula between Whitianga and Coroglen. *R.D. 1 Whitianga, tel. 07/866–3808.*

Exploring the Coromandel Peninsula

This tour begins at **Thames** and follows Highway 25 in a clockwise direction as it circles the peninsula. If you leave Auckland early in the morning, it's possible to do the trip in a single day.

Numbers in the margin correspond to points of interest on the Coromandel Peninsula map.

Leave Thames and head north along Highway 25, which snakes along the seafront at the foot of the Coromandel Ranges, with expansive views across the Firth of Thames. At the former gold-mining town of Tapu, a narrow road turns inland to follow the Tapu River upstream along a narrow gorge that becomes prettier with every turn. About 6 kilometers (4 miles) from the start of this road, a sign on the right points to **Rapaura Falls Park,** a garden of native and exotic flowering species that has been sculpted from the wilderness. Paths wind through a riot of rhododendrons, lilies, azaleas, and orchids, while giant tree ferns and rata, remu, and kauri trees lock arms to form a green canopy overhead. The combination of delicacy and rugged grandeur has moved the hard-working gardener to philosophy, or at least to nuggets of wisdom painted on signs ("Keep your values in balance and you will always find happiness"). Be sure to take the 10-minute walk from the parking lot to the waterfall. *Admission: $5 adults, $1.50 children under 15. Open Oct.– Apr., daily 10–5.*

Return to Highway 25 and continue toward **Coromandel.** In 1852 the town became the site of New Zealand's first gold strike when Charles Ring, a sawmiller, found gold-bearing quartz at Driving Creek, just north of town. The find was important for New Zealand, since the country's manpower had been severely depleted by the gold rushes in California and Australia. Ring hurried to Auckland to claim the reward that had been offered to anyone finding "payable" gold. The town's population soared, but the reef gold could be mined only by heavy and expensive machinery, and within a few months Coromandel re-

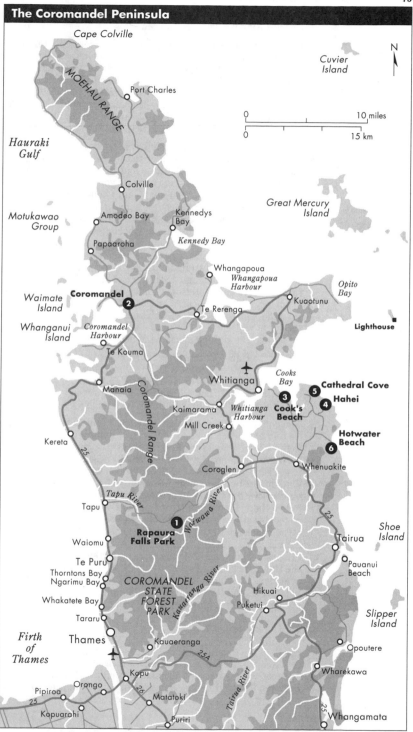

The Coromandel Peninsula

Cape Colville

Cuvier Island

N

Port Charles

MOEHAU RANGE

Hauraki Gulf

0   10 miles

0   15 km

Colville

Motukawao Group

Amodeo Bay

Kennedys Bay

Great Mercury Island

Papaaroha

Kennedy Bay

Whangapoua

Whangapoua Harbour

Opito Bay

Waimate Island

Coromandel ❷

Coromandel Harbour

Te Rerenga

Kuaotunu

Lighthouse

Whanganui Island

Te Kouma

Whitianga

Cooks Bay

Cathedral Cove ❺

Manaia

Cook's Beach ❸

❹ **Hahei**

Kaimarama

Whitianga Harbour

Mill Creek

Hotwater Beach ❻

Kereta

25

Coroglen

Whenuakite

Tapu River

Tapu

❶

Rapaura Falls Park

Waiwawa River

25

Shoe Island

Waiomu

Tairua

Te Puru

Coromandel Range

Pauanui Beach

Thorntons Bay

Ngarimu Bay

COROMANDEL STATE FOREST PARK

Hikuai

Whakatete Bay

Kauaeranga River

Puketui

Slipper Island

Tararu

Firth of Thames

Thames

Kauaeranga

Opoutere

25A

Kopu

Tairua River

Wharekawa

26

Pipiroa

Orongo

Matatoki

25

Kopuarahi

Puriri

Whangamata

25

sumed its former sleepy existence as a timber town—and Charles Ring was refused the reward.

Beyond Coromandel, Highway 25 winds across hilly terrain to the east coast of the peninsula, with marvelous sea views along the way. Beyond the village of Kuaotunu the road snakes around Mercury Bay, where Captain James Cook observed the transit of the planet Mercury in November 1769. Cook's landfall—the first by a European—is commemorated by a plaque ❸ on the southern side of the bay at **Cook's Beach;** however, the beach itself is one of the less attractive in the area.

Turn left on the southern side of Mercury Bay where a sign ❹ points to **Hahei.** At the entrance to the town, Pa Road turns to the right off Hahei Beach Road and, after 1½ kilometers (1 mile), ends at a small parking area. If you're feeling fit, follow the red arrow down the hill, and after about 50 yards take the right fork, which leads through a grove of giant pohutukawa trees, then through a gate and across a grassy, open hillside. The track is steep in places and becomes increasingly overgrown as you climb, but persist until you reach the summit, and then head toward the pohutukawas off to your right at the southern end of the headland. This is the site of an old Maori *pa*, a fortified hilltop, though no trace remains of the defensive terraces and wooden spikes that once ringed the hill. Another, much larger pa was located on the hilltop overlooking this site. If you happen to be there at high tide, the blowhole at the foot of the cliffs will add its booming bass note to the crash of the waves and the sighing of the wind in the grass.

Return to Hahei Beach Road, turn right toward the sea, and then, just past the shops, turn left into Grange Road and follow ❺ the signs to **Cathedral Cove.** The road ends at a parking lot with dramatic coastal views. Cathedral Cove, a vast sea cavern accessible at low tide, is a 45-minute walk each way.

❻ The popular **Hotwater Beach** lies a few kilometers to the south. To find the beach from Hahei, retrace your route toward the highway and watch for the signposts that point left. A thermal spring seeps beneath the beach, and by scooping a shallow hole in the sand you can create a pool of warm water; the deeper you dig, the hotter the water becomes. (The phenomenon occurs only at low to mid-tide.) For a swim without the spa treatment, follow Hahei Beach Road to its end at a well-protected cove, one of the finest along this coastline. The sands of this islandsheltered beach are tinted pink with crushed shells.

Time Out   **Calenso Orchard and Herb Garden,** on Highway 25 just south of the Hahei turnoff, is a relaxed cottage café set in a garden full of lavender. The menu lists fresh juices, vegetable soup, quiche with salad, and Devonshire teas—simple, wholesome fare that goes with the droning of the bees and the sound of the wind chimes. Prices are low. *Main Rd., Whenuakite, tel. 07/866–3275. Open daily 10–5.*

South of the coastal resort of Tairua, Highway 25 turns inland to skirt Tairua Harbour and then continues west across the spine of the peninsula to Thames—a short, dramatic journey between forested peaks. From Thames, the journey to Waitomo Caves or Rotorua takes about three hours.

What to See and Do with Children

Driving Creek Railway is one man's magnificent folly. Barry Brickell is a local potter who discovered that the clay on his land was perfect for his work. The problem was that the deposit lay in a remote area at the top of a steep slope; so he hacked a path through the forest and built his own miniature railroad. Visitors to his studio began asking if they could go along for the ride, and Brickell now takes passengers on a daily tour aboard his toy train. The route that the diesel-powered, narrow-gauge locomotive follows incorporates a cutting, a double-decker bridge, two tunnels, a spiral, and a switchback. The round-trip takes about 50 minutes. *Kennedy's Bay Rd., Coromandel, tel. 07/866–8703. Tickets: $6 adults, $3 children 5–15. Departs Dec.–Mar., 10:30, 2, 5; Apr.–Oct., 2, 4; Nov., 2, 5.*

Sports and the Outdoors

Hiking **Coromandel State Forest Park** has more than 30 walking trails which offer anything from a 30-minute stroll to a three-day trek. The most accessible starting point is the delightful Kauaeranga Valley Road, where the Coromandel Forest Park Headquarters provides maps and information (tel. 07/866–6869; open weekdays 8–4). To reach the Kauaeranga Valley, head south from Thames and on the outskirts of the town turn left on Banks Street, then right on Parawi Road, which becomes Kauaeranga Valley Road.

Dining

The Coromandel Peninsula is not well endowed with restaurants. In most towns the choice is between coffee shops and pubs, which usually offer cooked meals such as steaks and fish-and-chips, and sometimes salads. An outstanding exception is the dining room at the **Puka Park Lodge** (*see* Lodging, below), which brings an international menu and a dash of glitter to this remote part of the world. *Reservations required. Jacket required. AE, DC, MC, V. No lunch. Very Expensive.*

Lodging

Price categories for hotels are the same as in the Auckland Lodging section, above. Highly recommended lodgings are indicated by a star ★.

Very Expensive **Puka Park Lodge.** This stylish lodge, which attracts a largely
★ European clientele, lies immersed in native bushland on Pauanui Beach, at the seaward end of Tairua Harbour on the east coast of the peninsula. (The turnoff from Highway 25 is about 6 kilometers/4 miles south of Tairua.) The timber chalets are smartly furnished with black cane tables and wooden Venetian blinds; the gauze mosquito nets draped over the beds are there for effect rather than practical reasons. Sliding glass doors lead to a balcony perched up among the treetops. The bathrooms are well equipped but small. The lodge offers a full range of activities for those who want to take advantage of the splendor of the surrounding beaches and forests. The tariff is comparatively low for accommodation of this standard. The food and service in the international restaurant are outstanding. *Private Bag, Pauanui Beach, tel. 07/864–8088, fax 07/*

864–8112. 32 rooms with bath. Facilities: heated outdoor pool, tennis court, bicycles, restaurant, bar. AE, DC, MC, V.

Moderate **Brian Boru Hotel.** Built in the middle of last century when Thames was a booming gold town, this handsome hotel offers a choice of single or double rooms or motel units. All have a reasonable standard of comfort, but a bigger attraction is the vivacious owner, Barbara Doyle, who will arrange tours to little-known parts of the peninsula. Rooms without en suite bathrooms are also available at a significant discount. Every second weekend of the month, the hotel's Murder Mystery Weekends attract visitors from Auckland. *200 Richmond St., Thames, tel. 07/868–6523, fax 07/868–9760. 23 rooms, 8 motel units, all with bath. Facilities: restaurant, bar. AE, DC, MC, V.*

★ **Coromandel Colonial Cottages.** These six immaculate timber cottages offer spacious and comfortable self-contained accommodation for about the same price as a standard motel room. Each has two bedrooms, a lounge room with convertible beds, a large, well-equipped kitchen, and a dining area. Arranged with military precision in two ranks, the cottages face each other across a tailored lawn surrounded by green hills on the northern outskirts of Coromandel. During vacation periods, they must be booked several months in advance. *Rings Rd., Coromandel. tel. 07/866–8857. 6 cottages. Facilities: spa, croquet lawn, minigolf, guest laundry. AE, DC, MC, V.*

4 Rotorua to Wellington

By Michael Gebicki

The first part of this chapter covers the central area of the North Island, from the Waitomo Caves to the surroundings of Lake Taupo. In this area, focused on the town of Rotorua, nature has crafted a gallery of surreal wonders that includes limestone caverns, volcanic wastelands, steaming geysers, and hissing ponds. From the shores of Lake Taupo—the country's biggest lake and the geographic bull's-eye of the North Island—Mount Ruapehu, the island's tallest peak, is plainly visible. The mountain is the site of New Zealand's largest ski area and is the dominant feature of Tongariro National Park, a haunting landscape of craters, volcanoes, and lava flows that ran with molten rock as recently as 1988.

Southeast of Lake Taupo, on the shores of Hawke's Bay, lies the town of Napier, an unexpected oasis of Art Deco architecture. Napier is also the center of an excellent wine region. Our tour of the North Island ends at its southern tip, in the charming—if windy—city of Wellington, the nation's capital.

Rotorua, the Waitomo Caves, and Lake Taupo

It's one of the most extraordinary sights in the country. Everywhere you turn the earth bubbles, boils, spits, and oozes. Drainpipes steam, flowerbeds hiss, rings tarnish, cars corrode; the rotten-egg smell of hydrogen sulfide hangs in the air, and even the local golf course has its own mud-pool hot spots where a lost ball stays lost forever.

New Zealand's most famous tourist attraction, Rotorua, sits smack on top of the most violent segment of the Taupo Volcanic Zone, which runs in a broad belt from White Island in the Bay of Plenty to Tongariro National Park, south of Lake Taupo. While the spurting geysers and sulfur springs are perfectly good reasons to visit, there's a lot more to the area than hellfire and brimstone. Drive outside the city limits and you'll find yourself in magnificent, untamed country, where spring-fed streams sprint through native forests into lakes that are home to some of the biggest rainbow trout on earth. Not only are these trout large and abundant, they seem to be genetically programmed for suicide: Anglers still regularly pull 10-pound rainbow trout from Lake Tarawera, and there are fishing guides who guarantee that no client will come home empty-handed.

Rotorua also has a well-established Maori community tracing its ancestry back to the great Polynesian migration of the 14th century. Maori culture is stamped indelibly on the town, although the majority of visitors will have their most intimate contact with that culture at a *hangi*—a traditional feast—followed by a Maori concert.

Important Addresses and Numbers

Tourist Information

Rotorua Visitor Information Centre. *67 Fenton St., Rotorua, tel. 07/348–5179. Open daily 8–5:30*

Taupo Visitor Information Centre. *13 Tongariro St., Taupo, tel. 07/378–9000. Open daily 8:30–5.*

Waitomo Caves Visitor Information Centre. *Waitomo Museum of Caves, tel. 07/878-7640. Open daily 9-5:30.*

Emergencies Dial 111 for **fire**, **police**, and **ambulance** services.

Arriving and Departing

By Plane **Mount Cook Airline** (tel. 0800/80-0737) schedules daily flights between Rotorua and Auckland, Wellington, Christchurch, and Queenstown. **Rotorua Airport** stands about 10 kilometers (6 miles) from the city center. Taxi fare to the city is $15.

By Car From Auckland, take Highway 1 south, following the signs to Hamilton. From Hamilton, follow Highway 3. The Waitomo Caves are located 6 kilometers (4 miles) east of the highway. Driving time for the journey is about three hours.

By Bus **InterCity** (tel. 09/358-4085) has four bus services daily between Auckland and Rotorua. InterCity also operates a daily service between Auckland and Waitomo Caves and between Waitomo Caves and Rotorua. **Newmans** (tel. 09/309-9738) operates twice daily on the Auckland-Rotorua route.

Guided Tours

Gray Line (tel. 09/377-0904) offers one- and two-day tours of the Waitomo Caves and Rotorua from Auckland. The one-day tour costs $120 for adults, $60 for children 5-15. The two-day tour costs $318 for adults, $222 for children 5-15. Both are half-price for children 4-15.

The **Waimangu Round Trip** is probably the most complete and spectacular tour of Rotorua. The full-day tour includes an easy 5-kilometer (3-mile) hike through the Waimangu Thermal Valley to Lake Rotomahana, where a cruiser takes visitors past steaming cliffs to the narrow isthmus that divides the lake from Lake Tarawera. After crossing the lake on a second cruiser, the tour visits a village that was buried by a volcanic eruption and ends with a dip in the Polynesian Pools in Rotorua. Lunch is included. *Bookings at Rotorua Visitor Information Centre, or tel. 07/347-1199. Tickets: $90 adults, $50 children 6-14.*

Rotorua Sightseeing Shuttle is a bus service making a circuit of the city's 23 major attractions. Passengers may leave at any stop and catch any following bus. The first bus departs from Rotorua Visitor Centre at 8:15, and the service terminates at 5:10. *Visitor Information Centre, 67 Fenton St., Bookings at Rotorua tel. 07/348-5179. Tickets: $14 for half-day, $20 for full-day, half-price for children 4-14.*

Rotorua Helicopters offers a choice of scenic flights, from a six-minute city flight ($40 per person) to a half-hour spectacular over the crater of Mount Tarawera ($140). A minimum of two passengers is required. *Box 634, Rotorua, tel. 07/357-2512.*

Tour Magic (tel. 07/345-6080) has a choice of half- and full-day minibus tours of Rotorua's prime attractions, with pick-up and drop-off at your accommodation. These tours are recommended for their personal, attentive style. Tour parties are limited to six; half-day tours cost $45-$50 per person.

The **MV *Wairaka*** (tel. 07/374-8338) is a vintage riverboat that cruises from Taupo to Huka Falls daily at 10 and 2. The two-hour cruise costs $15 for adults, $5 for children under 12. A barbecue cruise departs at 12:30 and costs $35 for adults, $15 for children.

The Waitomo Caves

This itinerary begins at Auckland and travels south through Hamilton to the Waitomo Caves, east to Rotorua, and finally south again to Lake Taupo. It's possible to complete the journey in three days, but for anyone who wants to experience the vast range of activities in the area, four days is a practical minimum.

Numbers in the margin correspond to points of interest on the Central North Island map.

❶ The **Waitomo Caves** are an ancient seabed that has been lifted and then spectacularly eroded into a surreal landscape of limestone formations and caves, many of them still unexplored. Only two caves are open to the public for guided tours: the Aranui and the Waitomo, or Glowworm Cave. The **Waitomo Cave** takes its name from the Maori words *wai* and *tomo*, water and cave, since the Waitomo River vanishes into the hillside here. Visitors are taken through by boat, and the highlight is the **Glowworm Grotto.** The glowworm is the larva of *Arachnocampa luminosa*, a member of the gnat family, which looks like a small daddy longlegs later when it emerges from its cocoon. The larva, measuring between one and two inches, lives on the roof of caves and snares its prey by dangling filaments of tiny, sticky beads; insects attracted to the light it emits through a chemical oxidation process get trapped in the deadly necklace. In one of nature's crueler ironies, it is often the adult *Arachnocampa luminosa* that is caught and eaten by the infant of the species. A single glowworm produces far less light than any firefly, but when massed in great numbers, the effect is electrifying. **Aranui Cave,** 2 kilometers (1¼ mile) beyond the Glowworm Cave, is a very different experience. Eons of dripping water have sculpted a delicate garden in pink and white limestone. The cave is named after a local Maori, Te Rutuku Aranui, who discovered the cave in 1910 when his dog disappeared inside in pursuit of a wild pig. Each cave tour lasts 45 minutes. The Glowworm Cave is high on the list of every coach tour, so try to avoid visiting between 11 and 2, when many tour groups arrive from Auckland. *Te Anga Rd., tel. 07/ 878–8227. Admission to Aranui Cave: $13.50 adults, $6.75 children under 12. Admission to both caves: $21 adults, $10.50 children under 12. Glowworm Cave tours: every hour on the hour 9–4, with late tours at 4:30 and 5:30 Nov.–Easter. Aranui Cave tours: 10, 11, 1, 2, 3.*

In the center of the caves village, the **Museum of Caves** provides an entertaining and informative look at the formation of the caves and the life cycle of the glowworm, with a number of interactive displays designed especially for children. *Waitomo Caves Village, tel. 07/878–7640. Admission: $3 adults, children under 15 free. Open daily 9–5:30.*

The **Waitomo Walkway** is a 5-kilometer (3-mile), 2½-hour walk that begins across the road from the Museum of Caves and follows the Waitomo River. The track, which passes through forests and impressive limestone outcrops, provides many visitors with their fondest memories of Waitomo. It is relatively easy and highly recommended, but there is no transport from the

BOO.

See Down Under. Spend Way Under.

Vacation Cars. Vacation Prices. Wherever your destination in Australia or New Zealand, there is sure to be one of more than 250 Budget locations nearby. Budget offers you considerable values on a wide variety of quality cars from economy size to camper vans and even 4-wheel drives. And with the flexibility of the Budget World Travel Plan[SM] rate packages, you'll always find the right car at the right price. For information and reservations, contact your travel consultant or call Budget in the U.S. at **800-472-3325**, in Australia at **132-848**, and in New Zealand at **(9) 309-6737**.

THE SMART MONEY IS ON BUDGET.

We feature Ford and other fine cars.   *A system of corporate and licensee owned locations.*

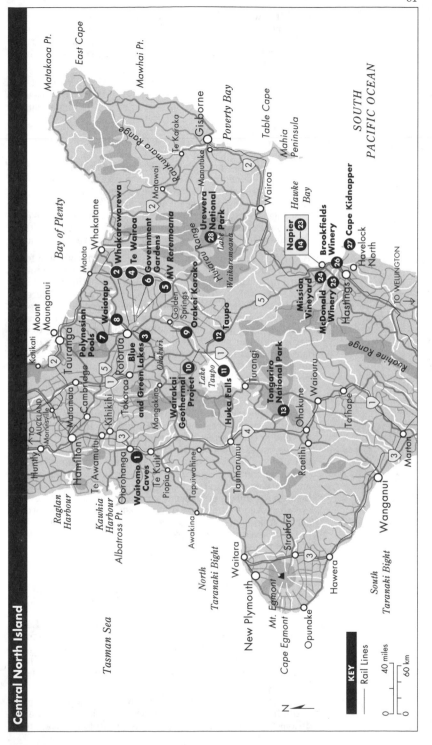

Central North Island

end of the walk back to Waitomo Caves Village. If you prefer an alternative to the complete walk, take Te Anga Road from the village, turn left onto Tumutumu Road, park at Ruakuri Reserve, and walk the short final section of the track through this delightful reserve.

From Waitomo Caves Village, return to Highway 3 and turn right to the town of Te Kuiti, where Highway 30 turns east to Rotorua. Driving time for the 150-kilometer (95-mile) journey is 2½ hours.

Rotorua and Lake Taupo

This driving tour begins at the Visitor Information Centre on Fenton Street and takes a day. (If you take the 11 AM cruise on Lake Tarawera, which is highly recommended, it will mean rearranging the tour to reach Tarawera Landing in time for the boat's departure.) From Rotorua, allow 25 minutes for the drive to Tarawera Landing. Limited picnic supplies are available from the café at the Buried Village, about 1 mile before the landing.

From the front door of the Visitor Centre, turn right and follow Fenton Street for 3 kilometers (2 miles) to **Whakarewarewa**— a mouthful of a name that the locals reduce to "Whaka." (In Maori names, "wh" is pronounced as "f," and "Whaka" is therefore spoken as "Faka.") This is easily the most accessible and popular of Rotorua's thermal areas, and also the most varied, since it gives an insight into Maori culture. Visitors are free to wander at their own pace, but you'll gain far more from the experience if you take one of the guided tours, which leave at frequent intervals from the Arts and Crafts Institute, near the ticket office. The trails that wind through the complex pass sinister, steaming pools, spitting mud ponds, and smooth silica terraces that appear to be coated in melted candle wax. The highlight is **Pohutu** ("the big splash"), a geyser that sometimes shoots to a height of over 80 feet; however, its eruptions are erratic. At the top end of the complex is a reconstructed Maori village with houses, gates, and a *marai*, a meeting house. At the lower end is a modern Maori village, but its people still cook in the traditional manner by placing meat and vegetables in flax baskets and dunking them in the steaming pools at the back of the village. At the village entrance is a graveyard in which the graves are all above ground, since it's impossible to dig down into the earth. A one-hour Maori concert takes place daily at 12:15 in the Arts and Crafts Institute. *Hemo Rd., Rotorua, tel. 07/348–9047. Admission: $9.30 adults, $8.15 children 5–14, $23 family. Concert: $8.80 adults, $2.50 children, $21 family. Open daily Nov.–Easter, 8–6; Easter–Oct. 8–5.*

Return to the city along Fenton Street and turn right into Amohau Street, which is easy to identify by the McDonalds on the left corner. After almost 3 kilometers (2 miles), turn right where a sign points to Tarawera and the **Blue and Green Lakes.** This road loops through forests and past a parking lot that overlooks the two lakes. The color contrast is most striking when Blue Lake is in sunlight and Green Lake shaded by clouds; when both are in either full sun or cloud, the difference is hard to detect.

Just past the lakes is **Te Wairoa,** the buried village. At the end of the 19th century this village was the starting point for expeditions to the pink and white terraces of Rotomahana, on the slopes of Mount Tarawera. These silica terraces were formed by the mineral-rich water from a geyser. As the water cascaded down the mountainside, it formed a series of baths, which became progressively cooler as they neared the lake. In the latter half of the last century these fabulous terraces were the country's major tourist attraction, but they were completely destroyed when Mount Tarawera erupted in 1886. The explosion, which was heard as far away as Auckland, killed 153 people and buried the village of Te Wairoa under a sea of mud and hot ash. The village has been excavated, and today a path makes a circuit of this fascinating and deceptively tranquil spot, complete with grazing deer. Of special interest is the *whare* (hut) of the *tohunga* (priest) Tuhoto Ariki, who predicted the destruction of the village. Eleven days before the eruption, two separate tourist parties saw a Maori war canoe emerge from the mists of Lake Tarawera and disappear again—a vision the tohunga interpreted as a sign of impending disaster. Four days after the eruption, the hundred-year-old tohunga was dug out of his buried whare still alive, only to die in hospital a few days later. The path, after circling the village, dives down the hill alongside Te Wairoa Falls, then passes through a cave, crosses a bridge, and ascends the moist, fern-covered slope on the far side. The walk is a delight, although the lower section of the track is steep and slippery in places. *Tarawera Rd., tel. 07/362–8287. Admission: $7 adults, $2 children 6–15, $16 family. Open daily 9–4:30, summer 8:30–5:30.*

Four kilometers (2½ miles) beyond the village a sign points right to Tarawera Landing. This road leads to a parking lot on the shores of Lake Tarawera, where a restored lake cruiser, ❺ the MV *Reremoana,* makes regular scenic runs. Especially recommended is the two-hour cruise, which departs at 11 AM and stops for 30 minutes at the foot of Mount Tarawera, where passengers can picnic, swim, or walk across the isthmus to Lake Rotomahana. Forty-five-minute cruises depart from the landing every hour from 1 to 4. Tarawera Launch Cruises, tel. 07/362–8595. Tickets: $15 adults, $7.50 children under 15, $35 family.

Return to Rotorua by the same route and turn right into Hinemaru Street, then right again through the gates of the ❻ **Government Gardens.** The Maoris call this area *Whangapiro,* "evil-smelling place"—a far more appropriate name for these bizarre gardens, where sulfur pits bubble and fume behind the manicured rose beds. The focus of interest here is the extraordinary neo-Tudor **Bath House.** Built as a spa at the turn of the century, this building is now Rotorua's Art and History Museum. One room on the ground floor is devoted to the eruption of Mount Tarawera, with a number of artifacts that were unearthed from the debris and a remarkable collection of photographs that show the terraces of Rotomahana before the eruption. *Government Gardens, Arawa St., tel. 07/348–4199. Open weekdays 10–4:30, weekends 1–4:30.*

Leave the gardens by the main gate, turn left into Hinemaru Street, and take the first left, Hinemoa Street. This road ends ❼ at the **Polynesian Pools.** A trip to Rotorua would hardly be complete without a dip in these soothing, naturally heated mineral baths. A wide choice of baths is available, from large communal pools to family pools to small, private baths for two. Massage and saunas are also available. *Hinemoa St., tel. 07/348–1328. Admission: Children's pool: $6 adults, $2 children 4–14; adult*

pool: $6; private pool (per half-hr.): $7 adults, $2 children.
Open 9 AM–10 PM.

Leave Rotorua by Fenton Street, which becomes Highway 5, and follow the signs to Taupo. After 30 kilometers (19 miles), turn left where a sign points to **Waiotapu.** This is a complete thermal wonderland—a freakish, fantastic landscape of deep, sulfur-crusted pits, jade-colored ponds, silica terraces, and a steaming lake edged with red algae and bubbling with tiny beads of carbon dioxide. The most spectacular feature is the **Lady Knox Geyser,** which erupts precisely at 10:15 daily—but not through some miracle of Mother Nature's. Five pounds of soap powder poured into the vent of the geyser causes the water to boil, and the vent is then blocked with rags until the pressure builds sufficiently for the geyser to explode. The phenomenon was discovered early this century. Wardens from a nearby prison farm would bring convicts to a pool here to wash their clothes. They found that when the water became soapy the pool would boil fiercely, and one of the wardens built a rock cairn to serve as a nozzle, concentrating the force of the boiling water and making the geyser rise even higher. *State Hwy. 5, tel. 07/366–6333. Admission: $7.50 adults, $2.50 children 5–15, $18 family. Open daily 8:30–5.*

Continue toward Taupo along Highway 5. At Mihi Bridge, just past Golden Springs, turn right along a road signposted "Orakei Korako." If by now you think you've seen enough bubbling mud pools and fuming craters to last a lifetime, this captivating thermal valley will change your mind. On the shores of Lake Ohakuri, a jet boat waits to take passengers across to **Orakei Korako,** where geyser-fed streams hiss and steam as they flow into the waters of the lake. One of the most impressive features of this area is the multicolored silica terrace, believed to be the largest in the world since the destruction of the terraces of Rotomahana. At the bottom of Aladdin's Cave, the vent of an ancient volcano, is a jade-green pool that was once used exclusively by Maori women as a beauty parlor, which is where the name Orakei Korako—"a place of adorning"—originated. *Tel. 07/378–3131. Admission: $9 adults, $4 children 5–15, $25 family. Open daily 8:30–4:30, winter 8:30–4.*

Return to Highway 5 and proceed toward Taupo. Just past the junction with Highway 1 you can see the **Wairakai Geothermal Project** in the distance, wreathed in swirling clouds of steam. The steam, tapped through underground shafts, drives generators that provide about 5% of New Zealand's electrical power. There are no guided tours of the plant, but the Geothermal Information Centre close to the highway has an informative display of the process by which steam is converted into electricity. *State Hwy. 1, tel. 07/374–8216. Admission free. Open daily 9–noon, 1–4.*

Beyond the power station a road turns left off the highway toward **Huka Falls,** where the Waikato River thunders through a narrow chasm and over a 35-foot rock ledge before it pours into Lake Taupo. The view from the footbridge is superb.

The town of **Taupo** is the services base for Lake Taupo, the largest lake in New Zealand. You can take your pick here from a wide range of water sports—sailing, cruising, waterskiing, swimming, but most of all, fishing: Taupo is the rainbow-trout capital of the universe. The average Taupo trout weighs in at around 4 pounds, and there is no closed season. For nonanglers, several sailing boats, modern catamarans, and vintage riverboats offer sightseeing cruises. From Taupo, the driving time back to Rotorua is about 90 minutes.

🔞 At the southern end of Lake Taupo is **Tongariro National Park,** the country's first, established on land donated by a Maori chief. The park is dominated by the peaks of three active volcanoes, one of which, Mount Ruapehu, is, at 2,752 meters (9,175 feet), the tallest mountain on the North Island. Ruapehu last erupted in 1988, spewing a shower of volcanic rocks. Tongariro's spectacular combination of dense rimu forests, crater lakes, stark, barren lava fields, and bird life makes it the most impressive and popular of the North Island's national parks. It has many walking trails, from the 40-minute Ridge Track to the Mount Tongariro Traverse, which crosses the mountain from one side to the other and is one of the finest one-day walks in the country. The longest walk in the park is the six-day Round the Mountain track. The Whakapapa ski area, on the north side of Mount Ruapehu, is New Zealand's largest. On the southern side of the mountain is a second ski area, Turoa, which generally offers a longer ski season than Whakapapa's June to October.

Highway 1 skirts the eastern side of the park, but the easiest access is from Highway 47, on the western side. For more information, contact the Department of Conservation Field Centre at Wkahapapa Village off Highway 47 (mailing address: Whakapapa Visitor Centre, Private Bag, Mount Ruapehu, tel. 07/892–3729). Accommodation in the village ranges from the **THC Tongariro Hotel** (Mount Ruapahu, tel. 07/892–3809; Very Expensive) to the cabins and campsites in the motor camp. The park has nine huts for trampers.

What to See and Do with Children

Agrodome. Most of this sprawling complex is dedicated to the four-footed wooly New Zealander. Shows daily at 9:15, 11, and 2:30 demonstrate the different breeds of sheep, shearing techniques, and sheepdogs at work. Children can participate by feeding lambs and milking a cow. In another part of the complex, **Trainworld,** scale-model trains rumble through a miniature slice of English countryside. The complex is part of a 320-acre farm, a 10-minute drive northwest of Rotorua. *Riverdale Park, Western Rd., Ngongotaha, tel. 07/357–4350. Admission to Agrodome: $8 adults, $4 children 5–15; Trainworld: $7 adults, $3.50 children. Open daily 9–4:30.*

Leisure World. This giant complex includes waterslides, three-wheeler dirt bikes, slot cars, a minigolf course, and video games. *Marguerita St., Rotorua, tel. 07/348–9674. Admission: free. Rides cost $3–$6 per person. Open weekdays 10–5, weekends 10–6.*

Rainbow Springs. Situated some 5 kilometers (3 miles) from Rotorua, this leafy park is home to many species of New Zealand wildlife, including deer, kiwis and other native birds, wild pigs, and most of all, trout. The trout that congregate for feeding sessions at the Rainbow and Fairy Springs are the King Kongs of the trout world. On the other side of State Highway 5 is the second part of the complex, Rainbow Farm, which demonstrates New Zealand farming life. A show similar to the one at the Agrodome takes place daily at 10:30, 1, and 2:30. *Fairy Springs Rd., tel. 07/347–9301. Admission (Rainbow Springs or Rainbow Farm): $9.70 adults, $3 children 5–15. Open daily 8–5.*

Off the Beaten Track

At the northern end of Rotorua, on the shores of the lake, stands **St. Faith's,** the Anglican church for the Maori village of Ohinemutu. Before the present Tudor-style church was built in 1910, one of the ministers was Seymour Spencer Mills, of Hartford, Connecticut, who preached to the Arawa people for 50 years. He is commemorated in a small window above the organ chancel, preaching to a group of Maoris as he holds his habitual umbrella. The interior of the church, which is richly decorated with carvings inset with mother-of-pearl, deserves attention at any time, but it's at its best during Sunday services, when the rich, melodic voices of the Maori choir rise in hymns. The service at 8 AM is in the Maori language; the 10 AM service is in both Maori and English. *Memorial Dr., Rotorua.*

Sports and the Outdoors

Fishing The lakes of the Rotorua/Taupo region are one of the few places where tales of the big one can be believed. If you want to keep the trout of a lifetime from becoming just another fishy story, it pays to have a boat with some expert advice on board. Expect to pay about $70 per hour for a fishing guide and a 20-foot cruiser that will take up to six passengers. The minimum charter period is two hours, and fishing gear and bait are included in the price. A one-day fishing license costs $8 per person and is available on board the boat. In Rotorua, fishing operators include **Clark Gregor** (tel. 07/347–1730), **Bryan Colman** (tel. 07/348–7766), and **Brian Ruby** (tel. 07/347–6436). In Taupo, contact **Richard Staines** (tel. 07/378–2736) or **Punch Wilson** (tel. 07/378–5596). At the other end of the scale, a luxury cruiser on Lake Taupo costs about $150 per hour; for more information, contact **Chris Jolly Boats** (Box 1020, Taupo, tel. 07/378–0623).

Hiking The **Rainbow Mountain Track** is a two-day, 26-kilometer (16-mile) walking track south of Rotorua that takes in the most active thermal areas in the country, the Waimangu Thermal Valley and Waiotapu, as well as the summit of Rainbow Mountain, an active volcano. The walk is moderately strenuous, but the reward is the chance to see secluded areas of intense thermal activity. *For information, contact the Forestry Corporation Visitors Centre, Long Mile Rd., Rotorua, tel. 07/346–2028.*

Rafting The center of the North Island has a number of rivers with grade-3 to grade-5 rapids that make excellent white-water rafting. For scenic beauty, the Rangitaki River is recommended. For experienced rafters who want a challenge, the Wairoa and the Mohaka rivers have exhilarating grade-5 rapids. In Taupo, contact **Rapid Descents** (tel. 07/377–0419); in Rotorua, **White Water Raft Adventures** (tel. 07/345–7182). Transport, wet suits, and meals are provided. The price of a one-day trip is about $65 per person.

Black-Water Rafting This is an unusual way to see the caves, and a lot of fun. Participants must first prove themselves with a giant leap into the Huhunoa Stream; the next three hours are spent dressed in wet suits and equipped with cavers' helmets and inflated inner tubes, floating through underground caverns. While the combination of darkness and freezing water might sound like a refined form of torture, the trip is an exhilarating one that will live vividly in your memory long after the goose bumps have disappeared. The cost is $50 per person. Departure times vary, depending on daily demand. *Information and bookings: Black Water Rafting, Box 13, Waitomo Caves, tel. 07/878-7640.*

Dining

Rotorua offers a unique New Zealand dining experience, the *hangi*, or Maori feast. Traditionally, meat and vegetables placed in flax baskets were gently steamed in an earth oven lined with heated stones and wet leaves. Several of the larger hotels in Rotorua offer a hangi, and although the food is still cooked by steam it's unlikely that it will be buried in the traditional earth oven. Lamb, pork, and seafood are usually available at the buffet-style meals, together with pumpkin and *kumara* (sweet potato), a staple of the Maori diet. Almost without exception, hangis in Rotorua are followed by a Maori concert, a performance of traditional songs and dances. The hangis at the **Sheraton** (tel. 07/348-7139) and the **Travelodge** (tel. 07/348-1174) enjoy long-standing reputations as two of the best in town. Expect to pay about $35 per person.

Price categories for restaurants are the same as in the Auckland Dining section in Chapter 3.

Expensive **Poppy's Villa Restaurant.** In an Edwardian villa about a mile from the town center, this elegant restaurant is synonymous with fine dining in Rotorua. First courses on the modern European-style menu include smoked salmon in a mousse of horseradish, capers, and crab on lemon coulis, and sweetbreads in a walnut brioche. The selection of eight main courses includes rack of lamb with kiwi sauce, veal in a brandy and apple sauce, and salmon with a mustard hollandaise. *4 Marguerita St., Rotorua, tel. 07/347-1700. Reservations required. Dress: casual but neat. AE, DC, MC, V. No lunch.*

Moderate **Incas Cafe.** This casual café caters to most tastes, with salads, grills, pasta, and fish dishes, but despite the name, nothing south-of-the-border appears on the menu. The restaurant's 1 AM closing time draws the night owls. *Pukaki and Fenton Sts., Rotorua, tel. 07/348-3831. Reservations not required. Dress: casual. AE, DC, MC, V. No lunch Sat.-Tues.*
Zanelli's Italian Cafe. Rotorua's favorite Italian restaurant offers a predictable range of dishes—spaghetti bolognese, lasagna, cannelloni, and fettuccine with various sauces; but the food is well flavored and the service is efficient. The decor—red walls, stone floor, plastic-topped tables—and the up-tempo Italian music create a slightly hectic atmosphere. *23 Amohia St., Rotorua, tel. 07/348-4908. Reservations not required. Dress: casual. DC, MC, V. No lunch.*

Inexpensive **Orchid Gardens Cafe.** If you are staying close to the city and want an alternative to hotel breakfasts, this is just the place. The café is located at the end of the Government Gardens, and diners are treated to a breakfast surrounded by palm trees and the sound of bird calls and trickling water. The breakfast menu lists fruit juices, cereals, toast, eggs, and bacon. Later in the day the menu expands to include soup, quiche, shrimp cocktail, and steaks. The café opens at 8 on weekdays, 7 on weekends. *Government Gardens, Hinemaru St., Rotorua, tel. 07/347–6182. No reservations. Dress: casual. MC, V. No dinner.*

Street Cafe. Situated beneath the veranda of the Princes Gate Hotel, this outdoor café is the perfect place for warm-weather eating. The menu lists beef on rye, croissants, burgers, BLTs, salads, and a fresh-fruit platter. *1 Arawa St., Rotorua, tel. 07/348–1179. No reservations. Dress: casual. AE, DC, MC, V. No dinner.*

Lodging

The accommodation scene in Rotorua is highly competitive. For most of the year there are many more hotel beds than visitors, and a number of hotels and motels offer significant discounts on their standard rates. The Visitor Centre on Fenton Street acts as a clearinghouse for discount accommodation, and you can often save up to half the published rate for a particular hotel by booking through the center on arrival in Rotorua. The exception is school holidays, when accommodation should be booked in advance.

Price categories for hotels are the same as in the Auckland Lodging section in Chapter 3. Highly recommended lodgings are indicated by a star ★.

Very Expensive   **Huka Lodge.** Buried in parklike grounds at the edge of the
★   frisky Waikato River, this superb lodge is the standard by which New Zealand's other sporting lodges are judged. It is run in the European style, however, and the atmosphere of aristocratic privilege may be a little overwhelming for some tastes. The large, lavish guest rooms, decorated in muted grays and whites, are arranged in blocks of two or three. All have sliding glass doors that open to a view across lawns to the river. In the interest of tranquility, guest rooms are not equipped with telephones, televisions, or radios. The five-course formal dinners are gourmet affairs served at a communal dining table. The wine list is a showcase of the very best New Zealand has to offer. Breakfasts include such luxuries as fresh croissants, brioche, and pastries. Children are accommodated by arrangement. *Huka Falls Rd., Taupo (mailing address: Box 95, Taupo), tel. 07/378–5791, fax 07/378–0427. 17 rooms with bath. Facilities: tennis court, fishing, spa, bar, restaurant. Tariff includes breakfast and dinner. AE, DC, MC, V.*

Sheraton Rotorua. Close to the Whakarewarewa thermal area on the outskirts of town, this hotel offers the chain's usual high standard of comforts and amenities. Request a room on one of the top two floors overlooking the golf course. The hotel's nightly hangi is one of the best in town. *Fenton and Sala Sts., Rotorua, tel. 07/348–7139, fax 07/348–8378. 130 rooms with bath. Facilities: outdoor pool, spa, sauna, gym, tennis court, 2 restaurants, bar. AE, DC, MC, V.*

Solitaire Lodge. It would be difficult to imagine a finer backdrop than the lakes, forests, and volcanoes that surround this plush retreat. Set high on a peninsula that juts out into Lake Tarawera, the lodge has been designed as a sophisticated hideaway where a few guests at a time can enjoy the scenery in a relaxed, informal atmosphere—a mood that has been cultivated by its ebullient owner, Reg Turner. All the suites are luxuriously equipped, though the bathrooms in the junior suites are modest in size. The best room is the Tarawera Suite, which has panoramic views. The surrounding lakes and forests hold many possibilities for hiking, boating, and fishing. Lake Tarawera is well known for its king-size rainbow trout, and the lodge has boats and fishing gear. Smoking is not permitted indoors. *Ronald Rd., Lake Tarawera, Rotorua, tel. 07/362–8208, fax 07/362–8445. 10 rooms with bath. Facilities: spa, bar, restaurant, sailing boats, motorboat, fishing. Tariff includes all meals. AE, DC, MC, V.*

Moderate **Cascades Motor Lodge.** Set on the shores of Lake Taupo, these
★ attractive brick and timber rooms are large, comfortable, and furnished and decorated in a smart contemporary style. The two-story "luxury" apartments, which sleep up to seven, have a lounge room, bedroom, kitchen, and dining room on the ground floor in an open-plan design, glass doors leading to a large patio, and a second bedroom and bathroom on the upper floor. Studio rooms have only one bedroom. All rooms are equipped with a spa bath. Room 1 is closest to the lake and the small beach. *Lake Terr., Taupo, tel. 07/378–3774, fax 07/378–0372. 24 rooms with bath. Facilities: heated outdoor pool. AE, DC, MC, V.*

★ **Cedar Lodge Motel.** These spacious modern units, about a half-mile from the city center, are exceptional value, especially for families. All the double-story units have a modern, well-equipped kitchen and lounge room on the lower floor and a bedroom on the mezzanine floor above. All have at least one queen-size and one single bed, and some have a queen-size bed and three singles. Every unit has its own spa pool in the private courtyard at the back. The grey-flecked carpet, smoked-glass tables, and recessed lighting have a clean, contemporary flavor. Request a room at the back, away from Fenton Street. *296 Fenton St., Rotorua, tel. 07/349–0300, fax 07/349–1115. 15 rooms with bath. Facilities: guest laundry. AE, DC, MC, V.*

Princes Gate Hotel. This ornate timber hotel occupies a prime position across the road from the Government Gardens. It was built in 1897 on the Coromandel Peninsula and brought here in 1917, and efforts have been made to re-create a turn-of-the-century flavor inside. The rooms are large and comfortable, and all have *en suite* facilities and french doors leading to the balcony. Motel rooms, located in a separate complex, were totally renovated in 1991, but they lack the atmosphere of those in the hotel. *1 Arawa St., Rotorua, tel. 07/348–1179, fax 07/348–6215. 29 hotel rooms, 12 motel units. Facilities: spa pool, mineral baths, tennis court, 2 restaurants, bar. AE, DC, MC, V.*

Inexpensive **Eaton Hall.** This well-kept, friendly guest house has an outstanding location one street from the heart of Rotorua. Guest rooms are homey and comfortable and maintained to a standard well above that in most guest houses. Room 4, a twin-bedded room with its own shower, is available at no extra charge. *39 Hinemaru St., Rotorua, tel. 07/347–0366. 8 rooms share 2 baths. Facilities: spa. Tariff includes breakfast. AE, DC, MC, V.*

Napier and Hawke's Bay

New Zealand is a country that prides itself on natural wonders, but Napier is an exception: This city of 50,000, situated about two-thirds of the way down the east coast of the North Island, is best known for its architecture. After an earthquake devastated Napier in 1931, the citizens rebuilt it in the Art Deco style fashionable at the time. Today the city is an Art Deco treasure.

The mild climate and beaches of Hawke Bay make this a popular vacation area for New Zealanders. (*Hawke* Bay is the body of water; *Hawke's* Bay is the region.) Another attraction is wine: The region produces some of New Zealand's best.

Important Addresses and Numbers

Tourist Information Napier Visitor Information Centre. *Marine Parade, Napier, tel. 06/835–4949. Open weekdays 8:30–5, weekends 9–5.*

Emergencies Dial 111 for **fire, police,** and **ambulance** services.

Arriving and Departing

By Plane **Air New Zealand** (tel. 06/835–3288) has several flights daily between Napier and Auckland, Wellington, and Christchurch.

By Car The main route between Napier and the north is Highway 5. Driving time from Taupo is 2½ hours. Highway 2 is the main southern route. Driving time to Wellington is five hours.

By Bus **Newmans** (tel. 09/309–9738) and **InterCity** (tel. 09/358–4085) both operate daily bus services between Napier and Auckland, Rotorua, and Wellington.

Guided Tours

Bay Tours features a four-hour tour of the various wineries in the area. It offers a chance to sample some of the boutique wines unavailable to independent travelers. *Napier Visitor Information Centre, tel. 06/843–6953. Tickets: $34 adults, first child and children under 10 free, other children $17. Sun.–Fri. 10:30, Sat. 1:15.*

Twin City Tours offers several guided tours, including city sightseeing, wine tasting, and trips to the gannet colony at Cape Kidnappers. *102 Harold Holt Ave., Napier, tel. 06/843–2318.*

The Art Deco Trust offers an excellent and informative guided walking tour of Napier. The 1-mile walk takes two hours. *Hawke's Bay Museum, 9 Herschell St., tel. 06/835–0022. Cost: $5 adults, children under 13 free. Tours Sun., Wed. 2 PM.*

Exploring Napier and Hawke's Bay

Number in the margin corresponds to point of interest on the Central North Island map.

⑭ This tour begins with a short walk around the center of **Napier,** focusing on the city's Art Deco buildings. Art Deco, the style born at the 1925 Exposition of Modern and Decorative Arts in Paris, can be recognized by its stylized decorative motifs—

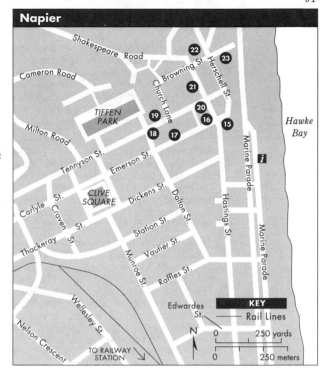

chevrons, zigzags, sunbursts, deer or dancers silhouetted in mid-leap. In some cases, Napier's Art Deco heritage has been spoiled by the addition of garish advertising or unsympathetic alterations to shopfronts. The classic Art Deco features that remain are often found above ground-floor level, and the first part of this tour might well result in a stiff neck. The walk is followed by a brief wine-tasting tour. The visit to the gannet colony at the end of the tour is possible only between October and March.

Numbers in the margin correspond to points of interest on the Napier map.

Begin at the **Napier Visitor Information Centre** in Marine Parade. Walk north along Marine Parade with the sea on your right and turn left at the clocktower of the A & B Building. The first notable building is the **Bank of New Zealand** on the left. The Maori theme on the lintels above the main entrance is echoed in the ceiling inside the building.

Continue along Emerson Street and cross into the pedestrian mall. The **Criterion Hotel** on the right is typical of the Spanish Mission style, whose popularity in the reconstructed Napier was due largely to its success in Santa Barbara, California, which had been devastated by its own earthquake just a few years before. Buildings along both sides of this mall number among Napier's finest examples of Art Deco, including **Hannahs,** the **Bowman's Building, McGruers,** the **Hawke's Bay Chambers,** and below the chambers, **Ju Ju's Restaurant.** Detour left into Dalton Street and look across the road to the balcony of the pink **Countrywide Bank Building,** one of Napier's Art Deco masterpieces.

Return to the intersection of Emerson Street and continue along Dalton Street to the next corner. Cross to the left side of ⑱ the street to view the decorative frieze on **Hildebrand's,** the building on the corner of Tennyson Street. Hildebrand was a German who migrated to New Zealand—thus the German flag at one end, the New Zealand at the other, and the wavy lines in the middle to symbolize the sea passage between the two countries.

Turn right into Tennyson Street; just past the next corner on ⑲ the left is the **Daily Telegraph Building,** an Art Deco classic. On ⑳ the right is the **Market Reserve Building,** the first to rise from the rubble following the earthquake. Turn left at the next cor-㉑ ner into Hastings Street. The facade of **Alsop's Bar,** on the left, has altered little since its previous incarnation as Hartson's Music Shop, which survived the quake.

Turn right into Browning Street; on the opposite corner is the ㉒ **Ministry of Works** building with its decorative lighthouse pillar at the front, still considered Art Deco despite its slightly forbidding appearance. On the next corner, on the right, is the ㉓ **Hawke's Bay Art Gallery and Museum.** Using newspaper reports, photographs, and audiovisuals, the museum re-creates the suffering caused by the earthquake. The museum also houses a unique display of artifacts of the Ngati Kahungunu people of the east coast. *65 Marine Pde., Napier, tel. 06/835–9668. Admission: adults $2, children under 14 free. Open weekdays 10–4:30, weekends 10–5.*

Numbers in the margin correspond to points of interest on the Central North Island map.

Leave Napier by Kennedy Road, which runs southwest from the city center toward Taradale. Just past Anderson Park, turn right into Auckland Road and left at the end into Church Road. ㉔ On the right is the **Mission Vineyard,** the oldest in the country. The vineyard at Taradale was established by Catholic Marist brothers in the late 1850s, after an earlier vineyard farther to the north at Poverty Bay was abandoned. Legend has it that in 1852 one of the brothers made a barrel of sacramental wine and shipped it to Napier; the seamen broached the cargo, drank the wine, and filled the empty cask with seawater. The pinot noir and semillon/sauvignon blanc blend both deserve attention. *Church Rd., Taradale, tel. 06/844–2259. Open Mon.–Sat. 8–5, Sun. 1–4.*

㉕ Continue along Church Road and turn right at the **McDonald Winery.** This long-established vineyard benefited from an injection of capital and expertise when it became part of the Montana wine making group in 1989. The Church Road Chardonnay and Pinot Noir have excited oenophiles. The winery operates free tours daily at 11, 1, 2, and 3. *200 Church Rd., Taradale, tel. 06/844–2053. Open summer Mon.–Thurs. 9–5, Fri.–Sat. 10–6, Sun. 11–5; Mar.–Nov., Mon.–Sat. 9–5, Sun. 11–4.*

Farther along Church Road, turn left at the intersection of Puketapu Road; follow it as it changes its name to Meeanee Road, and after about 6 kilometers (4 miles) turn right into ㉖ Brookfields Road and follow the signs to **Brookfields Winery.** This is one of the most attractive wineries in the area, befitting its status as a premier producer. The estate chardonnay and the pinot gris are usually outstanding, but the showpiece is the cabernet-merlot blend, characterized by intense fruit and assertive oak. *Brookfields Rd., Meeanee, tel. 06/834–4615. Open Mon.–Sun. 9–5.*

Return toward Napier along Brookfields Road, and at the intersection with State Highway 2 turn right and then left, following the signs to Te Awange and Clifton. The road follows the southern curve of Hawke Bay and ends at **Cape Kidnapper.** Named by Captain James Cook after local Maoris tried to kidnap the servant of Cook's Tahitian interpreter, the cape is the site of a large **gannet colony.** The gannet is a big white sea bird with black-tipped flight feathers, a golden crown, and wings that can reach a span of up to 6 feet. When the birds find a shoal of fish, they fold their wings and plunge straight into the sea at tremendous speed. Their migratory pattern ranges from western Australia to the Chatham Islands, about 800 kilometers (500 miles) east of Christchurch, but they generally nest only on remote islands. The gannet colony at Cape Kidnappers is believed to be the only mainland sanctuary in existence. Between October and March, about 15,000 gannets build their nests here, hatch their young, and prepare them for their long migratory flight. It is possible to walk to the sanctuary along the beach from Clifton, which is about 24 kilometers (15 miles) south of Napier, but the journey cannot be made at high tide. The 8-kilometer (5-mile) walk must begin no earlier than three hours after high tide; the return journey must begin no later than four hours before the next high tide. Tidal information is available at Clifton. A rest hut with refreshments is available near the colony. A far easier alternative is to ride aboard one of the **Garret Beach Adventures** (tel. 06/875–0898) tractor-trailers that are pulled along the beach at Te Awanga, 21 kilometers (13 miles) south of Napier. The fare is $14 for adults, $11 for children 12–17, $9 for children under 12; the tractors depart two hours before low tide. The trip takes 4–4½ hours. If tides prevent the trip along the beach, the only other access is across private farmland. However, **Gannet Safaris** (tel. 06/875–0511) operates a four-wheel-drive bus to Cape Kidnappers from Summerlee Station, just past Te Awanga. A minimum of four is required for this tour, and the fare is $35 adults, $17 children 4–15.

Northeast of Napier is **Urewera National Park,** a vast, remote region of forests and lakes straddling the Huiarau Range. The park's outstanding feature is the glorious **Lake Waikaremoana** ("Sea of Rippling Waters"), a forest-girded lake with good swimming, boating, fishing, and walks. The lake is circled by a 50-kilometer (31-mile) walking track; the three- to four-day walk is popular and in the summer months the lakeside tramping huts are often heavily used. There are many other short walks nearby. The one-hour walk to Lake Waikareiti Track is especially recommended. For information, contact the Department of Conservation Field Centre at Aniwaniwa, on the eastern arm of Lake Waikaremoana (mailing address: Aniwaniwa, Private Bag, Wairoa, tel. 06/837–3803). The motor camp on the lakeshore has cabins, chalets, and motel units. In the summer months a launch operates sightseeing and fishing trips from the motor camp.

What to See and Do with Children

Kiwi House. New Zealand's national symbol is the star attraction at this nocturnal wildlife house. After the half-hour educational and environmental show at 1, visitors may handle the kiwis. *Marine Pde., Napier, tel. 06/835-7553. Admission: $3 adults, $1 children 5-15, $7 family. Open daily 11-3.*

Napier Aquarium. Sharks, rays, tropical fish, saltwater crocodiles, turtles, and piranha are displayed in this drum-shaped building on the waterfront. *Marine Parade, Napier, tel. 06/ 835-7579. Admission: $6.50 adults, $3.25 children 5-15, $17 family. Open daily 9-5.*

Dining

Price categories for restaurants are the same as in the Auckland Dining section in Chapter 3. Highly recommended restaurants are indicated by a star ★.

Expensive **Bayswater on the Beach.** The changing, international menu at
★ this waterfront restaurant features some creative combinations of ingredients, such as chargrilled scallops with champagne and lemon sauce, rack of lamb with a black-olive tapenade, and for a first course, brioche with pâté, and tomato and roast pepper salad with shavings of Parmesan. The voguish, mostly white restaurant with tartan chairs has a strong local following and is especially popular for lunch on weekends. The moderately priced wine list offer some of the best that Hawke's Bay produces. In warm weather, request a table on the deck outside; otherwise, a table at the window. *Hardinge Rd., Napier, tel. 06/835-8517. Reservations recommended. Dress: casual. AE, DC, MC, V.*

Beaches. The strength of this bayside restaurant is its imaginative seafood dishes, such as the scallops sautéed with ginger, cashews, spring onions, and saki, or the delicious crayfish with vermouth, garlic, and fresh herbs baked in pastry. Decorated in pink and white, the restaurant has views across Hawke Bay. *War Memorial Bldg., Marine Pde., Napier, tel. 06/835-8180. Reservations recommended. Dress: casual. AE, DC, MC, V. No lunch Sat.-Tues. Closed Sun.*

★ **Bucks Great Wall Restaurant.** Housed in a landmark building on Napier's Marine Parade, this opulent and sophisticated restaurant is a real treat for anyone who enjoys Cantonese cooking. The menu lists almost 100 dishes, from Peking duck to crayfish to sautéed prawns with crispy rice, and while it rarely ventures into unfamiliar territory, the food is delicious and beautifully presented. The earthen-pot dishes are particularly good. In addition to the à la carte menu, there are three fixed-price selections, from $30 to $40 per person. The gregarious owner imports her chefs and even installed a laundry on the premises when the local service sent back tablecloths that were not quite whiter than white. *Marine Pde. and Emerson St., Napier, tel. 06/835-0088. Reservations not required. Dress: casual. AE, DC, MC, V. No lunch weekends.*

Moderate **Vidal's Barrel Room Restaurant.** Set in a vineyard on the southern outskirts of Hastings, this restaurant has a relaxed country atmosphere that's perfect for family dining. The menu relies heavily on steaks, but there is usually a choice of grilled salmon, spareribs, and pasta dishes, plus a changing blackboard menu. Old wine barrels, chunky furniture, and stained-glass windows give the restaurant an earthy appeal. In the winter there are open fires; in summer, a courtyard for open-air dining. If time allows, visit the wine shop and take a vineyard tour. *913 St. Aubyn St., East Hastings, tel. 06/876–8105. Reservations recommended weekends. Dress: casual but neat. DC, MC, V. Closed Sun.*

Lodging

Price categories for hotels are the same as in the Auckland Lodging section in Chapter 3. Highly recommended lodgings are indicated by a star ★.

Expensive **Ormlie Lodge.** This ornate, sprawling timber house offers a
★ taste of gracious country living at a reasonable price. Guest rooms, located on the upper level of the double-story house, are large, comfortable, and furnished with antiques. Room 4 has a Jacuzzi and french doors onto the balcony. To one side of the lodge is a group of four comfortable, modern timber chalets, an especially good value for a family. The hosts are warm and welcoming people who will happily point out golf courses or prime fishing spots in the area. The lodge is located in pastoral wine-growing country, about a 15-minute drive south of Napier. *Omarunui Rd., Waiohiki, Taradale, tel. 06/844–5774, fax 06/844–5499. 4 lodge rooms, 4 chalets. Facilities: restaurant, bar. AE, DC, MC, V.*

Moderate **Edgewater Motor Lodge.** These motel rooms are about average in size, facilities, and character, but they offer a central location and sea views. Rooms on the upper level have balconies, and there are several room styles to suit couples or families. *359 Marine Pde., Napier, tel. 06/835–1140, fax 06/835–6600. 20 rooms with bath. Facilities: spa pool, outdoor pool, guest laundry. AE, DC, MC, V.*

★ **Mon Logis Guesthouse.** The French owner of this seafront house has modeled his accommodation on the *logis* of his homeland—a refined version of traditional bed-and-breakfast accommodation. Rooms are large and prettily decorated in a Continental style with eiderdowns and feather pillows. Although they lack the sea view, the two rooms at the back of the house are quieter: Buttes Chaumont has an *en suite* bathroom, while Paris's bathroom is located off the hall. But what most sets this place apart from the standard B&B is the food. In the morning guests have brioche or croissants, freshly baked in the house, plus a cooked dish and filter coffee. Children are not accommodated. A four-course dinner at $30 per person, including wine, is available by arrangement. *415 Marine Pde., Napier, tel. 06/835–2125, fax 06/435–4196. 4 rooms with bath. Tariff includes breakfast. AE, DC, MC, V.*

Wellington

Most visitors find themselves in the capital more by necessity than by choice. Perched at the southern tip of the North Island, Wellington is the jumping-off point for the ferry south, and many travelers, in their rush to the South Island, pass through without a second glance. Yet those who delay their departure for even a single day will discover a sociable city of real charm, small enough to be easily explored on foot, yet large enough to cater to cultured tastes.

The city was named after the Duke of Wellington, the conqueror of Napoleon in his final defeat at Waterloo, and originally settled by English pioneers who purchased land from the New Zealand Company. Shortly after the Treaty of Waitangi was concluded in 1840, Auckland was chosen as the site for the new national capital; but the prosperous and influential gold miners of the South Island waged a campaign for a more central capital, and in 1865 the seat of government was shifted to Wellington.

This city of 354,000 sits in a glorious location on the western shores of Port Nicholson, squeezed against the sea by peaks that rear up to almost 900 meters (3,000 feet). Behind it, suburbs of quaint timber houses spill down precipitous slopes. "Windy Wellington" is a nickname that springs readily to the lips of every New Zealander. Frequently the streets are roped to help pedestrians avoid being bowled over. The cause of this bitter wind is the air currents funneled through the narrow neck of Cook Strait, the 18-kilometer (11-mile) channel between the two islands.

Important Addresses and Numbers

Tourist Information **Wellington Visitor Information Centre.** *Civic Administration Bldg., Victoria and Wakefield Sts., tel. 04/801–4000. Open daily 9–5.*

Embassies and High Commissions **Australian High Commission.** *72–78 Hobson St., Thorndon, tel. 04/473–6411. Open weekdays 8:45–12:15.*

British High Commission. *44 Hill St., City, tel. 04/472–6049. Open weekdays 9:30–noon and 2–3:30.*

Canadian High Commission. *61 Molesworth St., Thorndon, tel. 04/473–9577. Open weekdays 8:30–4:30.*

United States Embassy. *29 Fitzherbert Terr., Thorndon, tel. 04/472–2068. Open weekdays 10–noon and 2–4.*

Emergencies Dial 111 for **fire, police,** or **ambulance** services.

Hospital Emergency Rooms **Wellington Hospital.** *Riddiford St., Newtown, tel. 04/385–5999.*

Late-Night Pharmacies **The After-hours Pharmacy.** *17 Adelaide Rd., Newtown, tel. 04/385–8810. Open weekdays 5 AM–11 PM, Sat. 9 AM–11 PM, Sun. 10–10.*

Travel Agencies **American Express Travel Service.** *203 Lambton Quay, tel. 04/473–1221.*

Thomas Cook. *108 Lambton Quay, tel. 04/473–5167.*

Arriving and Departing

By Plane **Wellington International Airport** lies about 8 kilometers (5 miles) from the city. **Super Shuttle** (tel. 04/387–8787) operates a 10-seater bus between the airport and any address in the city ($8 for one person, $10 for two). The bus meets all incoming flights; tickets are available from the driver. A slightly less expensive alternative is the **Tranzit Bus,** which operates between the airport and the railway station with stops at any bus stop along the way ($4.50 adults, $2.30 children 5–15). Weekdays the bus departs from the airport at 20-minute intervals 6 AM–9:30 PM; Saturday, every 30 minutes 8 AM–1:30 PM; Sunday, every 30 minutes noon–8 PM.

By Car The main access to the city is via the Wellington Urban Motorway, an extension of National Highway 1, which links the city center will all towns and cities to the north.

By Train The Wellington Railway Station (tel. 04/472–5409) is on Bunny Street, a half-mile from the city center.

By Bus InterCity buses (tel. 04/495–2443) arrive and depart from Wellington Railway Station. The terminal for **Newmans** buses (tel. 04/499–3261) is the InterIslander Ferry Terminal, 3 kilometers (2 miles) from the city center.

By Ferry The **InterIsland Line** (tel. 04/498–3999) operates vehicle and passenger ferries between Wellington and Picton, at the northern tip of the South Island. The one-way adult fare is $36 during school holidays, $28 at other times. Children aged 4–14 pay half price. The fare for a medium-size sedan is $112 during school holidays, $90 at other times. The crossing takes about three hours and can be very rough. There are at least two departures in each direction every day, and bookings should be made in advance, particularly during holiday periods. The ferry terminal is about 3 kilometers (2 miles) from the city. A free bus leaves Platform 9 at the Wellington Railway Station for the ferry terminal 35 minutes before sailings.

Getting Around

By Bus Wellington's public bus network is known as **Ridewell.** For trips around the inner city, the fare is $1 for adults and 50¢ for children 4–14. **Daytripper** tickets ($6.50), allowing unlimited travel for one adult and two children, are available from bus drivers after 9 AM. For maps and timetables, contact the information center (142–146 Wakefield St., City, tel. 04/801–7000).

By Bicycle If the sun is shining and the wind is still, a bicycle is an ideal way to explore the city and its surrounding bays. **Penny Farthing Cycles** (89 Courtenay Pl., City, tel. 04/385–2772) hires out mountain bikes for $25 per day or $100 per week, including helmet.

Guided Tours

City Scenic Tours, a division of Wellington City Transport, operates a 2½-hour guided bus tour of the city center and the Miramar Peninsula to the east. The bus departs daily at 10 and 2 from the corner of Victoria and Wakefield streets. *286 Wakefield St., tel. 04/385–9955. Tickets: $21 adults, $10.50 children under 15.*

Wally Hammond, a tour operator with a great anecdotal knowledge and a fund of stories about the city, offers a 2½-hour minibus tour of the city and Marine Drive. Tours depart from Travel World, Mercer and Victoria streets, at 10 and 2. Passengers can be picked up at their city hotels at no extra cost. Tel. 04/472–0869 or 04/528–2248. Tickets: $20 per person.

The **Wellington Harbour Ferry,** a commuter service between the city and Days Bay, on the eastern side of Port Nicholson, is one of the best-value tours in the city. Weekdays the catamaran departs from Queens Wharf at 7:10, noon, 2, 4:15, and 5:30; weekends, at 10:30, noon, 2, and 4:15. The trip takes about 25 minutes. *Queens Wharf, City, tel. 04/499–1273. Round-trip tickets: $12 adults, $6 children 3–15.*

Exploring Wellington

This walking tour of the city includes city views, formal gardens, literary history, some fine examples of 19th-century architecture, and the seat of government. Allow about three hours.

Numbers in the margin correspond to points of interest on the Wellington map.

❶ Begin at the **Kelburn Cable Car** terminus in Cable Car Lane off Lambton Quay, opposite Grey Street. The Swiss-built funicular railway makes a short but sharp climb to Kelburn Terminal, which offers views across parks and city buildings to Port Nicholson. Sit on the left side during the six-minute journey for the best scenery. *Cost: $1.50 adults, 70¢ children 4–15. Departures about every 10 minutes, weekdays 7 AM–6:30 PM, Saturday 9:20–6, Sunday 10:30–6.*

Leave the Kelburn Terminal and take the Northern Walkway, following the arrow that points to St. Mary Street. This path **❷** skirts the edge of the **Botanic Garden,** with city views on one side and the domes of the Dominion Observatory on the other. As you round the hilltop, you'll see an immense green hill with transmission towers on top; this is Tinakori Hill, known to the Maoris as Ahumairangi—"sloping down from the sky."

Continue along the path, which becomes quite steep as it **❸** plunges down toward the **Lady Norwood Rose Garden** and the **Begonia House.** There are more than 100 types of roses in the garden, which erupts in a blaze of color between November and the end of April.

Turn your back on the roses and walk to the right around the enclosed Anderson Park, following the sign to Bolton Street Memorial Park. At the end of this short road, make a detour to **❹** the monument on the right. The **John Seddon Memorial** is dedicated to the colorful and popular liberal politician who was prime minister from 1893 to 1906. Under Seddon's leadership, New Zealand became the first country to pay its citizens an old-age pension, and the first to give women the vote.

Close to the memorial a track zigzags down the hill beneath a stand of pohutukawa trees. At the bottom, cross Bowen Street, walk downhill, take the path to your left, and climb narrow **❺** **Ascot Street.** The tiny, doll-like cottages along this street were built in the 1870s, and this remains the finest example of a 19th-century streetscape in Wellington. At the top of the rise, stop for a breather on the bench that has been thoughtfully provided in the shady courtyard.

Turn right into **Tinakori Road.** The lack of suitable local stone combined with the collapse of most of Wellington's brick buildings in the earthquake of 1848 ensured that timber was used almost exclusively for building here in the second half of the 19th century. Most of the carpenters of the period had learned their skills as cabinetmakers and shipwrights in Europe, and

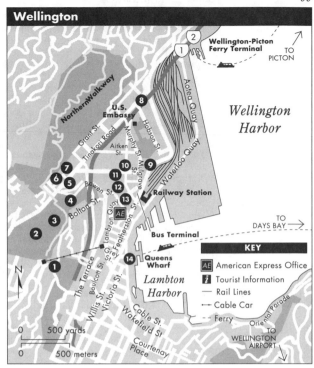

the sturdy houses in this street are a tribute to their craftsmanship.

6 Another fact of early life in Wellington is illustrated by **No. 306,** the pasta shop. Pressed for level ground, the citizens of early Wellington tended to build tall, narrow houses. This example—one room wide and five stories high—took things to extremes. Just below the house, make a short detour to see the three superbly restored timber houses side by side in Upton Terrace. Behind a green fence a few steps farther down Tinakori Road is **7** **Premier House,** the official residence of the prime minister until 1935, when the new Labour government, caught up in the reforming zeal of socialism, turned it into a dental clinic.

8 Continue down a relatively drab part of Tinakori Road to No. 25, just beyond the Hobson Street bridge. This is the **Katherine Mansfield House,** where the writer was born (as Kathleen Beauchamp) and lived the first five years of her life. Mansfield left to pursue her career in Europe when she was only 20, but many of her short stories are set in Wellington. A year before her death in 1923, she wrote, "New Zealand is in my very bones. What wouldn't I give to have a look at it!" The house, which has been restored as a typical Victorian family home, contains furnishings, photographs, videos, and tapes that elucidate Mansfield's life and times. *25 Tinakori Rd., Thorndon, tel. 04/473–9268. Admission: $4 adults, $1 children 4–15. Open Tues.–Sun. 10–4.*

Walk back along Tinakori Road to the Hobson Street overpass, and on the far side of the motorway turn right to walk through the elms of the Katherine Mansfield Memorial Park. Turn left around the rather stern compound of the U.S. Embassy, and walk down Murphy Street, which becomes Mulgrave Street, to

⑨ Old St Paul's Church. Consecrated in 1866, the church is a splendid example of the English neo-Gothic style executed in wood. Even the trusses that support the roof transcend their mundane function with their splendid craftsmanship. The hexagonal oak pulpit was a gift from the widow of Prime Minister Richard Seddon, in memory of her husband. *Mulgrave St., Thorndon, tel. 04/473-6722. Open Mon.-Sat. 10-4:30, Sun. 1-4:30.*

Walk down Mulgrave Street and turn right at Archives House into Aitken Street. The modern building on the right is the

⑩ National Library, which houses the largest collection of books in the nation as well as the remarkable Alexander Turnbull Library. This latter collection, named after the noted bibliophile who founded it, contains a particularly impressive Pacific history section, which includes accounts of every important European voyage of discovery since Magellan. The art collection includes many sketches of New Zealand made by early visitors; these are displayed in changing exhibitions. *Molesworth and Aitken Sts., tel. 04/474-3000. Open weekdays 9-5, Sat. 9-1.*

Cross Molesworth Street and walk through the gate to the

⑪ Parliament Buildings on the far side. The green Gothic structure on the right is the General Assembly Library, a soaring, graceful building compared with the ponderous gray bulk of the Parliament House next door. The layout of the House of Representatives, where legislation is presented, debated, and either passed or rejected by majority vote, is a copy of the British Houses of Parliament at Westminster, right down to the Speaker's mace and the despatch boxes. Tours of the building explain the parliamentary process in detail. *Molesworth St., tel. 04/471-9999. Admission free. Tours depart weekdays at varying times.*

It would be difficult to imagine a more complete contrast in ar-

⑫ chitectural styles than the **Executive Office** building to the left of the Parliament House, known for obvious reasons as "the Beehive"—though the people of Wellington will often add that it produces nothing sweet. This building houses the offices of parliamentarians and their staffs.

⑬ Walk down the hill from the Beehive to the **Cenotaph,** the memorial to New Zealanders killed in battle. New Zealand has a proud and distinguished war record. "Few Americans appreciate the tremendous sacrifices made by New Zealanders in the last two world wars," James A. Michener wrote in *Return to Paradise.* "Among the allies, she had the highest percentage of men in arms—much higher than the United States—the greatest percentage overseas, and the largest percentage killed."

The wide street that curves away to the back of the bronze lions is **Lambton Quay.** As its name suggests, this was once Wellington's waterfront. All the land between your feet and the present-day shoreline has been reclaimed. From this point, the shops of the city center are within easy walking distance along Lambton Quay.

Other Places of Interest

⑭ **Maritime Museum.** Housed in the handsome Harbour Board Building, this museum has paintings, figureheads, various nautical apparatuses, and some fine scale models of ships, including the *Wahine*, which sank in Cook Strait in 1968 with the loss of 51 lives. However, most of the displays belong to the old-fashioned, glass-cabinet school of museum design. *Queens Wharf, City, tel. 04/472-8904. Admission: by donation. Open weekdays 9:30-4, weekends 1-4:30.*

Southward Museum. The largest collection of vintage and veteran cars in the Southern Hemisphere, this amazing collection of more that 250 vehicles includes Bugattis, a Hispano-Suiza, one of only 17 Davis three-wheelers ever made, a De Lorean, a gull-wing 1955 Mercedes 300SL, gangster Micky Cohen's armor-plated 1950 Cadillac, and another Cadillac once owned by Marlene Dietriech. The motorcycle collection, which has a number of early Harley-Davidsons and Indians, a Brough Superior, and a Vincent V-twin, is almost as impressive. The museum is located just off Highway 1, about a 45-minute drive north of Wellington. *Otaihanga Rd., Paraparaumu, tel. 04/297-1221. Admission: $4 adults, $1 children 5-14. Open daily 9-4:30.*

Dining

Price categories for restaurants are the same as in the Auckland Dining section in Chapter 3. Highly recommended restaurants are indicated by a star ★.

Very Expensive **Pierres.** Prices at this smart, rather elegant restaurant are a
★ notch above those at most Wellington establishments, but the food is leaps ahead. Simplicity is the key word on a menu that shows an appreciation for the robust flavors of Mediterranean cooking. First course on the seasonal menu might be a dish of grilled eggplant, roast peppers, olives, and tomatoes on garlic toast with basil dressing. Mains include grilled chicken breast with sage, or a chargrilled fillet of beef with a béarnaise sauce. *342 Tinakori Rd., Thorndon, tel. 04/472-6238. Reservations recommended. Dress: casual. AE, DC, MC, V. No lunch Sat. Closed Sun.*

Expensive **Bellissimo Trattoria Italiana.** This is simply great Italian
★ food—served with far more style and panache than the name "trattoria" might suggest. First courses include carpaccio with olive oil, anchovies, and capers, and calamari in a chili sauce. Among the mains might be medaillon of veal in a marsala sauce, and breast of chicken in a brandy sauce with avocado and almonds. All the pasta is made on the premises by the Neapolitan owner/chef. *Dukes Arcade, Manners St., City, tel. 04/499-1154. Reservations not required. Dress: casual. AE, DC, MC, V. No lunch on weekends.*

★ **Brasserie Flipp.** Highly fashionable with Wellington's sophisticates, the innovative international menu makes this restaurant a good choice for lunch or dinner. Main courses include pasta with roast duck, mushrooms, and red currants, and a chargrilled steak with gremolada (garlic, grated lemon peel, and parsley) and olives. The decor is warehouse chic: stark white walls, glossy timber floors, and dazzling white napery. The wine list has a good selection of New Zealand wines, and a token bottle from just about everywhere else. Live entertainment is a feature on Friday and Saturday from 8:30. *RSA Bldg., 103 Ghunzee St., Wellington, tel. 04/385–9493. No reservations. Dress: casual. AE, DC, MC, V. Lunch and dinner daily.*

Tinakori Bistro. Set in a miniature Thorndon shopfront, this popular bistro has a modern, French-influenced menu and a long-standing reputation for reliability. Main courses include grilled salmon with a potato and bean salad, and chicken breast with a rosemary, garlic, and chili sauce. If the sun is shining, request an outside table. *328 Tinakori Rd., Thorndon, tel. 04/ 499–0567. Reservations recommended. Dress: casual but neat. BYOB. AE, MC, V. No lunch weekends. Closed Sun.*

Moderate **Chevy's.** With a name like that and a flashing neon cowboy out front, the burgers, nachos, chicken wings, BLTs, and barbecue spareribs come as little surprise. The salads are crisp, the fries are crunchy, the service is prompt, the quasi-American decor is bright and attractive, and the restaurant stays open until at least 10:30. *97 Dixon St., Wellington, tel. 04/384–2724. No reservations. Dress: casual. BYOB. AE, DC, MC, V. Lunch and dinner daily.*

The Sugar Club. This bistro/bar has a New Orleans honky-tonk flavor that's popular with Wellington's youth, and a menu that borrows from a wide range of cuisines. Main courses include Thai-style prawns cooked in coconut milk with chili and coriander, and pasta with mussels cooked in a tomato sauce. The chocolate fruit and nut terrine with chocolate mousse and cream is delicious. *105 Vivian St., City, tel. 04/384–6466. Reservations not required. Dress: casual. BYOB. AE, DC, MC, V. No lunch. Closed Sun.*

Inexpensive **Dixon Street Gourmet Deli.** This city-center delicatessen stocks
★ one of the best ranges of gourmet treats in the country. There are home-baked breads and bagels, an international choice of meats, cheeses, pickles, and preserves, plus local smoked fish and oysters—everything you need for a superior picnic. *45–47 Dixon St., City, tel. 04/384–2436. No credit cards. Open weekdays 9–5.*

Gourmet Lane. These half-dozen cafés on the basement of the Bank of New Zealand Building offer a choice of light meals, from spring rolls to fish and chips to pies, pastries, and salads. Try to avoid the 12:30 crush, when the place is crowded with office workers. *1 Willis St. No credit cards. Lunch only. Closed weekends.*

Lodging

Price categories for hotels are the same as in the Auckland Lodging section in Chapter 3. Highly recommended lodgings are indicated by a star ★.

Very Expensive **Parkroyal Wellington.** If you are looking for the luxury, facili-
★ ties, gloss, and glamour that only a big international hotel can deliver, this is the best in town—and possibly the best in the country. Opened in 1990, the bronze tower building has an art deco flavor in its public areas. Guest rooms are decorated in sea greens and blues with blond wood furnishings, and each has its own iron and ironing board. The bureau rooms, which have a desk and a queen-size bed instead of two doubles, are tailored especially for traveling executives. Request a room with ocean

views. Service by the young staff is excellent throughout the hotel. The Parkroyal is located in the city center, within walking distance of shops, restaurants, and the central business district. The Panama Street Brasserie is a favorite breakfast spot for the city's power brokers. *Featherston and Grey Sts., Wellington, tel. 04/72–2722, fax 04/472–4724. 232 rooms with bath. Facilities: spa pool, sauna, gym, heated indoor pool, guest laundry, 2 bars, 2 restaurants. AE, DC, MC, V.*

Moderate **Museum Hotel.** The location on a busy road in the dock area is uninspiring, and the standard rooms lack charm, but the Harbour View Deluxe rooms are large, moderately luxurious, and good value, especially between Friday and Sunday night, when rates are heavily discounted. *51–61 Cable St., Wellington, tel. 04/385–2809, fax 04/385–2483. 36 rooms with bath. AE, DC, MC, V.*

Inexpensive **Halswell Lodge.** Rooms at this hotel on the edge of the city center are compact and functional, but each has *en suite* facilities and a reasonable standard of comfort. The surroundings offer a wide choice of restaurants. Rooms at the front are affected by street noise during the daytime. *21 Kent Terr., Wellington, tel. 04/385–0196. 19 rooms with bath. AE, DC, MC, V.*

Tinakori Lodge. Situated in a historic suburb overlooking the city, this lodge offers atmospheric bed-and-breakfast accommodation in tranquil surroundings at a reasonable price. The rooms, which can sleep up to three, are simply furnished but comfortable. The city center is a 10-minute walk away, and there are several restaurants in the vicinity. The owners are extremely friendly and helpful. Children are accommodated by arrangement. *182 Tinakori Rd., Thorndon, tel. 04/473–3478, fax 04/472–5554. 10 rooms share 3 baths. Tariff includes breakfast. AE, DC, MC, V.*

The Arts and Nightlife

The Arts Wellington is the home of the **New Zealand Ballet Company** and the **New Zealand Symphony Orchestra.** The main venue for the performing arts is the **Michael Fowler Centre** (Wakefield Street, City, tel. 04/472–3088).

The **Downstage Theatre** holds frequent performances of stage classics. *Hannah Playhouse, Courtenay Pl. and Cambridge Terr., City, tel. 04/384–9639.*

Nightlife At the heart of the city, the **St. George Hotel** has several bars, live jazz music most nights of the week, and Legends of the George, a late-night restaurant. *Willis and Boulcott St., City, tel. 04/473–9139. Open 11 AM–midnight.*

North by Northwest is a restaurant/nightclub with live music that varies from jazz to pop classics. *15 Blair St., Courtenay Pl., City, tel. 04/385–3856. Open 5 PM–midnight.*

5 The South Island

By Michael
Gebicki

The South Island is separated from the North Island by Cook Strait, an expanse of just 17 kilometers (11 miles); yet the difference is far greater than the distance suggests. Whether you first glimpse the South Island from the deck of the ferry as it noses into Marlborough Sounds or through the window of a plane bound for Christchurch, the immediate impression is that the landscape has turned feral: The green, mellow beauty of the North Island has given way to jagged snow-capped mountains and rivers that charge down from them and sprawl across vast shingle beds. The locals will tell you that you haven't seen rain until you've been drenched by a rainstorm on the west coast—one of the wettest places on earth.

The headline attractions are Queenstown, the adventure-sport capital of the country; Mount Cook and its glaciers; and the sounds of Fiordland National Park. Beyond the well-defined tourist routes, the island's beech forests, lakes, trout streams, mountain trails, and beaches form a paradise for hikers, anglers, and just about anyone who enjoys a dose of fresh air. Sperm whales, dolphins, penguins, seals, and royal albatrosses can be seen in the wild along the coastline. And Stewart Island, off the southern tip of South Island, is remote enough to satisfy even the most determined escapist.

Marlborough, Nelson, and the West Coast

These three regions, which form the northern and western coasts of the South Island, offer an immense variety of scenery, from the siren seascapes of Marlborough Sounds to the mellow river valleys of the north coast to the icy world of the glaciers and the Southern Alps, where 12,000-foot peaks rise within 32 kilometers (20 miles) of the shore.

After the well-ordered serenity of the North Island, the wild grandeur of the west coast will come as a surprise. This is Mother Nature with her hair down, flaying the coastline with huge seas and drenching rains and littering its beaches with bleached driftwood sculptures. It is a country that creates a special breed, and the rough-hewn and powerfully independent people—known to the rest of the country as "coasters"—occupy a special place in New Zealand folklore.

For visitors who ferry across from Wellington, Marlborough Sounds will provide the first taste of the South Island. Together with the city of Nelson and Abel Tasman National Park to the west, this is a sporting paradise, with a mild climate that allows a year-round array of adventure activities.

Important Addresses and Numbers

Tourist Information Nelson Visitor Information Centre. *Trafalgar and Halifax Sts., tel. 03/548–2304. Open daily 9–5.*

Franz Josef Glacier Visitor Information Centre. *State Hwy. 6, Franz Josef, tel. 0288/31–796. Open daily 8–4:30.*

Greymouth Visitor Information Centre. *Regent Theatre Bldg., McKay and Herbert Sts., tel. 03/768–5101. Open weekdays 9–5.*

Emergencies Dial 111 for **fire, police,** or **ambulance** services.

Arriving and Departing

By Plane **Air New Zealand** (tel. 03/546–9300) links Nelson with Christchurch, Queenstown, Dunedin, the west coast town of Hokitika, and all major cities on the North Island. **Nelson Airport** lies 10 kilometers (6 miles) west of the city. **Super Shuttle** (tel. 03/547–5782) operates buses that meet all incoming flights and charge $6 to the city for one passenger, $5 each for two. The taxi fare to the city center is about $12.

By Car From Nelson, Highway 6 runs southwest to the west coast, down the coast to the glaciers, then south to Queenstown and Invercargill. Highway 1 follows the east coast to Christchurch and Dunedin. Allow at least seven hours for the 458-kilometer (284-mile) journey from Nelson to Franz Josef.

By Bus From Nelson, **InterCity** buses travel the length of both the west and east coasts daily. For bookings from Nelson, tel. 03/548–1539; Greymouth, tel. 03/768–1435; Franz Josef, tel. 03/752–0780.

By Ferry The berth for the **InterIsland Ferries** from Wellington is at Picton, 145 kilometers (90 miles) east of Nelson. At the ferry terminal, buses are readily available for travel either east to Blenheim and Christchurch or west to Nelson.

By Train The west coast in general is poorly served by the rail network, but one glowing exception is the **TranzAlpine Express,** which ranks as one of the world's great rail journeys. This passenger train crosses the Southern Alps between Christchurch and Greymouth, winding through beech forests and mountains that are covered by snow for most of the year. The bridges and tunnels along this line, including the 8-kilometer (5-mile) Otira Tunnel, represent a prodigious feat of engineering. The train is modern and comfortable, with panoramic windows as well as dining and bar service. Smoking is not permitted on board. The train departs Christchurch daily at 7:40 AM and arrives in Greymouth at 12:25 PM; the return train departs Greymouth at 1:40 PM and arrives at Christchurch at 6:30 PM. The one-way fare is $59 adults, $29.50 children 4–14.

Guided Tours

Abel Tasman National Park Enterprises operate launches that follow the majestic shoreline of the park. A popular option is to leave the boat at Bark Bay on the outward voyage, take a two-hour walk through the forests, and reboard the boat at Torrent Bay. The 6½-hour cruise departs daily from Kaiteriteri, a one-hour drive northwest of Nelson, at 9 AM. A bus connection from Nelson leaves the Visitor Information Centre at 7:35 AM. A cruise/flight option is also available. Passengers should buy a take-out lunch at Motueka—supplies on board are basic. *Old Cedarman House, Main Rd., Riwaka, tel. 03/528-7801. Cost: cruise (from Kaiteriteri), $40 adults, $12 children 4–14; cruise/flight (from Nelson): $104 adults, $90 children 4–14; bus (Nelson–Kaiteriteri round-trip), $16.*

The *Glenmore,* a small launch that makes a day-long trip ferrying mail and supplies around the reaches of Pelorus Sound, offers one of the best ways to discover this waterway and meet the people who live there. The boat departs from Havelock Tuesday to Thursday at 9:30 and returns about 5:30. *Glenmore Cruises, 73 Main Rd., Havelock, tel. 03/574-2276. Tickets: $45 adults, $22.50 children 4-14.*

The **Helicopter Line** operates several scenic flights over the glaciers from the heliport at Franz Josef. The shortest is the 20-minute flight over the Franz Josef Glacier ($40 per person); the longest is the Mountain Scenic Spectacular, a one-hour flight that includes a landing on the head of the glacier and a circuit of Mount Cook and Mount Tasman ($130 per person). *Box 45, Franz Josef, tel. 02/883-1767.*

The **Scenic Mail Run** is a five-hour tour aboard the bus that delivers the mail and supplies to isolated farming communities around Cape Farewell, at the northern tip of the South Island. The tour includes lunch on a 2,500-acre grazing property. The eight-seater bus departs from the Collingwood Post office. *Collingwood Bus Services, P.O. Collingwood, tel. 0524/48-188. Tickets: $25 adults, $15 children under 12. Tour departs 9:30 weekdays.*

Exploring Marlborough, Nelson, and the West Coast

This driving tour begins at Picton, where the InterIslander Ferries berth, and travels west to Nelson and Motueka, then south on Highway 6 along the coast. The detour through Motueka adds almost two hours; anyone who intends to make the seven-hour drive from Nelson to the glaciers in a single day should ignore this section of the tour and leave Nelson by Highway 6 instead.

Numbers in the margin correspond to points of interest on the Marlborough, Nelson, and the West Coast map.

❶ Picton is the base for cruising holidays in the **Marlborough Sounds,** the labyrinth of waterways that was formed when the sea invaded a series of river valleys at the northern tip of the South Island. Backed by forested hills that at times rise almost vertically from the water, the Sounds are a wild, majestic place edged with tiny beaches and rocky coves and studded with islands where such native wildlife as gannets and the primitive tuatara have remained undisturbed by introduced species. These waterways are the country's second-favorite cruising waters, after the Bay of Islands, but in terms of isolation and rugged grandeur they are in a class of their own. Much of the area is a national park; it has changed little since the 1770s, when Captain James Cook called in on five separate occasions to repair his ships and stock up with fresh provisions. There are rudimentary roads on the long fingers of land jutting into the Sounds, but the most convenient access is by water. One of the best ways to discover the area is hitching a ride at Havelock aboard the launch *Glenmore*, which delivers mail and supplies to outlying settlements scattered around Pelorus Sound (*see* Guided Tours, above).

❷ From the InterIslander ferry terminal, turn right and follow the signs to **Queen Charlotte Drive.** This road rises spectacularly along the edge of the sound, then cuts across the base of the peninsula that separates Queen Charlotte Sound from Pelorus Sound. Beyond Havelock the road winds through forested river

Marlborough, Nelson, and the West Coast

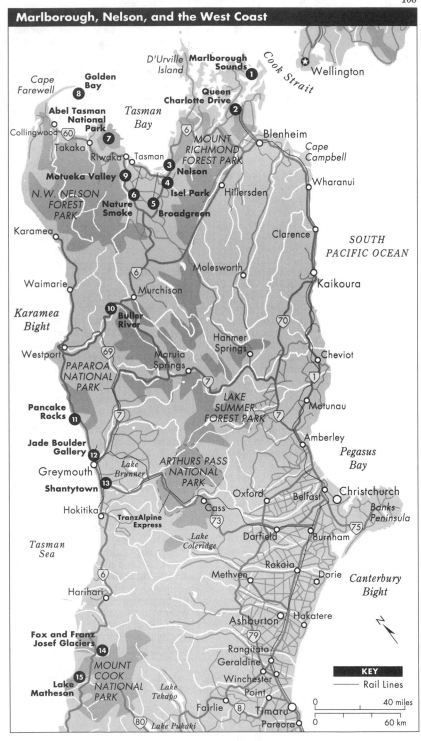

Cook Strait

★ Wellington

D'Urville Island

Marlborough Sounds ❶

Queen Charlotte Drive ❷

Cape Farewell

Golden Bay ❽

Tasman Bay

Blenheim

Cape Campbell

Abel Tasman National Park ❼

Collingwood (60)

Takaka

Riwaka Tasman

MOUNT RICHMOND FOREST PARK

(6)

Motueka Valley ❾

Nelson ❸

❹

Wharanui

Isel Park ❺

Broadgreen

Hillersden

N.W. NELSON FOREST PARK

❻

Nature Smoke

SOUTH PACIFIC OCEAN

Karamea

Clarence

Molesworth

Waimarie

(6)

Murchison

Kaikoura

Karamea Bight

❿ **Buller River**

Hanmer Springs

(70)

Westport (69)

Maruia Springs

Cheviot

PAPAROA NATIONAL PARK

(7)

LAKE SUMMER FOREST PARK

(7)

Motunau

Pancake Rocks ⓫

Amberley

Pegasus Bay

Jade Boulder Gallery ⓬

Lake Brunner

ARTHURS PASS NATIONAL PARK

Greymouth

⓭

Oxford Belfast Christchurch

Shantytown

Hokitika

Cass

Banks Peninsula

TranzAlpine Express

(73)

Darfield Burnham (75)

Tasman Sea

Lake Coleridge

Rakaia

Dorie

Canterbury Bight

Harihari

Methven

Fox and Franz Josef Glaciers ⓮

Ashburton Hakatere

MOUNT COOK NATIONAL PARK

(79)

⓯ **Lake Matheson**

Rangitata

Geraldine

Lake Tekapo

Winchester Point

Fairlie (8) Timaru

(80) *Lake Pukaki* Pareora

KEY

—— Rail Lines

0 ————— 40 miles

0 ————— 60 km

valleys before it rounds the eastern side of Tasman Bay and reaches Nelson.

Set on the broad curve of its bay with views of the Tasman Mountains on the far side, it would be hard to find a city and a ❸ climate better suited for year-round adventure than **Nelson.** To the east are the sheltered waters of Marlborough Sounds; to the west, the sandy crescents of the Abel Tasman National Park, and to the south, mellow river valleys and the peaks and glacial lakes of the Nelson Lakes National Park, a pristine wonderland for hikers, mountaineers, and cross-country skiers. Beyond those geographic splendors, Nelson has a mild climate with more hours of sunlight than any other city in the country. New Zealanders are well aware of these attractions, and in December and January the city is swamped with vacationers. Apart from this brief burst of activity, you can expect to have the roads and beaches almost to yourself.

Nelson is dominated by **Christ Church Cathedral,** which sits on a hilltop surrounded by gardens. Work on the cathedral began in 1925 and dragged on for the next 40 years. During construction the design was altered to withstand earthquakes, and despite its promising location, it looks like a church designed by a committee.

Leave Nelson by **Rutherford Street,** named in honor of the eminent nuclear physicist Ernest Rutherford, who was born nearby and educated at school here. On the outskirts of the city, take the right fork off this road, Waimea Road, and continue as it becomes Main Road. Turn left into Marsden Road, where a ❹ sign points to **Isel Park.** The **Nelson Provincial Museum** in the grounds of the park has a small but outstanding collection of Maori carvings. The museum also has a number of artifacts relating to the "Maungatapu murders," a grisly goldfields killing committed near Nelson in 1866. *Isel Park, Stoke, tel. 03/547–9740. Admission: Tues.–Fri. free, weekends 50¢. Open Tues.–Fri. 9:30–4:30, weekends 2–5.*

Isel House, near the museum, was built for Thomas Marsden, one of the region's prosperous pioneers. The Marsden family's impressive collection of porcelain and furniture is displayed inside. It was Marsden who laid out the magnificent gardens surrounding the house, which include a towering California redwood and a 42-meter (140-foot) Monterey pine. *Isel Park, tel. 03/547–9740. Admission to house: adults $2.50, children 5–15 $1. House open weekends 2–4. Closed June–Aug.*

Return to Main Road, turn right at the next set of traffic lights into Songer Street, turn right into Nayland Road, and stop at ❺ the park on the left. In the middle is **Broadgreen,** a fine example of a Victorian "cob" house. Cob houses, made from straw and horsehair bonded together with mud and clay, are commonly found in the southern English county of Devon, where many of Nelson's pioneers originated. The house is furnished as it might have been in the 1850s, with patchwork quilts and kauri furniture. *276 Nayland Rd., Stoke, tel. 03/546–0283. Admission: $2 adults, 50¢ children 5–15. Open Nov.–Apr., Tues.–Fri. 10:30–4:30, weekends 1:30–4:30; May–Oct., Wed. and weekends 2–4:30.*

Return to Main Road and turn right onto Highway 6. Unless time is short, turn right again onto Highway 60, following the "coastal route" signs to Motueka. Turn right where a sign points to Mapua and continue to Mapua Port. This road ends at a tiny dock with a couple of ramshackle warehouses; in the blue **6** corrugated iron building on the wharf is **Nature Smoke.** The business is operated by Dennis Crawford, who buys his fish right off the fishing boats, fillets it, marinates it according to a secret recipe, and smokes it. The result is delicious, and Crawford will happily offer samples. If you're headed south, you won't find a better lunch along the way than a slab of smoked snapper or albacore tuna with a loaf of crusty bread from the bakery in Motueka and apples from one of the roadside orchard stalls. *Mapua Wharf, tel. 03/540–2280. Open daily 9–5:30, longer in summer.*

West of Mapua, Highway 60 loops around quiet little sea coves that, for all but the warmest months of the year, mirror the snow-frosted peaks on the far shore. The tall vines along the roadside are hops, used to make beer.

Beyond the town of Motueka, Highway 60 passes close to the fine swimming beach at Kaiteriteri, then turns inland to skirt **7** the **Abel Tasman National Park,** the smallest of New Zealand's national parks. Its coastline is a succession of idyllic beaches backed by a rugged hinterland of beech forests, granite gorges, and waterfalls. The park has a number of walking trails, both from Totaranui at its northern end and Marahau in the south. The most popular is the two- to three-day **Coastal Track,** open year-round. Launches of the Abel Tasman National Park Enterprises (tel. 03/528–7801) will drop off and collect hikers from several points along the track. A popular way to explore the coastline is by sea kayak (*see* Sports and the Outdoors, below). The park information center is at the Department of Conservation Field Centre (1 Commercial St., Takaka, tel. 03/525–9136). The main accommodation base for the national park is Motueka.

Highway 60 returns to the sea near the town of Takaka. The **8** sweep of sand to the north is known, deservedly, as **Golden Bay,** but it once had a very different name. The Dutch navigator Abel Tasman anchored here briefly just a few days before Christmas 1642; his visit ended tragically when four of his crew were killed by Maoris. Bitterly disappointed, Tasman named the place Moordenaers, or Murderers' Bay, and sailed away without ever setting foot on New Zealand soil. For anyone who has time to explore, Golden Bay is a delight—a sunny 40-kilometer (25-mile) crescent of rocks and sand with a supremely relaxed crew of locals who firmly believe that they live in paradise.

Time Out   Next door to the Motueka Museum, **Annabelles Café** serves snacks and light, inexpensive meals: scones, muffins, salads, sandwiches, and great espresso. The café offers a choice of indoor or outdoor tables. *140 High St., Motueka, tel. 03/528–8696. Open daily 11–3.*

At the entrance to Motueka, at the Rothmans Clock Tower, turn south onto Highway 61, following the sign to Murchison. **9** The road snakes through **Motueka Valley** alongside the Motueka River, which is edged with poplars and yellow gorse, with the green valley walls pressing close alongside. If this river could talk, it would probably scream "Trout!" There are many deer farms in the area, easily identified by their high fences.

Fifty-seven kilometers (35 miles) beyond Motueka, Highway 61 joins Highway 6 for the journey south. Beyond Murchison, ⑩ the road parallels the broad **Buller River** as it carves a deep gorge from the jagged mountain peaks. Nineteen kilometers (12 miles) south of Murchison, the **Newtown Hotel,** no longer licensed, teeters on the brink of the gorge, surrounded by a fantastic junkyard of obsolete farm machinery. The Buller once carried a fabulous cargo of gold, but you have to use your imagination to reconstruct the days when places such as Lyell, 34 kilometers (21 miles) beyond Murchison, were bustling mining towns. **Hawk's Crag,** where the highway passes beneath a rock overhang with the river wheeling alongside, is the scenic climax of the trip along the Buller. Before the town of Westport, turn left to continue along Highway 6.

After a journey through coastal scrub, Highway 6 meets the sea; shortly thereafter it arrives at a tiny collection of shops called **Punakaiki.** From the visitor center, an easy 10-minute walk leads to a fantastic maze of limestone rocks stacked high ⑪ above the sea. These are commonly known as the **Pancake Rocks,** and they are the outstanding feature of the surrounding **Paparoa National Park.** At high tide, the blowhole spouts a thundering geyser of spray. Mount Cook is sometimes visible to the south. *Paparoa National Park, tel. 03/731–1895.*

The town of Greymouth is aptly named—a dull, dispirited strip ⑫ of motels and timber mills. Yet the **Jade Boulder Gallery** is a great place to pick up a distinctive souvenir. The gallery exhibits the work of Ian Boustridge, one of the country's most accomplished sculptors of greenstone, the jade that was highly prized by the Maoris. Earrings start at about $35, and sculptures can cost anything up to $1,000. *Guiness St., Greymouth, tel. 03/768–0700. Open daily 8–5.*

⑬ On the southern outskirts of Greymouth, **Shantytown** is a lively reenactment of a gold-mining town of the 1880s. Except for the church and the town hall, most of the buildings are replicas, but the gold diggings are authentic and fascinating. Displays include a water jet for blasting the gold-bearing quartz from the hillside, water sluices, and a stamper battery or crusher powered by a 30-foot water wheel. Visitors can pan for gold, and since the creek is salted with gold dust, there is a good chance of striking "color." *Rutherglen, Greymouth, tel. 03/762–6634. Admission: $7 adults, $4 children 5–15. Open daily 8:30–5.*

South of Greymouth the highway threads through farming country as it heads toward the Southern Alps and the glaciers of **Westland National Park.** The glaciers are formed by the massive rainfall of the west coast—up to 300 inches per annum—which descends as snow on the névé, or head, of the glacier. The snow is compressed into ice, which flows downhill under its own weight. There are more than 60 glaciers in the park; the most ⑭ famous and accessible are **Fox** and **Franz Josef,** the only glaciers on earth that grind through a rain forest. They lie about 24 kilometers (15 miles) apart. You can park a 15-minute walk away from the terminal face of Fox Glacier, and a 30-minute walk from the Franz Josef terminal. Both parking lots are terrorized by keas—mountain parrots—which specialize in destroying the rubber molding around car windows. (Keas are harmless to humans, and a coating of insect repellent around the window frames should safeguard your vehicle.)

Trails from the parking lots wind across the valley floor to the glacier faces, where a tormented vocabulary of squeaks, creaks, groans, and gurgles can be heard as the glacier creeps down the mountainside at an average rate of 5 feet per day. Care must be taken here, since rocks and chunks of ice frequently drop from the melting face. These being New Zealand glaciers, there is much to do besides admire them. You can fly over them and land on their névé, walk on them, even make a bloodcurdling and very cold white-water rafting trip down the Waiho River where it emerges from the base of Franz Josef (*see* Guided Tours, above, and Sports and the Outdoors, below). Flights should be made early in the morning, when the visibility is better. Fox Glacier is slightly larger and longer than Franz Josef, but you'll miss nothing important if you see only one. Both glaciers have separate townships, and if you are spending the night, Franz Josef is marginally preferable.

At the town of Fox Glacier, turn toward the sea where a sign ⑮ points to Gillespies Beach, then turn right toward **Lake Matheson** for one of the country's most famous views. A walking trail winds along the lakeshore, and the snowcapped peaks of Mount Cook and Mount Tasman are reflected in the water. Allow at least an hour for the complete walk to the "View of Views." The best time is early morning, before the mirrorlike reflections are fractured by the wind.

Beyond the glaciers Highway 6 continues along the south coast to Haast, where it turns inland to Wanaka and Queenstown. The driving time between Fox Glacier and Wanaka is six hours. The best accommodation along this road is the Lake Moeraki Wilderness Lodge, just north of Haast (*see* Lodging, below).

Sports and the Outdoors

Hiking **Abel Tasman Enterprises** operates a four-day guided trek along the southern half of the Abel Tasman Track. Travelers spend all three nights in a comfortable lodge at Torrent Bay; during the days they explore the coastline and forests of the national park. Walkers carry only a light day pack, and all meals are provided. The guided walk, which has an "easy" grading, departs each Tuesday and Friday. *Old Cedarman House, Main Rd., Riwaka, tel. 03/528-7801. Cost: $645 adults, $570 children 8-14.*

Alpine Guides offers guided walks on Fox Glacier, the only way to safely experience the ethereal beauty of the ice caves, pinnacles, and crevasses on top of the glaciers. The three-hour walks travel about 2 kilometers (1 mile) up the glacier. The climb is quite strenuous and extremely slippery, despite the metal-pointed staves and spiked boots supplied to hikers. *Box 38, Fox Glacier, tel. 02/883-1825. Cost: $30. Tours depart daily at 9:30 and 2.*

Boating and **Abel Tasman Kayaks** has one- and two-person kayaks for hire at
Rafting Marahau, at the southern end of Abel Tasman National Park, which gives paddlers ready access to beaches and campsites that are often inaccessible to hikers. The company does not rent to solo kayakers, and a minimum two-day rental is required. The cost is $80 for two days. Guided kayak tours cost

American Express offers Travelers Cheques built for two.

American Express® Cheques *for Two*. The first Travelers Cheques that allow either of you to use them because both of you have signed them. And only one of you needs to be present to purchase them.

Cheques *for Two* are accepted anywhere regular American Express Travelers Cheques are, which is just about everywhere. So stop by your bank, AAA* or any American Express Travel Service Office and ask for Cheques *for Two*.

$75 for one day, $260 for three days. *Marahau, RD2 Motueka, tel. 03/527–8022.*

The **Marlborough Sounds Adventure Company** offers one- and four-day guided kayak tours of the Sounds, as well as kayak rentals for experienced paddlers. The cost is $50 for a one-day guided tour, $350 for a four-day guided tour. A kayak rental costs $35 per day. *1 Russell St., Picton, tel. 03/573–6078.*

Nelson Raft Company has various trips along the Motueka and Buller Rivers, from $28 for two hours to $95 for a full day. Transport to and from Nelson is included. *Lodder La., RD 3, Motueka, tel. 03/546–6212.*

Cycling   **Cycle Treks** offers several escorted cycle tours, from a two-day trip through mountains and lakes ($185) to a seven-day tour of Marlborough Sounds ($1379). Cyclists are supplied with 21-speed mountain bikes, group size is limited to 10, a back-up van is provided, and trips begin and end at either Nelson or Picton. *Box 733, Nelson, tel. 03/547–9122.*

Dining

Apart from Nelson, gourmet highlights are rare in this area. Price categories for restaurants are the same as in the Auckland Dining section in Chapter 3. Highly recommended restaurants are indicated by a star ★.

Expensive   **La Bonne Vie.** This attractive seafood restaurant is a favorite
★   with the locals for its lively atmosphere, brisk service, and a menu that pairs the excellent local seafood with delicate sauces. Main courses include salmon fillet with lime and coriander, and a whole flounder, either poached or baked, and served with a lemon sauce. Outdoor seating is available in summer. Vegetarians and steak-eaters are also provided for. *75 Bridge St., Nelson, tel. 03/548–0270. Reservations recommended. Dress: casual. AE, DC, MC, V. No lunch.*

Moderate   **Chez Eelco Coffee House.** The menu, with its array of steaks, burgers, seafood, and salads, may not try too hard, but it's impossible to ignore this cheerful sidewalk café at the foot of the cathedral in Nelson's main street. In warm weather, the outside tables are recommended; otherwise, try elsewhere. *296 Trafalgar St., Nelson, tel. 03/548–7595. No reservations. Dress: informal. BYOB. No credit cards. Lunch and dinner daily.*
Pomeroy's. This smart, popular bistro brings a modern European selection and a touch of class to Nelson's dining scene. The menu offers croissants, focaccia, bagels, and more substantial fare such as lamb stuffed with sun-dried tomatoes and served with a spinach salad. *276 Trafalgar St., Nelson, tel. 03/548–7524. Reservations not required. Dress: casual. BYOB. AE, DC, MC, V. No dinner Mon.–Wed. Closed Sun.*

Lodging

Price categories for hotels are the same as in the Auckland Lodging section in Chapter 3. Highly recommended lodgings are indicated by a star ★.

Very Expensive   **Lake Brunner Sporting Lodge.** Set on the southern shore of
★   Lake Brunner a 40-minute drive southeast of Greymouth, this sprawling lodge offers excellent fishing, a variety of activities,

and a high level of comfort at a price that is relatively low by the standards of New Zealand's elite lodges. Guest rooms are large and well equipped, with the emphasis on comfort rather than opulence. The best rooms are at the front of the house, overlooking the lake. The lodge is known for its "clear water stalking," since the brown trout can be easily seen in the clear waters of the surrounding rivers. Hunting, hiking, boating, mountain biking, and bird-watching are also available. Children are welcome, a rare concession at sporting lodges. *Mitchells, RD1, Kumara, Westland, tel. 03/738–0163, fax 03/ 738–0163. 9 rooms with bath. Facilities: fishing, mountain bikes, nature tours, hunting. Tariff includes all meals. AE, DC, MC, V. Closed July–Sept.*

Motueka River Lodge. A recent addition to New Zealand's list of exclusive fishing retreats, this lodge offers tranquility, marvelous scenery, and a superb standard of comfort. Owned and operated by a former Auckland adman, the lodge is set on a hillside with views across a deer farm to the valley of the Motueka River. Inside, the rustic flavor of the house is accented with folk art collected around the world. Guest rooms are luxuriously equipped but do not have telephones or TVs. The lodge offers a range of activities—tramping, river rafting, golf, tennis; but its specialty is fishing, especially dry-fly fishing for brown trout in the wild river country, which can be reached only by helicopter. The activities are restricted outside the October–April fishing season. *Hwy. 61, Ngatimoti, Motueka, tel. 03/ 526–8668, fax 03/526–8668. 4 rooms with bath. Facilities: fishing, tennis court. Tariff includes all meals. AE, DC, MC, V.*

Expensive ★ **Cambria House.** Built for a sea captain, this 1860 house has been sympathetically modernized to offer B&B accommodation with personality and a dash of luxury. The furnishings mix antiques and floral-print fabrics, and the rooms are very comfortable. Each has an en suite bathroom. The house is located in a quiet street within easy walking distance of the center of Nelson. Children are not accommodated. *7 Cambria St., Nelson, tel. 03/548–4681, fax 03/546–6649. 5 rooms with bath. Tariff includes breakfast. MC, V.*

Doone Cottage. This serene, homey farmstay is set in a pretty part of the Motueka River Valley, within easy reach of five trout streams and a 40-minute drive from Nelson. The hosts are a relaxed, hospitable middle-aged couple who have farmed in this valley for many years. Guest accommodation is comfortable and crowded with family memorabilia. Dinners are likely to feature organically grown vegetables, local meat, and fish fresh from the rivers. Children are not accommodated. *RD1, Motueka, tel. 03/526–8740. 2 rooms with bath. Tariff includes breakfast and dinner. V.*

Moderate **Ashley Motor Inn.** This motor inn has modern, comfortable rooms, though Greymouth and its surroundings, compared with other parts of the west coast, have little to justify an overnight stop. *70 Tasman St., Greymouth, tel. 03/768–5135. 60 rooms with bath. Facilities: indoor pool, spa, guest laundry, restaurant, bar. AE, DC, MC, V.*

★ **California Guest House.** Set at the end of a garden brimming with flowers, this country charmer is recommended for anyone looking for a bed-and-breakfast with character. Guest rooms are moderately large and comfortable and furnished with antiques. The best rooms are the slightly more expensive Victorian Rose and Everett. Breakfasts include muffins, filter coffee, ham-and-sour-cream omelets, fresh fruit, and pancakes with strawberries and cream. Children are not accommodated. Smoking is not permitted indoors. *29 Collingwood St., Nelson, tel. 03/548–4173. 4 rooms with bath. Tariff includes breakfast. MC, V.*

★ **Lake Moeraki Wilderness Lodge.** While these simple motel suites lack the luxurious frills of many other lodges, the natural splendor of the surroundings is the equal of any—and the price is a bargain. The lodge is located on Lake Moeraki, just north of the west coast town of Haast. There are penguins and seals along the beaches, a feisty river on the doorstep, canoes and kayaks for paddling the lake, and forest trails that echo with the sound of rushing streams and birdcalls. The lodge is owned and operated by Dr. Gerry McSweeney and his family. Dr. McSweeney, a leading voice in New Zealand's conservation movement, took over the lodge with the intention of demonstrating that tourism was an economic alternative to logging in the forests of South Westland. His knowledge of and feeling for the area contribute much to any visit. *Private Bag, Hokitika, tel. 02/883–2881, fax 03/750–0882. 20 rooms with bath. Facilities: nature tours, canoes, fishing, restaurant, bar. AE, DC, MC, V.*

Westland Motor Inn. The largest motel in the glacier region, this complex at the center of Franz Josef village offers rooms a cut above the average in size and furnishings. Larger suites with upgraded facilities are also available, and the motor lodge has a choice of dining facilities. *State Hwy. 6, Franz Josef, tel. 02/883–1729. 100 rooms with bath. Facilities: 2 spa pools, guest laundry, restaurant, bar. AE, DC, MC, V.*

Christchurch and Canterbury

The Canterbury region includes both the Canterbury Plains, the flattest land in the country, and the Southern Alps, the steepest. Its capital is New Zealand's third-largest city, Christchurch, which has a population approaching 300,000. Christchurch is the only South Island city with an international airport, and many travelers will begin or end their New Zealand journeys here.

Christchurch is something of a paradox—a city under the grand delusion that it is somewhere in southern England. The drive from the airport into town takes you through pristine suburbs of houses lapped by seas of flowers, past playing fields where children flail at one another's legs with hockey sticks. The heart of this pancake-flat city is dominated by church spires; its streets are named Durham, Gloucester, and Hereford; and instead of the usual boulder-leaping New Zealand torrent there bubbles, between banks lined with willows and oaks, the serene River Avon, suitable only for punting. The city is compact and easy to explore, and most of its major sights can be seen on a half-day walking tour.

The big attraction in this region is Mount Cook National Park, a wonderland of snow and ice; but if you have an extra day, the sperm whales that spout off the coast at Kaikoura make a memorable trip. For a rewarding half-day excursion through delectable country scenery and seascapes, journey out to Akaroa, a pretty little town on a big blue bay.

Important Addresses and Numbers

Tourist Information Christchurch Visitor Information Centre. *Worcester St. and Oxford Terr., Christchurch, tel. 03/379–9629. Open weekdays 8:30–6, weekends 8:30–5.*

Mount Cook Visitor Information Centre. *Mount Cook Village, tel.03/435–1818. Open daily 8–5.*

Emergencies Dial 111 for **fire, police,** or **ambulance** services.

Arriving and Departing

By Plane **Ansett New Zealand** (tel. 03/371–1146) and **Air New Zealand** (tel. 03/379–5200) link Christchurch with cities on both the North and South islands. **Mount Cook Airline** (tel. 03/379–0690) flies from Christchurch to Queenstown and Mount Cook. **Christchurch Airport** is located 10 kilometers (6 miles) northwest of the city. **Avon City Shuttle** buses (tel. 03/379–9999) meet all incoming flights and charge $7 per passenger to city hotels. **CANRIDE** buses operate between the airport and Cathedral Square from 6 AM to 11 PM daily. The fare is $2.40 for adults, $1.20 for children 4–14. A **taxi** to the city costs about $15.

By Car Highway 1 links Christchurch with Kaikoura and Blenheim in the north and Dunedin in the south. Driving time for the 330-kilometer (205-mile) journey between Christchurch and Mount Cook Village is five hours; between Christchurch and Dunedin, 5½ hours.

By Bus **Mount Cook Landline** (tel. 03/379–0690) and **InterCity** (tel. 03/379–9020) operate daily bus services between Christchurch and Dunedin, Mount Cook, Nelson, and Queenstown.

Getting Around

The city of Christchurch is flat and compact, and the best way to explore it is on two legs. It's unlikely that visitors will have occasion to use the public bus system, which is just as well since the once efficient, city-owned system has recently been divided among several different companies and is now a mess. Timetables and maps are unobtainable. The only reliable way to find out whether a bus is going your way is to ask the drivers at the terminal in Cathedral Square. Another option is bicycle. **Trailblazers** hires out mountain bikes for $20 per day. *96 Worcester St., tel. 03/366–6033. Open weekdays 9–5:30, weekends 10–4.*

Guided Tours

Guided walking tours of the city depart daily at 10 and 2 from the red-and-black booth in Cathedral Square. The cost of the two-hour tour is $8 per person.

Punting on the Avon is perfectly suited to the languid motion of Christchurch. Punts with expert boatmen may be hired from the Worcester Street bridge, near the corner of Oxford Terrace, from 10 to 6 in summer and 10 to 4 the rest of the year. The price of a 20-minute trip is $8 per adult, $4 for children under 12.

The **Gray Line** (tel. 03/343–3874) operates a half-day Morning Sights tour ($23) and a full-day tour of Akaroa ($45), both daily at 9 AM. A tour to Mount Cook ($124) departs at 7:45 AM and returns at 11:30 PM. All tours leave from the Christchurch Visitor Information Centre. Children 5–14 pay half fare.

Exploring Christchurch

This is a gentle stroll from the Visitor Centre through the heart of the city. Aim to finish at 1 PM, in time to catch the Wizard in Cathedral Square.

Numbers in the margin correspond to points of interest on the Christchurch map.

❶ From the front door of the Visitor Centre, cross Worcester Street to the **statue of Captain Robert Falcon Scott** (1868–1912), "Scott of the Antarctic," who visited Christchurch during his two Antarctic expeditions. The statue was sculpted by his widow, Kathleen Lady Kennett, and inscribed with his last words, written as he and his party lay dying in a blizzard on their return journey from the South Pole.

❷ Follow the curve of the River Avon past the arched **Bridge of Remembrance.** The bridge was built in memory of the soldiers who crossed the river here from King Edward Barracks, just down Cashel Street, on their way to the battlefields of Europe during the First World War.

❸ A little farther along the riverbank is the white timber **St. Michael and All Saints Anglican Church.** Christchurch was founded in 1850 by the Canterbury Association, a group of leading British churchmen, politicians, and peers who envisioned a settlement that would serve as a model of industry and ideals, governed by the principles of the Anglican faith. The first settlers the Association sent out were known as the "Canterbury Pilgrims," and their churches were a focal point for the whole community. Built in 1872, St Michael's is an outstanding example. One of the bells in the wooden belfry came from England aboard one of the four ships that carried the Canterbury Pilgrims. *Oxford Terr. and Durham St. Open daily noon–2 PM.*

❹ Follow the Avon upstream, cross to the far bank at the next bridge, and turn immediately left along the avenue of chestnuts and silver birches to the **Antigua Boatshed.** Built for the Christchurch Boating Club, this is the only boat shed that remains of the half-dozen that once stood along the Avon. Canoes may be hired for short river trips. *Rolleston Ave., tel. 03/366–5885. Single canoes $4/hr, double $8/hr. Open daily 9:30–4:30.*

❺ Walk along Rolleston Avenue and turn left at the first gate into the **Botanic Gardens,** a green jewel of woodland and rose gardens that might easily have been transplanted from the home counties of England. *Rolleston Ave., tel. 03/366–1701. Open daily dawn–dusk.*

❻ At the northern end of the gardens is the **Canterbury Museum.** Of special interest here are the reconstruction of an early Christchurch streetscape and the display of Maori artifacts. The Hall of Antarctic Discovery charts the links between the city and the U.S. bases on the frozen continent from the days of Captain Scott; Christchurch is still used as a forward supply depot for U.S. Antarctic bases. *Rolleston Ave., Christchurch,*

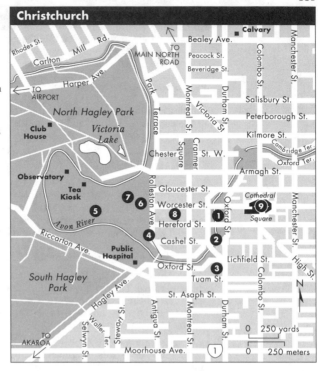

tel. 03/366–8379. Admission by donation. Open daily 9:30–4:30.

7 Behind the museum is the **Robert McDougal Art Gallery,** built in the 1930s by a prominent businessman. The gallery has works by 19th-century New Zealand artists and an international collection of painting and sculpture, including two Rodins. *Rolleston Ave., tel. 03/365–0915. Admission free. Open daily 10–4:30.*

8 From the museum, cross Rolleston Avenue into Worcester Boulevard and turn right into the **Arts Centre.** These gothic stone buildings once housed Canterbury University, whose most illustrious pupil was Ernest Rutherford (1871–1937). Just past the information desk inside is "Rutherford's Den," the modest stone chamber where the eminent physicist conducted experiments in what was at the time a new field, radioactivity. It was Rutherford who first succeeded in splitting the atom, a crucial step in the harnessing of atomic power. In 1908 Rutherford's work earned him the Nobel Prize—not for physics but for chemistry. *Worcester St., tel. 03/366–0989. Open weekdays 8:30–5, weekends 10–4.*

Time out Housed in a mock-Tudor building, **Dux de Lux** is a popular cafeteria-style restaurant that bills itself as "gourmet vegetarian." The blackboard menu offers quiches, crêpes, sandwiches, pies, fresh vegetable juices, and a range of crisp salads and breads. The courtyard is a great spot on a sunny day, especially with a beer from the brewery next door. *41 Hereford St., near Montre-*

al St., tel. 03/366-6919. No credit cards. Lunch and dinner daily. Inexpensive.

Continue along Worcester Boulevard and cross the river to **Cathedral Square.** The square is the city's focal point, functioning as a bus terminal and a venue for an arts and crafts market, food stalls, and street musicians, as well as a hangout for the city's unemployed youth. **Christchurch Cathedral,** the city's dominating landmark, was begun in 1864, 14 years after the arrival of the Canterbury Pilgrims, but not consecrated until 1904. Carvings inside commemorate the work of the Anglican missionaries, including Tamihana Te Rauparaha, the son of a fierce and, for the settlers, troublesome Maori chief. Free guided tours begin daily at 11 and 2. For a view across the city to the Southern Alps, climb the 133 steps to the top of the bell tower. The cathedral is known for its boys choir, which can be heard singing evensong at 4:30 Friday, except during school holidays. *Cathedral Sq. Open daily 8:30 AM–9 PM. Admission to tower: $2 adults, $1 children 5–15.*

If it's close to 1 PM when you emerge from the cathedral, look for the bearded gentleman with long hair, who is easy to spot because of the crowd that instantly forms around him. This is **the Wizard,** who makes funny and irreverent dissertations on just about any controversial subject—especially religion, politics, sex, and women's issues. Originally a freelance soapbox orator, the Wizard (whose real name is Ian Channel) became so popular that he is now employed by the city council—one of his frequent targets. *1 PM, Cathedral Sq. No performances May–Oct.*

Shopping

Inside the Christchurch Arts Centre is the **Galleria,** a dozen shops and studios for artisans and craftworkers. The quality of the work, however, is not representative of the finest of New Zealand's craftsmanship. Most of the shops are open 10 to 4; some are closed weekends. Most do not take credit cards. *Worcester Blvd., tel. 03/379-7573.*

Bivouac sells a complete range of outdoor gear and maps. *76 Cashel St., tel. 03/366-3197. Open weekdays 9–5:30, Sat. 10–1.*

Dining

Price categories for restaurants are the same as in the Auckland Dining section in Chapter 3. Highly recommended restaurants are indicated by a star ★.

Very Expensive **Sign of the Takahe.** Set in a splendid baronial castle that overlooks the city and the Southern Alps from the heights of the Cashmere Hills, this mock gothic restaurant is well known for its game and lobster, the house specialty. The buffet lunch is a less expensive option, but it lacks the stiff white napery, silver service, and candlelit tables that make the dinners magic. The restaurant is a 20-minute drive from the city center. Dinners are heavily booked by Japanese tour groups, and other diners may face long delays. *Dyers Pass and Hackthorne Rds., Cashmere Hills, tel. 03/332-4052. Reservations required. Jacket and tie required at dinner. AE, DC, MC, V. Lunch and dinner daily.*

Expensive **Bardellis.** The name says it all—a bar, a deli, and an Italian accent. Stylish and medium-loud, this bar/brasserie is where Christchurch's chic crowd comes for marinated octopus salads and Coronas straight from the beer bottle. The international menu, which changes frequently, is heavy on seafood, salads, pizza, and pasta. Typical dishes are seafood pasta with fresh fish; and pizza with fresh tomato sauce, prawns, pesto, sun-dried tomatoes, and salad greens. Steaks and the standard New Zealand rack of lamb also make an appearance. This is a good choice for casual outdoor eating on a warm summer evening. *98 Cashel Mall, tel. 03/353-0001. Reservations advised for dinner. Dress: casual. AE, DC, MC, V. Lunch and dinner daily.*

★ **Espresso 124.** This smart modern restaurant is a good bet for mid-morning coffee or midnight snacks. Simplicity is the key on a menu that features chargrilled steaks, lamb, and seafood, and salads dressed with olive oil and balsamic vinegar. The restaurant has a high-energy atmosphere generated by the fashionable crowd that frequents it. The river and the heart of the city are both conveniently close. Next door to the restaurant is a lunch deli, which offers inexpensive sandwiches, focaccia, pasta, and savory pies, and a choice of indoor or outdoor dining. *124 Oxford Terr., tel. 03/365-0547. Reservations advised for dinner. Dress: casual but neat. AE, DC, MC, V. Lunch and dinner daily.*

Moderate **Lone Star Cafe.** Quarterback-size servings of steaks, chicken, ribs, burgers, and french fries are the specialty at this big, pleasant restaurant within a five-minute walk of the city center. *26 Manchester St., tel. 03/365-7086. No reservations. Dress: casual but neat. BYOB. AE, DC, MC, V. No lunch.*

Lodging

Price categories for hotels are the same as in the Auckland Lodging section in Chapter 3. Highly recommended lodgings are indicated by a star ★

Very Expensive **Parkroyal Christchurch.** This plush hotel, in a prime location
★ overlooking Victoria Square and the river, brings a touch of glamour to the city's accommodation scene. The rooms are large, luxurious, and styled in a powder-blue and cream color scheme. Be sure to request one overlooking Victoria Square. The hotel is especially well equipped with restaurants and bars. The Canterbury Tales dining room and the Japanese restaurant, Yamagen, are among the city's finest. *Kilmore and Durham Sts., tel. 03/365-7799, fax 03/365-0082. 297 rooms with bath. Facilities: gym, sauna, bicycles, 4 restaurants, 3 bars. AE, DC, MC, V.*

Moderate **Pacific Park.** Rooms at this attractive peach-and-white complex on the northern fringe of the city are marginally better than at the average motel; all were refurbished during 1991–1992. Two-bedroom executive suites are available. Special rates apply on weekends and during winter. The motel is about 2 kilometers (1¼ miles) from the city center. *263 Bealey Ave., tel. 03/379-8660, fax 03/366-9973. 66 rooms with bath. Facilities: restaurant, bar. AE, DC, MC, V.*

★ **Riverview Lodge.** This grand Edwardian manor overlooking the Avon is the pick of the bed-and-breakfast accommodation in Christchurch. Completely restored in 1991, it offers superbly comfortable, historic accommodation and a cooked breakfast at about the same price as a motel room. The best room is the Turret Room, which has access to the front balcony. Children are accommodated by arrangement. The city center is a 15-minute walk along the river. *361 Cambridge Terr., tel. 03/365–2860. 3 rooms share 2 baths. Facilities: canoe, bicycles, golf clubs. Tariff includes breakfast. MC, V.*

Turret House. This century-old lodge has comfortable, well-maintained rooms and a friendly atmosphere that makes it a standout among Christchurch's bed-and-breakfast accommodation. All the rooms are different, and prices vary accordingly. The largest, the Apartment, has a lounge room, a separate bedroom, and a kitchen, and could easily sleep four. For a couple, the medium-size rooms offer a good combination of space and value. Despite its location close to a major intersection, noise is not a problem. *435 Durham St., tel. 03/365–3900. 8 rooms with bath. Tariff includes breakfast. AE, DC, MC, V.*

Excursion to Akaroa

Allow at least a half-day for this trip to the scenic Banks Peninsula.

Getting There The main route to Akaroa is Highway 75, which leaves the southwest corner of Christchurch as Lincoln Road. The 82-kilometer (50-mile) drive takes about 90 minutes. **Akaroa Tours** (tel. 03/379–9629) operates a shuttle service between the Christchurch Visitor Information Centre and Akaroa; buses depart Christchurch weekdays at 10:30 and 4, Saturday at noon, and Sunday at noon and 6:45; buses depart Akaroa weekdays at 8:20 and 2:20, weekends at 10:30 ($24 adults, $10 children 5–15 round-trip).

Exploring *Numbers in the margin correspond to points of interest on the Canterbury map.*

Dominated by tall volcanic peaks, the **Banks Peninsula**—the knobbly landform that juts into the Pacific Ocean south of Christchurch—has a wonderful coastline indented with small bays where sheep graze almost to the water's edge. Its main ❶ source of fame is the town of **Akaroa,** which was chosen as the site for a French colony in 1838. The first French settlers arrived in 1840 only to find that the British had already established sovereignty over New Zealand by the Treaty of Waitangi. Less than 10 years later, the French abandoned their attempt at colonization, but the settlers remained and gradually intermarried with the local English community. Apart from the street names and a few surnames, there is little sign of a French connection any more, but the village has a splendid setting, and on a sunny day it makes a marvelous trip from Christchurch.

The best way to get the feel of the town is to stroll along the waterfront from the lighthouse to Jubilee Park. The focus of historic interest is the **Akaroa Museum,** which has a display of Maori greenstone and embroidery and dolls dating from the days of the French settlement. The museum includes Langlois-Eteveneaux House, the two-room cottage of an early French settler, which bears the imprint of his homeland in its architecture. *Rue Lavaud and Rue Balguerie, tel. 03/304–7614. Admission: $2.50 adults, 50¢ children 5–15. Open daily 10:30–4:30.*

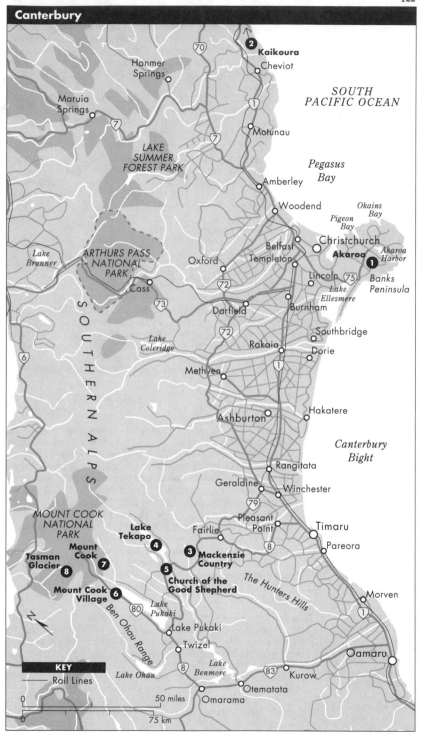

The picture-book **Church of St. Patrick,** near the museum, was built in 1864 to replace two previous Catholic churches—the first destroyed by fire, the second by tempest. *Rue Pompallier. Open daily 8–5.*

Lodging   **Glencarrig.** Buried in greenery on a hillside a three-minute
Moderate   walk from Akaroa, this charming lodge offers a high standard
★   of B&B accommodation at a reasonable price. Built in 1851, the house is filled with antiques and kilims, which complement its rustic character. The best of the three rooms is the Aylmer, which opens onto the veranda. The rambling country garden, bordered by a stream with its own waterwheel, is a real delight. This is a nonsmoking house. *7 Percy St., Akaroa, tel. 03/ 304–7008. Facilities: outdoor pool. 2 rooms with bath. Tariff includes breakfast. No credit cards.*

Excursion to Kaikoura

This excursion from Christchurch up the coast to Kaikoura requires a full day.

Getting There   The 190-kilometer (120-mile) drive up Highway 1 takes 3½ hours. InterCity (tel. 03/72–8297) and Mount Cook Landline (tel. 03/79–0690) operate daily buses between Christchurch and Kaikoura.

Exploring   The town of **Kaikoura** lies to the north of Christchurch. The
2   name means "to eat crayfish" in Maori, and while the crayfish sold from roadside stalls are an excellent reason to go, an even better one is the sperm whales that can be seen off the coast in greater numbers than anywhere else on earth. The sperm whale, the largest toothed mammal, can reach a length of 60 feet and a weight of 70 tons. The reason for the whales' concentration in this area is the abundance of squid, their main food, in the deep trench just off the continental shelf, barely a kilometer off Kaikoura. Sperm whales are most likely to be seen between October and August. **Whale Watch Kaikoura Ltd.** (tel. 0800/65–5121) operates three-hour whale-spotting trips at varying times, depending on weather ($85 adults, $50 children aged 5–15). Even in calm weather, the sea often has a sizable swell.

Christchurch to Mount Cook

The 330-kilometer (205-mile) drive from Christchurch straight through to Mount Cook Village takes five hours.

The **Canterbury Plains,** which ring Christchurch, are the country's finest sheep pastures, as well as its largest area of flat land. But while this may be sheep heaven, the drive south along the plain is mundane by New Zealand standards—until you leave Highway 1 and head toward the Southern Alps.

At Rangitata, on the south bank of the wide Rangitata River, Highway 79 turns inland from Highway 1 and travels toward the distant mountains through the town of Geraldine to Fairlie, where Highway 8 takes up the journey. When the highway crosses Burkes Pass, the woodland is suddenly replaced by the high-country tussock grassland, which is dotted with lupines in
3   the summer months. This is known as the **Mackenzie Country** after James ("Jock") Mackenzie, one of the most intriguing and enigmatic figures in New Zealand history. Mackenzie was a

Scot who may or may not have stolen the thousand sheep that were found with him in these secluded upland pastures in 1855. Arrested, tried, and convicted, he made several escapes from jail before he was granted a free pardon nine months after his trial—and disappeared from the pages of history. Regardless of his innocence or guilt, there can be no doubt that Mackenzie was a master bushman and herdsman.

Cradled by snowy mountain peaks, the long, narrow expanse of ❹ **Lake Tekapo** is one of the most photographed sights in New Zealand. Its extraordinary milky-turquoise color comes from rock-flour—rock ground by glacial action and held in a soupy suspension. On the eastern side of the lakeside power station is ❺ the tiny **Church of the Good Shepherd,** which strikes a dignified note of piety in these majestic surroundings. A nearby memorial commemorates the sheepdogs of the area. Before fences were erected around their runs, shepherds would tether dogs at strategic points to stop their sheep from straying.

At Lake Pukaki, Highway 80 turns north between the lake and the Ben Ohau Range, a scenic spectacular that reaches its cli- ❻ max when the road ends at **Mount Cook Village.** The village consists of a visitor center, a grocery store, and a couple of hotels, one of which, the Hermitage, is probably the most famous in the country (*see* Lodging, below). Surrounding the village is Mount Cook National Park. The park includes 22 peaks topping the 3,000-meter (10,000-foot) mark, the tallest of which is ❼ **Mount Cook**—at approximately 3,684 meters (12,283 feet), the highest peak between Papua New Guinea and the Andes. The mountain was dramatically first scaled in 1894 by three New Zealanders, Fyfe, Graham, and Clarke, just after it was announced that an English climber and an Italian mountain guide were about to attempt the summit. In a frantic surge of national pride, the New Zealand trio resolved to beat them to it, which they did on Christmas Day. Mount Cook is still considered a difficult ascent. In the summer of 1991 a chunk of it broke away, but fortunately there were no climbers in the path of the massive avalanches. High Peak, the summit of the mountain, is now about 20 meters (66 feet) lower, but a much more difficult ascent. Provided the sun is shining, the views are spectacular and the walks are inspiring. If the cloud ceiling is low, however, you may wonder why you came—and the mountain weather is notoriously changeable. Since a lengthy detour is required to reach Mount Cook Village, it is advisable to contact the Visitor Information Centre (tel. 03/435–1818) to check weather conditions.

Radiating from the visitor center is a network of trails offering walks of varying difficulty, from the 10-minute Bowen Track to the 5½-hour climb to the 1,445-meter (4,818-foot) summit of Mount Sebastapol. Particularly recommended is the walk along the Hooker Valley, a two-to-four-hour round trip. There are frequent ranger-guided walks from the visitor center, with informative talks on flora, fauna, and geology along the way.

The other main activity at Mount Cook is **flightseeing.** From the airfield at Mount Cook Village, helicopters and fixed-wing aircraft make spectacular scenic flights across the Southern Alps. One of the most exciting is the one-hour trip aboard the ski- ❽ planes that touch down on the **Tasman Glacier** after a dazzling scenic flight. The 10-minute stop on the glacier doesn't allow time for much more than a snapshot, but the sensation is tremendous. The moving tongue of ice beneath your feet—one of the largest glaciers outside the Himalayas—is 29 kilometers (18 miles) long and up to 600 meters (2,000 feet) thick in places. The intensity of light on the glacier can be dazzling, and sunglasses are a must. Generally, the best time for flights is early morning. During winter the planes drops skiers on the glacier at 3,000 meters (10,000 feet), and they ski down through 13 kilometers (8 miles) of powder snow and fantastic ice formations. With guides, this run is suitable even for intermediate skiers. Skiplane flights cost about $184 for adults, $138 for children under 12; helicopter flights range from $108 to $252. Skiplane flights are operated by **Mount Cook Line** (tel. 03/435–1848), helicopters by the **Helicopter Line** (tel. 03/435–1801). **Alpine Guides Ltd.** (Box 20, Mount Cook, tel. 03/435–1834) can assist with guides for all treks and ski trips in the national park.

Dining

Expensive **Panorama Room.** It's the view rather than the food that dazzles at the dining room of the Hermitage Hotel (*see* Lodging, below). The service is efficient and the food well presented, but the meals are vastly more expensive than in the neighboring Alpine Restaurant. Choices from the menu include fillet of sole stuffed with spinach, crayfish thermidor, and venison cutlets with a blueberry glaze. *Mount Cook Village, tel. 03/627–1809. Reservations required. Jacket required. AE, DC, MC, V. No lunch.*

Lodging

Lodging at Mount Cook Village is controlled by a single company that operates the three hotels there. Although it is the most expensive of the three, only The Hermitage can be said to offer reasonable value.

Very Expensive **The Hermitage.** Famed for its stupendous mountain views, this rambling hotel is the luxury option at Mount Cook Village. The guest rooms are gradually being remodeled and decorated with green plaid–upholstered wood furniture and brass accents to enhance the rustic-lodge atmosphere. Request one of these renovated rooms. *Mount Cook Village, tel. 03/435–1809, fax 03/435–1879. 104 rooms with bath. Facilities: sauna, 3 restaurants, bar. AE, DC, MC, V.*

Expensive **Mount Cook Travelodge.** The views here are similar to those at the Hermitage, but the drop in the quality of rooms and facilities is far greater than the drop in price. *Mount Cook Village, tel. 03/627–1809, fax 03/435–1879. 55 rooms with bath. Facilities: restaurant. Tariff includes breakfast. AE, DC, MC, V. Closed winter.*

Kimbell Colonial Cottages. These neat, self-contained cottages are located in the Mackenzie Country north of Fairlie, about midway between Christchurch and Mount Cook. Prettiest of the three is Laurel, a simple timber cottage in the midst of flower beds and sheep pastures. Furnishings in each are simple and appropriately rustic. The surroundings offer trout fishing and deer hunting, and the Kimbell pub is a great source of local color. *RD 17, Fairlie, South Canterbury, tel. 03/658–8170, fax 03/685–8179. 3 cottages with bath. Tariff includes breakfast. AE, MC, V.*

Moderate **Mount Cook Chalets.** These metal-roofed A-frames with cooking facilities are the budget option at Mount Cook Village. Each has two small bedrooms plus a fold-down couch and can sleep up to six. *Mount Cook Village, tel. 03/627–1809, fax 03/435–1879. 18 chalets. AE, DC, MC, V.*

Southland, Otago, and Stewart Island

These areas make up the lower third of the South Island. Most of Southland (to the west) is taken up by two giant national parks, Fiordland and Mount Aspiring. Fiordland, the name generally given to the southwest coast, is a majestic wilderness of rocks, ice, and beech forests, where glaciers have carved deep notches into the coast. The scenic climax of this area—and perhaps of the whole country—is Milford Sound. The cruise on the Sound is a must, but anyone who wants to experience Fiordland in all its raw grandeur should hike along one of the many trails in the area, among them the famous four-day Milford Track, "the finest walk in the world." The accommodation base and adventure center for the region is Queenstown.

To the southeast is the flatter area known as Otago. Its capital, Dunedin, is one of the unexpected treasures of New Zealand: a harbor city of steep streets and prim Victorian architecture, with a royal albatross colony on its doorstep. Invercargill, at the southern tip of this region, is essentially a farm service community that few travelers will find any reason to visit unless they are traveling on to Stewart Island, the southernmost of New Zealand's three main islands.

Queenstown to Milford Sound

Important Addresses and Numbers **Queenstown Visitor Information Centre.** *Clocktower Centre, Shotover and Camp Sts., tel. 03/442–8238. Open daily 7–7.*

Dial 111 for **fire, police,** and **ambulance** services.

Arriving and Departing

By Plane Queenstown is linked with Auckland, Christchurch, Rotorua, and Wellington by both **Ansett New Zealand** (tel. 03/442–6161) and **Mount Cook Airlines** (tel. 03/442–7650), which also flies several times daily to Mount Cook. **Queenstown Airport** is 9 kilometers (6 miles) east of town. The **Johnston's Shuttle Express** (tel. 03/442–3639) meets all incoming flights and charges $5 per person to hotels in town. The taxi fare is about $13.

By Car Highway 6 enters Queenstown from the west coast; driving time for the 350-kilometer (220-mile) journey from Franz Josef is eight hours. From Queenstown, Highway 6 continues south to Invercargill—a 190-kilometer (120-mile) distance that takes about three hours to drive. The fastest route from Queenstown to Dunedin is via Highway 6 to Milton, then north along Highway 1, a distance of 280 kilometers (175 miles) that can be covered in five hours.

By Bus From Queenstown, both **Mount Cook Landline** (tel. 03/442–7650) and **InterCity** (tel. 03/442–8238) operate daily bus services to Christchurch, Mount Cook, and Dunedin. **InterCity** buses operate daily to Nelson via the west coast glaciers.

Guided Tours

Fiordland Travel has a wide choice of fly/drive tour options to Milford and Doubtful sounds from Queenstown. The cost of a one-day bus tour and cruise on Milford Sound is $128, $64 for children 4–14. *Steamer Wharf, Queenstown, tel. 03/442–7500.*

Milford Sound Adventure Tours offers a bus/cruise trip to Milford Sound from Te Anau ($69) that includes a cycling option. From the Homer Tunnel, passengers can leave the bus and coast 13 kilometers (8 miles) down to the Sound on mountain bikes. *Box 134, Te Anau, tel. 03/249–7227. Tour departs Te Anau 8 AM.*

The **T.S.S.** *Earnslaw* is vintage lake steamer that has been restored to brassy, wood-paneled splendor and put to work cruising Lake Wakatipu from Queenstown. A lunch cruise, an afternoon cruise across the lake to a sheep station, and a dinner cruise are available from July to May. *Steamer Wharf, Queenstown, tel. 03/442–7500.*

The **Double Decker** (tel. 03/442–6067) is an original London bus that makes a 2½-hour circuit from Queenstown to Arrowtown and the bungy-jumping platform on the Kawarau River. Tours ($25 adults, $10 children 5–15) depart Queenstown daily at 10 and 2 from the Mall and the Earnslaw wharf.

Exploring Queenstown and Fiordland National Park

Numbers in the margin correspond to points of interest on the Southland, Otago, and Stewart Island map.

Set on the edge of a glacial lake beneath the saw-toothed peaks of the Remarkables, **Queenstown** is the most popular tourist destination on the South Island. Once prized by the Maoris as a source of greenstone, the town boomed when gold was discovered in the Shotover, which quickly became famous as "the richest river in the world." Queenstown could easily have become a ghost town when the gold gave out—except for its location. With ready access to mountains, lakes, rivers, ski fields, and the glacier-carved coastline of Fiordland National Park, Queenstown has become the adventure capital of New Zealand. Its shop windows are crammed with skis, Gore-tex jackets, Asolo walking boots, and Marin mountain bikes. Along Shotover Street, the travel agents offer white-water rafting, jet boating, caving, trekking, heliskiing, parachuting, and bungy jumping.

Despite its marvelous location, Queenstown is basically a comfortable, cosmopolitan base camp. The best views of the town ❶ are from the **Queenstown Gardens,** on the peninsula that encloses Queenstown Bay, and from the heights of Bob's Peak, ❷ 435 meters above the lake. The **Skyline Gondola** whisks passengers to the top for a panoramic view of the town and the Remarkables on the far side of the lake. The summit terminal has a cafeteria, a carvery restaurant, and *Kiwi Magic*, a 25-minute aerial film tour of the country with stunning effects. *Brecon St., Queenstown, tel. 03/442–7540. Gondola: $9 adults,*

Southland, Otago, and Stewart Island

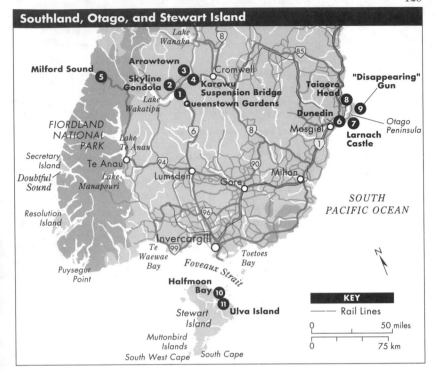

$3 children 4–15. Open daily 10–10. Kiwi Magic screens every hour on the hour, 11–9. Admission: $6 adults, $3 children under 15.

❸ Another gold-mining town, **Arrowtown,** lies 20 kilometers (13 miles) to the northeast. It had long been suspected that there was gold along the Arrow River, and when Edward Fox, an American, was seen selling large quantities of the precious metal in nearby Clyde, the hunt was on. Others attempted to follow the wily Fox back to his diggings, but kept giving his pursuers the slip, on one occasion even abandoning his tent and provisions in the middle of the night. Eventually a large party of prospectors stumbled on Fox and his team of 40 miners. The secret was out, miners rushed to stake their claims, and Arrowtown was born.

After the gold rush ended, the place was just another sleepy rural town until tourism created a new boom. Lodged at the foot of the steep Crown Range, this atmospheric little village of weathered-timber shop fronts and white stone churches shaded by ancient sycamores was simply too gorgeous to escape the attention of the tour buses. These days it has become a tourist trap, but a highly photogenic one, especially when autumn gilds the hillsides.

In a less visited part of the town is the former **Chinese settlement.** Chinese miners were common on the goldfields in the late 1860s, but local prejudice forced them to live in their own separate enclave. A number of their huts and Ah Lum's Store, one of the few Chinese goldfield buildings to survive intact, have

So, you're getting away from it all.

Just make sure you can get back.

AT&T Access Numbers
Dial the number of the country you're in to reach AT&T.

AMERICAN SAMOA	633 2-USA	**INDIA**◆	**000-117**	NEW ZEALAND		000-911
AUSTRALIA	0014-881-011	**INDONESIA**◆	**00-801-10**	***PHILIPPINES**		**105-11**
*CAMBODIA	**800-0011**	*JAPAN	0039-111	**SAIPAN**†		**235-2872**
CHINA, PRC◆◆	**10811**	**KOREA**	**009-11**	SINGAPORE		800-0111-111
COOK ISLANDS	09-111	**KOREA**◇◇	**11 ✱**	SRI LANKA		430-430
GUAM	**018-872**	MACAO	0800-111	***TAIWAN**		**0080-10288-0**
HONG KONG	**800-1111**	***MALAYSIA**	**800-0011**	THAILAND◆		0019-991-1111

Countries in bold face permit country-to-country calling in addition to calls to the U.S. *Public phones require deposit of coin or phone card. ◆ Not available from public phones. ◆◆ Not yet available from all areas. ◇◇ From public phones only, push the red button, wait for dial tone and then dial. †May not be available from every phone. © 1993 AT&T.

Here's a travel tip that will make it easy to call back to the States. Dial the access number for the country you're visiting and connect right to AT&T **USADirect**® Service. It's the quick way to get English-speaking operators and can minimize hotel surcharges.

If all the countries you're visiting aren't listed above, call **1 800 241-5555** before you leave for a free wallet card with all AT&T access numbers. International calling made easy—it's all part of **The _i_ Plan.**℠

THE _i_ PLAN℠

AT&T

All The Best Trips Start with **Fodor's**

been preserved. *Bush Creek, at the western end of town. Open daily 9–5.*

④ On Highway 6 not far from Arrowtown is the **Karawau Suspension Bridge,** where the bungy jumpers make their leaps—a spectacle well worth the short detour. As a promotional stunt, the AJ Hackett company (*see* Sports and the Outdoors, below) once offered a free jump to anyone who would jump nude, but there were so many takers that the scheme had to be abandoned.

From Queenstown, the road to Milford Sound passes through the town of Te Anau, then winds through deep, stony valleys where waterfalls cascade into mossy beech forests as it enters **Fiordland National Park.** Allow at least 2½ hours for the 119-kilometer (74-mile) journey from Te Anau to Milford Sound. Fiordland, the largest national park in New Zealand, takes its name from the deep sea inlets, or sounds, on its western flank. This is the most rugged part of the country. Parts of the park are so remote that they have never been explored, and visitor activities are mostly confined to a few of the sounds and the walking trails. The nearest services base is the town of Te Anau, which offers a choice of motel, hotel, or motor camp accommodation. For information, contact the Fiordland National Park Visitor Centre (Box 29, Te Anau, tel. 03/249–7921).

⑤ For most visitors, Fiordland's greatest attraction is **Milford Sound**—the sort of overpowering place where photographers run out of film. Hemmed in by walls of rock that rise, almost sheer, from the sea up to 4,000 feet, the 16-kilometer- (10-mile-) long inlet was carved by a succession of glaciers as they gouged a track to the sea. Its dominant feature is the 5,560-foot pinnacle of Mitre Peak, which is capped with snow for all but the warmest months of the year. Opposite the peak, Bowen Falls tumbles 520 feet before exploding into the sea. Milford Sound is also spectacularly wet: The average annual rainfall is around 20 feet. An inch an hour for 12 hours straight isn't uncommon, and two days without rain is reckoned to be a drought. In addition to a raincoat you'll need insect repellent—the Sound is renowned for its sandflies. From the road end, a number of cruise boats depart frequently, from about 11 AM to 3 PM, for trips around the Sound; expect to pay about $40 for adults, $15 for children. During the summer holiday period it's essential to book ahead. *Fiordland Travel, Steamer Wharf, Queenstown, tel. 03/442–7500.*

Sports and the Outdoors

Bungy Jumping **AJ Hackett Bungy,** the pioneer in the sport, offers two jumps in the area. Kawarau Bridge is the original jump site, 23 kilometers (14 miles) from Queenstown on State Highway 6. Daredevils who graduate from the 143-foot plunge might like to test themselves on the 230-foot Skippers Canyon Bridge. The price is $89 for the Kawarau jump, $145 for Skippers Canyon. *Box 488, Queenstown, tel. 03/442–1177. Open winter, daily 8:30–5; summer, daily 8–7.*

Horse Trekking **Moonlight Stables** offers a choice of full- or half-day rides along the scenic Moonlight Trail, which follows the Shotover Gorge. No previous riding experience is necessary. Transport from Queenstown is provided. *Box 784, Queenstown, tel. 03/442 8892. $45 per person for ½-day trip.*

Jet Boat Rides The **Dart River Jet Boat Safari** is a 2½-hour journey 20 miles upstream into the ranges of the Mount Aspiring National Park. This rugged area is one of the most spectacular parts of the South Island, and the trip is highly recommended. Buses depart Queenstown daily at 8, 11, and 2 for the 45-minute ride to the boats. *Box 76, Queenstown, tel. 03/442–9992. Tickets: $99 adults, $55 children 5–16.*

The **Shotover Jet** is the most famous jet boat ride in the country (and one of the most exciting): a high-speed, heart-stopping adventure on which the boat pirouettes within inches of canyon walls. If you want to stay relatively dry, sit beside the driver. The boats are based at the Shotover Bridge, a 10-minute drive from Queenstown, and depart frequently between 8 AM and 7 PM from December to April, 9:30–4:30 the rest of the year. *Shotover River Canyon, Queenstown, tel. 03/442–8570. Tickets: $55 adults, $24 children under 15.*

Rafting **Kawarau Raft Expeditions** offers various half-, full-, and two-day white-water rafting trips in the Queenstown area. For intrepid rafters, the grade 4-to-5 rapids of the Shotover River provide an unforgettable journey, which ends with the rafts shooting through the 560-foot Oxenbridge Tunnel. *35 Shotover St., Queenstown, tel. 03/442–9792. Cost: $89 to $229 per person.*

Dining

Price categories for restaurants are the same as in the Auckland Dining section in Chapter 3.

Moderate **Avanti.** This restaurant at the heart of Queenstown serves better-than-average Italian dishes at a far lower price than most in this resort area. Pastas and pizzas are prominent on the extensive menu, but so are more substantial meals such as venison goulash and chicken parmigiano. Servings are designed for appetites honed on the mountain slopes. *The Mall, Queenstown, tel. 03/442–8503. No reservations. Dress: casual. AE, DC, MC, V. BYOB.*

The Continental. At the lake end of Queenstown Mall, this clublike bar/bistro is a notch up the smartness stakes from most of the town's restaurants. Among the main courses you might choose venison with a mushroom and red wine sauce, or rack of lamb with a sesame and soy sauce. The service is professional and friendly. *5 The Mall, Queenstown, tel. 03/442–8372. No reservations. Dress: casual. AE.*

The Cow. The pizzas and pastas at this tiny, stone-walled restaurant are some of the best-value meals in town, but the place is immensely popular, so be prepared to wait for a table. A roaring fire makes for a cozy atmosphere on chilly evenings, but patrons aren't encouraged to linger over dinner, and you may be asked to share your table. *Cow La., Queenstown, tel. 03/442–8588. No reservations. Dress: casual. MC, V. BYOB. No lunch.*

Inexpensive **Gourmet Express.** The food may not reach gourmet standards, but the service is certainly express. A popular breakfast spot, this casual diner at the front of a shopping arcade serves pancakes with maple syrup, eggs any way you want, and heart-starting coffee. A variety of inexpensive grills and burgers is available for lunch and dinner. *Bay Centre, Shotover St.,*

Queenstown, tel. 03/442–9619. No reservations. Dress: casual. AE, DC, MC, V. BYOB.

Stonewall Cafe. There is nothing remarkable about the sandwiches, salads, soups, and pasta at this center-of-town café, but the outdoor tables are a good choice for lunch on a sunny day. *The Mall, Queenstown, tel. 03/442–6429. No reservations. Dress: casual. AE, MC, V. Closed weekends.*

Lodging

Price categories for hotels are the same as in the Auckland Lodging section in Chapter 3. Highly recommended lodgings are indicated by a star ★.

Very Expensive **Millbrook Resort.** A 20-minute drive from Queenstown, this ★ glamorous new resort offers luxurious, self-contained accommodation with special appeal for golfers. The resort is an elevated cluster of big, comfortable, two-story villas surrounded by an 18-hole golf course that was designed by New Zealand professional Bob Charles. The villas are decorated in country style: pine tables, textured walls, shuttered windows, and a cream-and-cornflower-blue color scheme. Each has a fully equipped kitchen, laundry facilities, a large lounge/dining room, ski closet, and two bedrooms, each with an *en suite* bathroom, and the price is a bargain. *Malaghans Rd., Arrowtown, tel. 03/442–1563, fax 03/442–1145. 20 villas with bath. Facilities: golf course, tennis court, bar, restaurant. AE, DC, MC, V.*

★ **Nugget Point.** Poised high above the Shotover River, this modern, stylish retreat offers the finest accommodation in the Queenstown area. Rooms are cozy and luxuriously large, and each has a balcony, a kitchenette, and a bedroom separate from the lounge area. The lodge is a 10-minute drive from Queenstown on the road to Coronet Peak, one of the top ski areas in the country. *Arthurs Point Rd., Queenstown, tel. 03/442–7630, fax 03/442–7308. 35 rooms with bath. Facilities: heated pool, sauna, spa, squash, tennis, restaurant, bar. AE, DC, MC, V.*

Queenstown Parkroyal. This modern resort complex sits in a prime position close to town. Guest rooms are large and luxuriously equipped, and about half overlook the steamer wharf. Request one on the top floor. *Beach St., Queenstown, tel. 03/442–7800, fax 03/442–8895. 139 rooms with bath. Facilities: heated pool, sauna, restaurant, bar. AE, DC, MC, V.*

Expensive **Hulbert House.** Set in tranquil gardens overlooking Queens★ town and the lake, this century-old timber home offers a high standard of bed-and-breakfast lodging. Rooms are large and comfortably furnished with antiques. Request one with lake and mountain views. The city center is a five-minute walk away down a very steep hill. *68 Ballarat St., Queenstown, tel. 03/442–8767. 5 rooms with bath. Tariff includes breakfast. MC.*

Moderate **Trelawn Place.** Perched on the brink of the Shotover Gorge 1½ miles (3 kilometers) from Queenstown, this stone and timber colonial-style house offers homely comforts and million-dollar views. The owners show a strong preference for strident colors and fussy furnishings that are at odds with the simple but dramatic surroundings. The most popular of the three spacious guest rooms is the blue room, on the ground floor. For guests who want more privacy and the option of making their own meals, the two-bedroom cottage, which costs $20 more, is recommended. *Box 117, Queenstown, tel. 03/442-9160. 3 rooms with bath, 1 cottage with bath. Facilities: spa. Tariff includes breakfast. No credit cards.*

Dunedin and Otago

Important Addresses and Numbers

Dunedin Visitor Information Centre. *48 The Octagon, tel. 03/474-3300. Open weekdays 8:30-5, weekends 9-5.*

Dial 111 for **fire, police,** and **ambulance** services.

Arriving and Departing

By Plane Dunedin is linked with all other New Zealand cities by **Ansett New Zealand** (tel. 03/477-4146) and **Air New Zealand** (tel. 03/477-5769). **Dunedin Airport** lies 20 kilometers (13 miles) south of the city. **Johnston's Shuttle Express** (tel. 03/476-2519), a shuttle service between the airport and the city, meets all incoming flights and charges $10 per person. Taxi fare to the city is about $30.

By Car Driving time along the 280 kilometers (175 miles) between Queenstown and Dunedin (via Highway 6 and Highway 1) is five hours. The main route between Dunedin and Invercargill is Highway 1—a 3½ hour drive. A slower scenic alternative is Highway 92 along the coast, which adds another 90 minutes to the journey.

By Bus Dunedin is served by **Mount Cook Landline** (tel. 03/474-0674) and **InterCity** buses (tel. 03/477-8860).

Guided Tours

Twilight Tours offer various minibus tours of Dunedin and its surroundings, including an afternoon tour that focuses on the albatrosses, penguins, and seals of the Otago Peninsula. The penguin sanctuary is a privately operated venture, and this tour is the only way to see the rare Yellow-eyed and Little Blue penguins. *Box 963, Dunedin, tel. 03/474-3300. Cost: $46 adults, $29 children under 15. Tours depart daily at 1:15 from Dunedin Visitor Information Centre.*

Exploring Dunedin

❻ Clinging to the walls of the natural amphitheater at the western end of Otago Harbour, the South Island's second largest city, **Dunedin,** combines wildlife, inspiring seascapes, and a handsome Victorian townscape. Dunedin also has a large number of university students who give the city a vitality far greater than its population of 120,000 might suggest.

Dunedin is the Gaelic name for Edinburgh, and the city's Scottish roots are obvious. It was founded in 1848 by settlers of the Free Church of Scotland, a breakaway group from the Presbyterian Church; today it has the only kilt shop in the country and the only whiskey distillery. A giant statue of Robert Burns presides over the heart of the city. The most compelling attraction for visitors is probably the royal albatross colony at Taiaroa Head, the only place on earth where these majestic seabirds can be seen with relative ease. The city is noted for its rhododendrons, which are at their best in October.

This walking tour begins at the Visitor Information Centre in the **Octagon,** the city's navel. Dunedin prospered mightily during the gold rush of the 1860s. For a while it was the largest city in the country, and the riches of the Otago goldfields are reflected in the bricks and mortar of Dunedin, most notably in the Italianate Municipal Chambers building.

Turn away from the figure of Burns, who sits in front of the cathedral "with his back to the kirk and his face to the pub," and walk down the hill along Stuart Street. On the corner of Dunbar Street you'll come to the late-Victorian **Law Courts.** Above the Stuart Street entrance stands the figure of Justice, scales in hand but without her customary blindfold (though the low helmet she wears probably has the same effect).

On the far side of Anzac Avenue is the **Dunedin Railway Station,** a cathedral to the power of steam. The massive bluestone structure in the Flemish Renaissance style is lavishly decorated with heraldic beasts, coats of arms, nymphs, scrolls, a mosaic floor, and even stained-glass windows portraying steaming locomotives. This extravagant building earned its architect, George Troup, the nickname "Gingerbread George" from the people of Dunedin, and a knighthood from the king. The station has far outlived the steam engine, and for all its magnificence it receives few trains these days. *Open daily 7–6.*

Walk away from the front of the station into High Street; on the corner of Cumberland Street stands the **Early Settlers Museum.** The museum preserves an impressive collection of artifacts, from the years when this was a whaling station to the days of the early Scottish settlers to the prosperous gold-rush era of the late 19th century. *220 Cumberland St., tel. 03/477–5052. Admission: $4 adults, children under 15 free. Open weekdays 10–5, weekends 1–5.*

Overlooking the museum is the spire of the **First Presbyterian Church,** perhaps the finest example of a Norman Gothic building the country. Turn into Burlington Street and walk to the left of the church, turn left into Moray Place, and cross the Octagon into George Street. Turn left into Pitt Street and left again at Royal Terrace to **Olveston.** This 35-room Jacobean-style mansion was built in 1904–06 for David Theomin, a wealthy businessman and patron of the arts, who amassed a handsome collection of antiques and contemporary furnishings. The house and its furnishings are undoubtedly a treasure from an elegant age, but apart from some paintings collected by Theomin's daughter there is very little in it to suggest that it's in New Zealand. Even the oak staircase and balustrade were prefabricated in England. The one-hour guided tour is recommended. *42 Royal Terr., tel. 03/477–3320. Admission: $9 adults, $3 children 5–15. Open daily 9–5. Tours daily 9:30, 10:45, 12, 1:30, 2:45, 4.*

The Otago Peninsula

The main areas of interest on the claw-shaped peninsula that extends northeast from Dunedin are the albatross colony and Larnach Castle. On the return journey to Dunedin, the Highcliff Road, which turns inland at the village of Portobello, is a scenic alternative to the coastal Portobello Road.

7 Set high on a hilltop with commanding views from its battlements, **Larnach Castle** is the grand baronial fantasy of William Larnach, an Australian-born businessman and politician. The castle was a vast extravagance even in the free-spending atmosphere of the gold rush. Larnach imported an English craftsman to carve the ceilings, which took 12 years to complete, and the solid marble bath, the marble fireplaces, tiles, glass, and even much of the wood came from Europe. The mosaic in the foyer depicts Larnach's family crest and the modest name he gave to his stately pile: The Camp. Larnach rose to a prominent position in the New Zealand government of the late 1800s, but in 1898, beset by a series of financial disasters and possible marital problems, he committed suicide in Parliament House. (According to one romantic version, Larnach's third wife, whom he married at an advanced age, ran off with his eldest son; devastated, he shot himself.) A café in the castle ballroom serves Devonshire teas and light snacks. *Camp Rd., tel. 03/476–1302. Admission: $9.50 adults, $3.50 children 5–15. Open daily 9–5.*

8 **Taiaroa Head,** the eastern tip of the Otago Peninsula, is the site of a breeding colony of royal albatrosses. Among the largest birds in the world, with a wingspan of 11 feet, the albatrosses can take off only from steep slopes with the help of a strong breeze. Outside of Taiaroa Head and the Chatham Islands to the east, they are found only on windswept islands deep in southern latitudes, remote from human habitation. The colony is open for viewing from October through August, with the greatest number of birds present shortly after the young hatch around the end of January. Between March and September the parents leave the fledglings in their nests while they gather food for them. In September the young birds fly away, returning about eight years later to start their own breeding cycle. From the visitor center, groups follow a steep trail up to the Albatross Observatory, from which the birds may be seen through narrow windows. They are only rarely seen in flight. Access to the colony is strictly controlled, and visitors must book in advance. The tour takes about an hour. *Taiaroa Head, Dunedin, tel. 03/478–0499. Admission: $15 adults, $7 children 5–16. Open Oct.–Aug., daily 10:30–4.*

9 In the same area as the colony is the **"Disappearing" Gun,** a six-inch artillery piece installed during the Russian Scare of 1888. When fired, the recoil would propel the gun back into its pit, where it could be reloaded out of the line of enemy fire. The gun has been used in anger only once, when it was fired across the bow of a fishing boat that had failed to observe correct procedures before entering the harbor during World War II. *Admission: $8 adults, $4 children 5–15. Combined albatross colony/gun admission: $18 adults, $9 children. Open 10:30–4.*

Dining

Price categories for restaurants are the same as in the Auckland Dining section in Chapter 3. Highly recommended restaurants are indicated by a star ★.

Very Expensive **95 Filleul.** This pink Victorian terrace house has long been regarded as the finest restaurant in town. The dining area is small and modestly elegant, and the modern, international menu includes such main courses as medium-rare venison accompanied by a grapeleaf filled with venison-liver mousse, and barbecued fish served with wasabi butter. *95 Filleul St., Dunedin, tel. 03/477–7233. Reservations advised. Jacket advised. AE, DC, MC, V. BYOB. No lunch.*

Expensive **Harbour Lights.** Poised on the shores of the Otago Peninsula
★ overlooking the harbor, this restaurant is an exception to the rule that good food and good views don't usually coincide. Fish and game dishes are prominent on a menu that features such main courses as smoked South Island salmon with fresh herbs, wild boar shnitzel, and grilled grouper steak with a béarnaise sauce. The balcony is a favorite spot for summer dining. *494 Portobello Rd., MacAndrew Bay, tel. 03/476–1604. Reservations advised. Dress: casual but neat. AE, DC, MC, V. No lunch Mon., Tues.*

Moderate **Palms Cafe.** Vegetarians are especially well served at this casu-
★ al, popular restaurant. The menu includes a casserole of olives, feta cheese, mushrooms, and tomatoes, and a Greek pastry roll filled with spinach and feta. Nonvegetarian mains include lamb kebabs with peanut sauce, a whole sole with garlic sauce, and fillet of lamb with a green peppercorn glaze. The restaurant has a no-smoking policy. *84 High St., Dunedin, tel. 03/477–6534. Reservations advised. Dress: casual but neat. No credit cards. BYOB. Closed Sun.–Mon. No lunch.*

Lodging

Price categories for hotels are the same as in the Auckland Lodging section in Chapter 3.

Moderate **Cargills Motor Inn.** In a convenient location close to the city center, this motor inn offers superior motel-style rooms as well as two-bedroom family suites. Reduced rates apply Friday to Sunday nights. *670 George St., Dunedin, tel. 03/477–7983, fax 03/477–8098. 51 rooms with bath. Facilities: bar, restaurant. AE, DC, MC, V.*

Inexpensive **Larnach Lodge.** A modern timber building on the grounds of Larnach Castle, 19 kilometers (12 miles) from Dunedin, the lodge offers comfortable motel suites with marvelous views. Dinners are available in the castle by arrangement; otherwise the nearest restaurant is a 10-minute drive away. Budget rooms with shared facilities are available in the converted coach house. *Camp Rd., Otago Peninsula, Dunedin, tel. 03/476–1302. 27 rooms with bath. AE, DC, MC, V.*
Magnolia House. Overlooking the city of Dunedin in a prestige suburb, this gracious B&B offers atmospheric accommodation. The spacious guest rooms are furnished with antiques, and the house is surrounded by a pretty garden that includes native bushland. The house has a no-smoking policy. Dinners are available by arrangement, and children are welcome. *18 Grendon St., Maori Hill, Dunedin, tel. 03/467–5999. 3 rooms share 1 bathroom. Tariff includes breakfast. No cards.*

Stewart Island

Important **Stewart Island Visitor Information Centre.** *Halfmoon Bay, tel.*
Addresses and *03/219–1218. Open weekdays 8–4:30.*
Numbers Dial 111 for **fire, police,** and **ambulance** services.

Arriving and Departing

By Plane **Southern Air** (tel. 03/218–9129) operates several flights daily between Invercargill and Halfmoon Bay. The round-trip fare for the 20-minute flight is $135 adults, $67.50 children 4–14. The free baggage allowance is 15 kilograms (33 pounds) per passenger.

By Boat **Stewart Island Marine** (tel. 03/219–8376) operates a ferry service between the island and the port of Bluff, the port for Invercargill. The one-way fare is $37 for adults, $18.50 for children under 15. Ferries depart Bluff on Monday, Wednesday, and Friday at 9:30 and 3:30 between May and November, daily at 9:30 and 3:30 during the rest of the year.

Guided Tours

For information on fishing trips, birdwatching trips to Ulva Island, and boat trips around Paterson Inlet, contact **Stewart Island Travel** (Box 26, Stewart Island, tel. 03/219–1269).

Exploring Stewart Island

The third and most southerly of New Zealand's main islands, Stewart Island is separated from the South Island by the 24-kilometer (15-mile) Foveaux Strait. Even by New Zealand standards, Stewart Island is remote, raw, and untouched. Electricity is a recent innovation, roads total about 20 kilometers (13 miles), and apart from the settlement of **Halfmoon Bay** on Paterson Inlet, the place is practically uninhabited. For most visitors, the attractions are its seclusion, its relaxed way of life, and—despite a once-busy sawmilling industry—its untouched quality.

The island, which covers some 1,700 square kilometers (650 square miles) and measures about 40 miles from north to south and about 40 miles across at its widest point, forms a rough triangle, with a deep indentation, Paterson Inlet, on its eastern flank. On the coastline, sharp cliffs rise from a succession of sheltered bays and beaches; in the interior, forested hills rise gradually toward the western side of the island. Seals and penguins frequent the coast, and the island's prolific birdlife includes a number of species rarely seen in any other part of the country. One of the best spots for bird-watching is **Ulva Island,** a one-hour launch trip from Halfmoon Bay (*see* Guided Tours, above).

Outdoor Activities

Hiking A network of walking trails has been established on the northern half of the island, leaving the south as a wilderness area. A popular trek is the **Northern Circuit,** a 10-day walk from Halfmoon Bay that circles the north coast and then cuts through the interior to return to its starting point. The island's climate is notoriously changeable, and walkers should be prepared for rain and mud. For information on walks, contact the **Department of Conservation** (Main Rd., Halfmoon Bay, tel. 03/219–1218).

Hunting Another major activity for visitors to the island is hunting. Red deer and Virginia or whitetail deer were introduced earlier this century and may be hunted all year round. Hunting permits are available from the Department of Conservation office at Halfmoon Bay (*see* Hiking, above).

Dining and Lodging

Price categories are the same as in the Auckland Dining and Lodging sections in Chapter 3.

Very Expensive   **Stewart Island Lodge.** The most luxurious accommodation on the island offers comfortable, centrally heated suites with private baths. The focal points of life at the lodge are the guest lounge and the dining room, both of which boast expansive views across the bay. The owners have a game fishing launch and can arrange scenic tours of the island. Local seafood is a specialty on the dinner menu. *Halfmoon Bay, Nichol Rd., Stewart Island, tel., fax 03/219–1085. Tariff includes all meals. 4 rooms with bath. AE, DC, MC, V.*

Inexpensive   **Rakiura Motel.** Within easy walking distance of Halfmoon Bay, the Rakiura offers standard motel units will sleep up to six. *Horseshoe Bay Rd., Halfmoon Bay, tel. 03/219–1096. 5 rooms with bath. MC.*

6 Adventure Vacations

*By David
McGonigal*

Visitors miss the best of New Zealand if they don't get away from the cities to explore the magnificent outdoors. The mountains in this green, clean land are made for hiking and climbing; the sparsely populated roads for bicycling; the rivers for rafting. The rugged coastline looks wonderful from the deck of a small vessel or, even closer to the water, a sea kayak. And this is the country that invented jetboating.

Adventure vacations are commonly split into soft and hard adventures. A hard adventure requires a substantial degree of physical participation, although you usually don't have to be perfectly fit; in a few cases, prior experience is a prerequisite. In soft adventures the destination rather than the means of travel is often what makes it an adventure. With most companies, the adventure guides' knowledge of flora and fauna—and love of the bush—is matched by a level of competence that ensures your safety even in dangerous situations. The safety record of adventure operators is very good. Visitors should be aware, however, that most adventure-tour operators require participants to sign waiver forms absolving the company of responsibility in the event of an accident or a problem. Courts normally uphold such waivers except in cases of significant negligence.

Far more adventure-tour operators exist than can be listed in this chapter. Most are small and receive little publicity outside their local areas, so contact the relevant local tourist office if you have a specific area of interest. Here are the addresses of the major adventure-tour operators mentioned in the following pages:

Adventure Center (1311 63rd St., #200, Emeryville, CA 94608, USA, tel. 415/654–1879); **Abel Tasman National Park Enterprises** (Old Cederman House, Main Rd., Riwaka, Motueka RD3, Nelson, tel. 03/528–7801); **Alpine Guides** (Box 20, Mt. Cook, tel. 03/435–1834); **Alpine Recreation Canterbury** (Box 75, Lake Tekapo, tel. 03/680–6736); **Danes Shotover Rafts** (Corner Shotover and Camp Sts., Queenstown, tel. 03/442–7318); **Hollyford Tourist and Travel Company** (Box 205, Waikaitipu, Central Otago, tel. 03/442–3760); **Karavan Adventure Treks** (117 Harris Crescent, Christchurch, tel. 03/352–2177); **Landsborough River Expeditions** (Box 410, Queenstown, tel. 03/442–3630); **New Zealand Pedaltours** (Box 37–575, Parnell, Auckland, tel. 09/302–0968); **New Zealand Travel Professionals** (Box 219, Auckland, tel. 09/377–0761); **Ocean River Adventure Company** (Main Rd., Marahau Beach, RD2, Motueka, tel. 03/527–8266); **The Rafting Company** (Box 2392, Rotorua, tel. 073/480–233); **Routeburn Walk Ltd.** (Box 568, Queenstown, tel. 03/442–8200); **Southern Heritage Tours** (Box 22, Waikari, North Canterbury, tel. 03/314–4393); **THC Te Anau Travelodge** (Box 185, Te Anau, tel. 03/249–7411); **Wilderness Expeditions** (3rd Floor, 411 Kent St., Sydney, NSW 2000, tel. 02/264–3721).

See also Special-Interest Tours and Sports and the Outdoors in Chapter 1.

Bicycling

Bicycles may seem an impractical way to travel, but cycling is actually an excellent way to explore a small region, allowing you to cover more ground than on foot and observe far more than from the window of a car or bus. And while a bike may not be much fun in the fumes of city traffic, riding down quiet country lanes is a great way to relax and get fit at the same time. Cycling rates as a hard adventure because of the level of exercise.

Season: October–March.
Locations: Both islands.
Cost: From $1,570 for eight days to $4,200 for 19 days, including accommodation, meals, and support vehicle. Bikes can be rented for about $15 a day.
Tour Operators: New Zealand Pedtaltours, Adventure Center.

The combination of spectacular scenery and quiet roads is ideal for cycle holidays. Traditionally the South Island, with its central alpine spine, has been more popular, but Auckland is where most people arrive, and the North Island has enough curiosities—the hot mud pools of sulfurous Rotorua, the Waitaimo Caves, and the old gold-mining area of the Coromandel Peninsula—to fill each day. The average daily riding distance is about 60 kilometers (37 miles), and the support vehicle is large enough to accommodate all riders and bikes if circumstances so demand. The rides on the South Island extend from the ferry port of Picton to picturesque Queenstown, the center of a thriving adventure day-trip industry.

Cross-country Skiing

Although cross-country skiing doesn't offer the same adrenaline rush as downhill skiing, there are no expensive lift tickets to buy—your legs must do the work. While the crowds build up on the groomed slopes, cross-country skiers have a chance to get away from the hordes and experience the unforgettable sensation of skiing through silent landscapes. Cross-country skiing is hard adventure, even though many tours are arranged so that skiers stay in lodges every night. The joy of leaving the first tracks across new snow and the pleasure afforded by the unique scenery of the snowfields is tempered by the remarkable fatigue that your arms and legs feel at the end of the day.

Season: June–September.
Location: Mt. Cook.
Cost: $1,550 for seven days, including guide fees, accommodation, food, transport, and aircraft access.
Tour Operator: Alpine Guides.

Mt. Cook and its attendant Murchison and Tasman glaciers offer wonderful ski touring, with terrains to suit all levels of skiers. The tour commences with a flight to the alpine hut that becomes your base; from here the group sets out each day for skiing and instruction.

Hiking and Climbing

Hiking—or trekking, as it's more commonly called by Kiwis—is something akin to a national sport in this land of varied and spectacular scenery. A trek is intensely satisfying, but it doesn't have to be hard work: An easy ramble with a picnic lunch can be every bit as rewarding as a challenging 20-kilometer hike to a muddy camp. Depending on the type of walk, therefore, trekking can be a soft or hard adventure. Mountaineering is an associated high-adrenaline hard adventure well-suited to some parts of the terrain.

If it seems from the list below that every New Zealand company is involved in trekking, wait till you see the trails—particularly in the peak months of January and February; they can be crowded enough to detract from the nature experience. An advantage of a guided walk is that companies have their own tent camps or huts, with such luxuries as hot showers—and cooks. For the phobic, it's worth mentioning one very positive feature: New Zealand has no snakes or predatory animals.

Season: October–March for high-altitude walks, year-round for others.
Location: South Island.
Cost: From $425 for four days to $2,500 for 13 days. The climbing school costs $1,525 for seven days (including aircraft access, meals, accommodation, and transport).
Tour Operators: Abel Tasman National Park Enterprises, Adventure Center, Alpine Guides, Alpine Recreation Canterbury, Hollyford Tourist and Travel Company, Karavan Adventure Treks, New Zealand Travel Professionals, Routeburn Walk, THC Te Anau Travelodge, Wilderness Expeditions.

The most famous New Zealand walk, the Milford Track—a four-day trek through Fiordland National Park—covers a wide variety of terrains, from forests to high passes, lakes, a glowworm grotto, and the spectacle of Milford Sound itself. There are other walks in the same area: the Greenstone Valley (three days) and the Routeburn Track (three days)—combined they form the Grand Traverse; and the Hollyford Valley (five days). For something different, the three-to-six-day walks along beaches of Queen Charlotte Sound and through forests and along beaches in the Abel Tasman National Park (northwest South Island) are very popular and relatively easy, well suited to family groups; your pack is carried for you, and you stay in lodges. Karavan Adventure Treks has a series of unusual walks throughout the South Island. One of the most appealing is a four-day trip in Nelson Lakes National Park, near the top of the island; for two nights your base is the Angelus Basin Hut, spectacularly located beside a beautiful mountain lake beneath towering crags. Another option is the Alpine Recreation Canterbury 13-day minibus tour of the South Island, with one-day walks along the way; it provides an extensive and scenic cross-section, but it misses the magic of completing a long single walk.

For the very enthusiastic, Alpine Guides has a world-renowned seven-day course on the basics of mountain climbing, in the area of Mt. Cook, the highest point in the New Zealand Alps. There is also a 10-day technical course for experienced climbers. New Zealand is the home of Sir Edmund Hillary, who, with Tenzing Norgay, made the first ascent of Mt. Everest; clearly the country has a fine mountaineering tradition, and Alpine Guides is the nation's foremost training school.

Rafting

The exhilaration of sweeping down into the foam-filled jaws of a rapid is always tinged with fear—white-water rafting is, after all, rather like being tossed into a washing machine. While this sort of excitement appeals to many people, the attraction of rafting in New Zealand encompasses much more. As you drift downriver during the lulls between the white water, it's wonderful to sit back and watch the wilderness unfold, whether it's stately river gums overhanging the stream, towering cliffs, or forests on the surrounding slopes. Rafting means camping by the river at night, drinking tea brewed over the campfire, drinking billy tea brewed over the campfire, going to sleep with the sound of the stream in the background or sighting an elusive platypus at dawn. The juxtaposition of action and serenity gives rafting an enduring appeal that leads anyone who has tried it to seek out more rivers with more challenges. Rivers here are smaller and trickier than the ones used for commercial rafting in North America, and rafts usually hold only four to six people. The rafting companies provide all rafting and camping equipment—you only need clothing that won't be damaged by water (cameras are carried in waterproof barrels), a sleeping bag (in some cases), and sunscreen. Rafting qualifies as a hard adventure.

Season: Mainly October–May.
Location: Both islands.
Cost: From $65 for one day to $650 for three days (with helicopter set-down), including all equipment (wetsuits, helmets, footwear).
Tour Operators: Danes Shotover Rafts, Landsborough River Expeditions, The Rafting Company.

There are several rafting rivers on both islands of New Zealand. Near Rotorua, the Rangitaiki offers exciting grade-4 rapids and some good scenery. Nearby, the Kaituna River has the highest raftable waterfall in the world: a 7-meter (21-foot) free fall. On the South Island, the great majority of activity centers on Queenstown; the most popular spot here is the upper reaches of the Shotover beyond the tortuous Skippers Canyon. In winter the put-in site for the Shotover is only accessible by helicopter, and wet suits are essential year-round, as the water is very cold. Some of the rapids are grade 5—the highest before a river becomes unraftable.

To combine the thrill of white water with a wilderness experience, take a two-day trip down the Landsborough River, which rises in Mt. Cook National Park and flows past miles of virgin forest and into some very exciting rapids.

Sailing

Sailing is an excellent way to take in the varied coastline of New Zealand. You are likely to participate in the sailing of the vessel a bit more than you would on a regular cruise line, but for all intents and purposes this is a soft adventure in paradise.

Season: Year-round.
Location: South Island
Cost: From $320 for three days in Doubtful Sound to $900 for a six-day trip around the tip of South Island to $2,650 for nine days in Fiordland National Park to $3,850–$10,350 for 11-18 days cruising the sub-Antarctic islands of Australia and New Zealand.
Tour Operator: New Zealand Travel Professionals, Southern Heritage Tours.

Southern Heritage Tours uses the eight-cabin, 65-foot MV *Affinity*, a diesel-powered New Zealand-built vessel, to take visitors to otherwise inaccessible parts of the coastline. From June to August it explores the deeply indented shores of Fiordland National Park. In September and October it heads for the top of the South Island and the warmer waters of Marlborough Sounds—a maze of waterways and islands of incredible beauty. Throughout the summer months (December–January), Southern Heritage Tours operates a 140-foot vessel, the MV *Pacific Ruby*, down to the sub-Antarctic islands of Australia and New Zealand. On these stark, rocky outcrops can be seen the ruins of early attempts at settlement and animals such as the royal albatross, Hookers sea lion, elephant seal, and penguins.

New Zealand Travel Professionals offers two cruises along the shores of the South Island aboard the 15-meter (50-foot) *Waverley*. Accommodations for eight passengers are on a twin-share basis. A three-day cruise goes around Doubtful Sound; a six-day trip follows Captain Cook's journey around the bottom of the South Island.

Sea Kayaking

Unlike rafting, where much of the thrill comes from negotiating white water, sea kayaking involves paddling through gentler waters. The enjoyment comes from the relaxing pace and the passing scenery. Sea kayaking is soft adventure.

Season: December–May.
Location: Abel Tasman National Park, South Island.
Cost: From $80 for one day to $300 for four days, including kayaks, tents, cooking and camping equipment, and park permits.
Tour Operator: Ocean River Adventure Company.

This tour along the sheltered waters of the Abel Tasman National Park provides a waterline view of a beautiful coastline. It allows you to explore otherwise inaccessible golden-sand beaches and remote islands and to meet fur seals on their home surf. When wind conditions permit, paddles give way to small sails, and the kayaks are propelled home by an inshore breeze.

Index

Personal Itinerary

Departure *Date*

Time

Transportation

Arrival *Date*   *Time*

Departure *Date*   *Time*

Transportation

Accommodations

Arrival *Date*   *Time*

Departure *Date*   *Time*

Transportation

Accommodations

Arrival *Date*   *Time*

Departure *Date*   *Time*

Transportation

Accommodations

Personal Itinerary

Arrival *Date*   *Time*

Departure *Date*   *Time*

Transportation

Accommodations

Arrival *Date*   *Time*

Departure *Date*   *Time*

Transportation

Accommodations

Arrival *Date*   *Time*

Departure *Date*   *Time*

Transportation

Accommodations

Arrival *Date*   *Time*

Departure *Date*   *Time*

Transportation

Accommodations

Personal Itinerary

Arrival *Date*   *Time*

Departure *Date*   *Time*

Transportation

Accommodations

Arrival *Date*   *Time*

Departure *Date*   *Time*

Transportation

Accommodations

Arrival *Date*   *Time*

Departure *Date*   *Time*

Transportation

Accommodations

Arrival *Date*   *Time*

Departure *Date*   *Time*

Transportation

Accommodations

Personal Itinerary

Arrival *Date*   *Time*

Departure *Date*   *Time*

Transportation

Accommodations

Arrival *Date*   *Time*

Departure *Date*   *Time*

Transportation

Accommodations

Arrival *Date*   *Time*

Departure *Date*   *Time*

Transportation

Accommodations

Arrival *Date*   *Time*

Departure *Date*   *Time*

Transportation

Accommodations

Personal Itinerary

Arrival *Date*   *Time*

Departure *Date*   *Time*

Transportation

Accommodations

Arrival *Date*   *Time*

Departure *Date*   *Time*

Transportation

Accommodations

Arrival *Date*   *Time*

Departure *Date*   *Time*

Transportation

Accommodations

Arrival *Date*   *Time*

Departure *Date*   *Time*

Transportation

Accommodations

Addresses

Name

Address

Telephone

Name

Address

Telephone

Name

Address

Telephone

Name

Address

Telephone

Name

Address

Telephone

Name

Address

Telephone

Name

Address

Telephone

Name

Address

Telephone

Name

Address

Telephone

Name

Address

Telephone

Name

Address

Telephone

Name

Address

Telephone

Name

Address

Telephone

Name

Address

Telephone

Name

Address

Telephone

Name

Address

Telephone

Addresses

Name

Address

Telephone

Name

Address

Telephone

Name

Address

Telephone

Name

Address

Telephone

Name

Address

Telephone

Name

Address

Telephone

Name

Address

Telephone

Name

Address

Telephone

Name

Address

Telephone

Name

Address

Telephone

Name

Address

Telephone

Name

Address

Telephone

Name

Address

Telephone

Name

Address

Telephone

Name

Address

Telephone

Name

Address

Telephone

Fodor's Travel Guides

Available at bookstores everywhere, or call 1–800–533–6478, 24 hours a day.

U.S. Guides

Alaska

Arizona

Boston

California

Cape Cod, Martha's
Vineyard, Nantucket

The Carolinas & the
Georgia Coast

Chicago

Colorado

Florida

Hawaii

Las Vegas, Reno,
Tahoe

Los Angeles

Maine, Vermont,
New Hampshire

Maui

Miami & the Keys

New England

New Orleans

New York City

Pacific North Coast

Philadelphia & the
Pennsylvania Dutch
Country

The Rockies

San Diego

San Francisco

Santa Fe, Taos,
Albuquerque

Seattle & Vancouver

The South

The U.S. & British
Virgin Islands

The Upper Great
Lakes Region

USA

Vacations in New York
State

Vacations on the
Jersey Shore

Virginia & Maryland

Waikiki

Walt Disney World
and the Orlando Area

Washington, D.C.

Foreign Guides

Acapulco, Ixtapa,
Zihuatanejo

Australia & New
Zealand

Austria

The Bahamas

Baja & Mexico's
Pacific Coast Resorts

Barbados

Berlin

Bermuda

Brazil

Brittany & Normandy

Budapest

Canada

Cancun, Cozumel,
Yucatan Peninsula

Caribbean

China

Costa Rica, Belize,
Guatemala

The Czech Republic
& Slovakia

Eastern Europe

Egypt

Euro Disney

Europe

Europe's Great Cities

Florence & Tuscany

France

Germany

Great Britain

Greece

The Himalayan
Countries

Hong Kong

India

Ireland

Israel

Italy

Japan

Kenya & Tanzania

Korea

London

Madrid & Barcelona

Mexico

Montreal &
Quebec City

Morocco

Moscow &
St. Petersburg

The Netherlands,
Belgium &
Luxembourg

New Zealand

Norway

Nova Scotia, Prince
Edward Island &
New Brunswick

Paris

Portugal

Provence & the
Riviera

Rome

Russia & the Baltic
Countries

Scandinavia

Scotland

Singapore

South America

Southeast Asia

Spain

Sweden

Switzerland

Thailand

Tokyo

Toronto

Turkey

Vienna & the Danube
Valley

Yugoslavia

Special Series

Fodor's Affordables

Caribbean

Europe

Florida

France

Germany

Great Britain

London

Italy

Paris

Fodor's Bed & Breakfast and Country Inns Guides

Canada's Great Country Inns

California

Cottages, B&Bs and Country Inns of England and Wales

Mid-Atlantic Region

New England

The Pacific Northwest

The South

The Southwest

The Upper Great Lakes Region

The West Coast

The Berkeley Guides

California

Central America

Eastern Europe

France

Germany

Great Britain & Ireland

Mexico

Pacific Northwest & Alaska

San Francisco

Fodor's Exploring Guides

Australia

Britain

California

The Caribbean

Florida

France

Germany

Ireland

Italy

London

New York City

Paris

Rome

Singapore & Malaysia

Spain

Thailand

Fodor's Flashmaps

New York

Washington, D.C.

Fodor's Pocket Guides

Bahamas

Barbados

Jamaica

London

New York City

Paris

Puerto Rico

San Francisco

Washington, D.C.

Fodor's Sports

Cycling

Hiking

Running

Sailing

The Insider's Guide to the Best Canadian Skiing

Skiing in the USA & Canada

Fodor's Three-In-Ones (guidebook, language cassette, and phrase book)

France

Germany

Italy

Mexico

Spain

Fodor's Special-Interest Guides

Accessible USA

Cruises and Ports of Call

Euro Disney

Halliday's New England Food Explorer

Healthy Escapes

London Companion

Shadow Traffic's New York Shortcuts and Traffic Tips

Sunday in New York

Walt Disney World and the Orlando Area

Walt Disney World for Adults

Fodor's Touring Guides

Touring Europe

Touring USA: Eastern Edition

Fodor's Vacation Planners

Great American Vacations

National Parks of the East

National Parks of the West

The Wall Street Journal Guides to Business Travel

Europe

International Cities

Pacific Rim

USA & Canada

WHEREVER YOU TRAVEL, HELP IS NEVER FAR AWAY.

From planning your trip to providing travel assistance along the way, American Express® Travel Service Offices* are always there to help.

New Zealand

North Island

AUCKLAND
101 Queen Street
9-379-8243

HAMILTON
Calder & Lawson Travel
455 Grey Street
7-856-9009

LOWER HUTT
Century 21 Travel
Queens Arcade, Queens Drive
4-569-3816

ROTORUA
Blackmores Galaxy United Travel
411 Tutanekai Street
7-347-9444

WELLINGTON
Century 21 Travel, 203 Lambton Quay
4-473-1221

WHANGAREI
Small World Travel
23 Rathbone Street
9-438-2939

South Island

CHRISTCHURCH
Guthreys Travel Centre
126 Cashel Street
3-379-3560

DUNEDIN
Brooker Travel
369 George Street
3-477-3383

NELSON
Nelson Holiday Shoppe
Corner Haven Rd. & Rutherford St.
3-548-9079

QUEENSTOWN
Mount Cook Line Travel Centre
Rees Street
3-442-7650

INTRODUCING

Fodor's WORLDVIEW
TRAVEL UPDATE

AT LAST, YOUR OWN PERSONALIZED LIST OF WHAT'S GOING ON IN THE CITIES YOU'RE VISITING.

KEYED TO THE DAYS WHEN YOU'RE THERE, CUSTOMIZED FOR YOUR INTERESTS, AND SENT TO YOU BEFORE YOU LEAVE HOME.

EXCLUSIVE FOR PURCHASERS OF FODOR'S GUIDES...

Introducing a revolutionary way to get customized, time-sensitive travel information just before your trip.

Now you can obtain detailed information about what's going on in each city you'll be visiting <u>before</u> you leave home—up-to-the-minute, objective information about the events and activities that interest you most.

Your Itinerary:
Customized reports available for 160 destinations

This is a special offer for purchasers of Fodor's guides – a customized Travel Update to fit your specific interests and your itinerary.

Travel Updates contain the kind of time-sensitive insider information you can get only from local contacts – or from city magazines and newspapers once you arrive. But now you can have the same information before you leave for your trip.

The choice is yours: current art exhibits, theater, music festivals and special concerts, sporting events, antiques and flower shows, shopping, fitness, and more.

The information comes from hundreds of correspondents and thousands of sources worldwide. Updated continuously, it's like having your own personal concierge or friend in the city.

You specify the cities and when you'll be there. We'll do the rest — personalizing the information for you the way no guidebook can.

It's the perfect extension to your Fodor's guide and the best way to make the most of your valuable travel time.

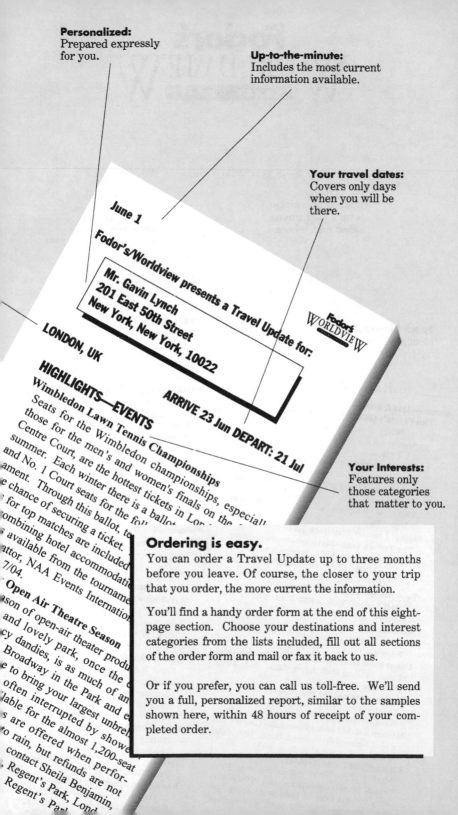

Personalized:
Prepared expressly for you.

Up-to-the-minute:
Includes the most current information available.

Your travel dates:
Covers only days when you will be there.

June 1

Fodor's/Worldview presents a Travel Update for:

Mr. Gavin Lynch
201 East 50th Street
New York, New York, 10022

Fodor's
WORLDVIEW

LONDON, UK

ARRIVE 23 Jun DEPART: 21 Jul

Your Interests:
Features only those categories that matter to you.

HIGHLIGHTS—EVENTS

Wimbledon Lawn Tennis Championships

Seats for the Wimbledon championships, especially those for the men's and women's finals on the Centre Court, are the hottest tickets in Lon... summer. Each winter there is a ballot... and No. 1 Court seats for the foll... ament. Through this ballot, te... e chance of securing a ticket... for top matches are included... ombining hotel accommodati... available from the tourname... ator, NAA Events Internation... 7/04.

Open Air Theatre Season

ason of open-air theater produ... and lovely park, once the... cy dandies, is as much of an... Broadway in the Park and e... e to bring your largest unbre... often interrupted by showe... able for the almost 1,200-seat... s are offered when perfor... o rain, but refunds are not... Regent's Park, Lon... Regent's Pa...

Ordering is easy.

You can order a Travel Update up to three months before you leave. Of course, the closer to your trip that you order, the more current the information.

You'll find a handy order form at the end of this eight-page section. Choose your destinations and interest categories from the lists included, fill out all sections of the order form and mail or fax it back to us.

Or if you prefer, you can call us toll-free. We'll send you a full, personalized report, similar to the samples shown here, within 48 hours of receipt of your completed order.

**Special concerts—
who's performing
what and where**

**One-of-a-kind,
one-time-only events**

**Special interest,
in-depth listings**

Children — Events

Angel Canal Festival
The festivities include a children's funfair, entertainers, a boat rally and displays on the water. Regent's Canal. Islington. N1. Tube: Angel. Tel: 267 9100. 11:30am-5:30pm. 7/04.

Blackheath Summer Kite Festival
Stunt kite displays with parachuting teddy bears and trade stands. Free admission. SE3. BR: Blackheath. 10am. 6/27.

Megabugs
Children will delight in this infestation of giant robotic insects, including a praying mantic 60 times life size. Mon-Sat 10am-6pm; Sun 11am-6pm. Admission 4.50 pounds. Natural History Museum, Cromwell Road. SW7. Tube: South Kensington. Tel: 938 9123. Ends 10/01.

Childminders
This establishment employs only women, providing nurses and qualified nannies to

Music — Jazz & Blues

Tito Puente's Golden Men of Latin Jazz
The father of mambo and Cuban rumba king comes to town. Royal Festival Hall. South Bank. SE1. Tube: Waterloo. Tel: 928 8800. 8pm. 7/15.

Georgie Fame and The New York Band
Riding a popular tide with his latest album, the smoky-voiced Fame and his keyboard are on a tour yet again. The Grand. Clapham Junction. SW11. BR: Clapham Junction. Tel: 738 9000 7:30pm. 7/07.

Jacques Loussier Play Bach Trio
The French jazz classicist and colleagues. Kenwood Lakeside. Hampstead Lane. Kenwood. NW3. Tube: Golders Green, then bus 210. Tel: 413 1443. 7pm. 7/10.

Tony Bennett and Ronnie Scott
Royal Festival Hall. South Bank. SE1. Tube: Waterloo. Tel: 928 8800. 8pm. 7/11.

Santana
Royal Festival Hall. South Bank. SE1. Tube: Waterloo. Tel: 928 8800. 8pm. 7/12.

Count Basie Orchestra and Nancy Wilson Trio
Royal Festival Hall. South Bank. SE1. Tube: Waterloo. Tel: 928 8800. 8pm. 7/14.

King Pleasure and the Biscuit Boys
Royal Festival Hall. South Bank. SE1. Tube: Waterloo. Tel: 928 8800. 6:30 and 9pm. 7/16.

Al Green and the London Community Gospel Choir
Royal Festival Hall. South Bank. SE1. Tube: Waterloo. Tel: 928 8800. 8pm. 7/13.

BB King and Linda Hopkins
Mother of the blues and successor to Bessie Smith, Hopkins meets up with "Blues Boy" King. Royal Festival Hall. South Bank. SE1. Tube: Waterloo. Tel: 928 8800. 6:30 and 9pm.

Music — Classical

Marylebone Sinfonia
Kenneth Gowen conducts music by Puccini and Rossini. Queen Elizabeth Hall. South Bank. SE1. Tube: Waterloo. Tel: 928 8800. 7:45pm. 7/16.

London Philharmonic
Franz Welser-Moest and George Benjamin conduct selections by Alexander Goehr, Messiaen, and some of Benjamin's own compositions. Queen Elizabeth Hall. South Bank. SE1. Tube: Waterloo. Tel: 928 8800. 8pm.

London Pro Arte Orchestra and Forest Choir
Murray Stewart conducts selections by Rossini, Haydn and Jonathan Willcocks. Queen Elizabeth Hall. South Bank. SE1. Tube: Waterloo. Tel: 928 8800. 7:45pm. 7/11.

Kensington Symphony Orchestra
Russell Keable conducts Dvorak's Dmitri. Queen Elizabeth Hall. South Bank. SE1.

Here's what you get . . .

Detailed information about what's going on — precisely when you'll be there.

Show openings
during your visit

Reviews by
local critics

Exhibitions & Shows—Antique & Flower
Westminster Antiques Fair
Over 50 stands with pre-1830 furniture and other Victorian and earlier items. Thu-Fri 11am-8pm; Sat-Sun 11am-6pm. Admission 4 pounds, children free. Old Royal Horticultural Hall. Vincent Square. SW1. Tel: 0444/48 25 14. 6-24 thru 6/27.

Royal Horticultural Society Flower Show
The show includes displays of carnations, summer fruit and vegetables. Tue 11am-7pm; Wed 10am-5pm. Admission Tue 4 pounds, Wed 2 pounds. Royal Horticultural Halls. Greycoat Street and Vincent Square. SW1. Tube: Victoria. 7/20 thru 7/21.

Hampton Court Palace International Flower Show
Major international garden and flower show taking place in conjunction with the British

Theater — Musical
Sunset Boulevard
In June, the four Andrew Lloyd Webber musicals which dominated London's stages in the 1980s (Cats, Starlight Express, Phantom of the Opera and Aspects of Love) are joined by the composer's latest work, a show rumored to have his best music to date. The 1950 Billy Wilder film about a helpless young writer who is drawn into the world of a possessive, aging silent screen star offers rich opportunities for Webber's evolving style. Soaring, aching melodies, lush technical effects and psychological thrills are all expected. Patti Lupone stars. Mon-Sat at 8pm; matinee Thu-Sat at 3pm. In-person sales only at the box office; credit card bookings, Tel: 344 0055. Admission 15-32.50 pounds. Adelphi Theatre. The Strand. WC2. Tube: Charing Cross. Tel: 836 7611. Starts: 6/21

Leonardo A Portrait of Love
A new musical about the great Renaissance artist and inventor comes in for a London premiere tested by a brief run at Oxford's Old Fire Station autumn. The work explores the relations Vinci and the woman

Spectator Sports — Other Sports
Greyhound Racing: Wembley Stadium
This dog track offers good views of greyhound racing held on Mon, Wed and Fri. No credit cards. Stadium Way. Wembley. HA9. Tube: Wembley Park. Tel: 902 8833.

Benson & Hedges Cricket Cup Final
Lord's Cricket Ground. St. John's Wood Road. NW8. Tube: St. John's Wood. Tel: 289 1611. 11am. 7/10.

Business-Fax & Overnight Mail
Post Office, Trafalgar Square Branch
Offers a network of fax services, the Intelpost system, throughout the country and abroad. Mon-Sat 8am-8pm, Sun 9am-5pm. William IV Street. WC2. Tube: Charing Cross. Tel: 930 9580.

Transworld

Albuquerque • Atlanta • Atlantic City • Ne Baltimore • Boston • Chicago • Cincinnati Cleveland • Dallas/Ft.Worth • Denver • De Houston • Kansas City • Las Vegas • Los Angeles • Memphis • Miami • Milwaukee • New Orleans • New York City • Orlando • Springs • Philadelphia • Phoenix • Pittsburg Portland • Salt Lake • San Antonio • San Di San Franc • Seattle • St Louis • Tamp Oslo • Wash • Honolulu • Island • Hawaii • Kauai • Maui • Abacos • Bimini Ber • Coco • Hamilton • Antigua & B • vis • Porto Gorda • Barbados • Dominica • Gren acia • St. Vincent • Trinidad & Tobago ymans • Puerto Plata • Santo Doming Aruba • Bonaire • Curacao • St. Ma ec City • Montreal • Ottawa • Toron Vancouver • Guadeloupe • Martiniqu helemy • St. Martin • Kingston • Ixta o Bay • Negril • Ocho Rios • Ponce n • Grand Turk • Providenciales • S St. John • St. Thomas • Acapulco • & Isla Mujeres • Cozumel • Guadal • Los Cabos • Manzinillo • Mazatl City • Monterrey • Oaxaca • Puerto do • Puerto Vallarta • Veracruz • Ix dam • Athens • Barcelona • Berlin • Budapest •

Fodor's WORLDVIEW
TRAVEL UPDATE

Interest Categories

For <u>your</u> personalized Travel Update, choose the categories you're most interested in from this list. Every Travel Update automatically provides you with *Event Highlights* – the best of what's happening during the dates of your trip.

1.	**Business Services**	Fax & Overnight Mail, Computer Rentals, Photocopying, Secretarial , Messenger, Translation Services

Dining

2.	**All Day Dining**	Breakfast & Brunch, Cafes & Tea Rooms, Late-Night Dining
3.	**Local Cuisine**	In Every Price Range—from Budget Restaurants to the Special Splurge
4.	**European Cuisine**	Continental, French, Italian
5.	**Asian Cuisine**	Chinese, Far Eastern, Japanese, Indian
6.	**Americas Cuisine**	American, Mexican & Latin
7.	**Nightlife**	Bars, Dance Clubs, Comedy Clubs, Pubs & Beer Halls
8.	**Entertainment**	Theater—Drama, Musicals, Dance, Ticket Agencies
9.	**Music**	Classical, Traditional & Ethnic, Jazz & Blues, Pop, Rock
10.	**Children's Activities**	Events, Attractions
11.	**Tours**	Local Tours, Day Trips, Overnight Excursions, Cruises
12.	**Exhibitions, Festivals & Shows**	Antiques & Flower, History & Cultural, Art Exhibitions, Fairs & Craft Shows, Music & Art Festivals
13.	**Shopping**	Districts & Malls, Markets, Regional Specialities
14.	**Fitness**	Bicycling, Health Clubs, Hiking, Jogging
15.	**Recreational Sports**	Boating/Sailing, Fishing, Ice Skating, Skiing, Snorkeling/Scuba, Swimming
16.	**Spectator Sports**	Auto Racing, Baseball, Basketball, Football, Horse Racing, Ice Hockey, Soccer

Please note that interest category content will vary by season, destination, and length of stay.

Destinations

The Fodor's/Worldview Travel Update covers more than 160 destinations worldwide. Choose the destinations that match your itinerary from this list. (Choose bulleted destinations only.)

United States (Mainland)
- Albuquerque
- Atlanta
- Atlantic City
- Baltimore
- Boston
- Chicago
- Cincinnati
- Cleveland
- Dallas/Ft. Worth
- Denver
- Detroit
- Houston
- Kansas City
- Las Vegas
- Los Angeles
- Memphis
- Miami
- Milwaukee
- Minneapolis/ St. Paul
- New Orleans
- New York City
- Orlando
- Palm Springs
- Philadelphia
- Phoenix
- Pittsburgh
- Portland
- St. Louis
- Salt Lake City
- San Antonio
- San Diego
- San Francisco
- Seattle
- Tampa
- Washington, DC

Alaska
- Anchorage/Fairbanks/Juneau

Hawaii
- Honolulu
- Island of Hawaii
- Kauai
- Maui

Canada
- Quebec City
- Montreal
- Ottawa
- Toronto
- Vancouver

Bahamas
- Abacos
- Eleuthera/ Harbour Island
- Exumas
- Freeport
- Nassau & Paradise Island

Bermuda
- Bermuda Countryside
- Hamilton

British Leeward Islands
- Anguilla
- Antigua & Barbuda
- Montserrat
- St. Kitts & Nevis

British Virgin Islands
- Tortola & Virgin Gorda

British Windward Islands
- Barbados
- Dominica
- Grenada
- St. Lucia
- St. Vincent
- Trinidad & Tobago

Cayman Islands
- The Caymans

Dominican Republic
- Puerto Plata
- Santo Domingo

Dutch Leeward Islands
- Aruba
- Bonaire
- Curacao

Dutch Windward Islands
- St. Maarten

French West Indies
- Guadeloupe
- Martinique
- St. Barthelemy
- St. Martin

Jamaica
- Kingston
- Montego Bay
- Negril
- Ocho Rios

Puerto Rico
- Ponce
- San Juan

Turks & Caicos
- Grand Turk
- Providenciales

U.S. Virgin Islands
- St. Croix
- St. John
- St. Thomas

Mexico
- Acapulco
- Cancun & Isla Mujeres
- Cozumel
- Guadalajara
- Ixtapa & Zihuatanejo
- Los Cabos
- Manzanillo
- Mazatlan
- Mexico City
- Monterrey
- Oaxaca
- Puerto Escondido
- Puerto Vallarta
- Veracruz

Europe
- Amsterdam
- Athens
- Barcelona
- Berlin
- Brussels
- Budapest
- Copenhagen
- Dublin
- Edinburgh
- Florence
- Frankfurt
- French Riviera
- Geneva
- Glasgow
- Interlaken
- Istanbul
- Lausanne
- Lisbon
- London
- Madrid
- Milan
- Moscow
- Munich
- Oslo
- Paris
- Prague
- Provence
- Rome
- Salzburg
- St. Petersburg
- Stockholm
- Venice
- Vienna
- Zurich

Pacific Rim Australia & New Zealand
- Auckland
- Melbourne
- Sydney

China
- Beijing
- Guangzhou
- Shanghai

Japan
- Kyoto
- Nagoya
- Osaka
- Tokyo
- Yokohama

Other
- Bangkok
- Hong Kong & Macau
- Manila
- Seoul
- Singapore
- Taipei

Fodor's WORLDVIEW Order Form

THIS TRAVEL UPDATE IS FOR (Please print):

Name _____

Address _____

City _____ State _____ ZIP _____

Country _____ Tel # (_____) _____ - _____

Title of this Fodor's guide: _____

Store and location where guide was purchased: _____

INDICATE YOUR DESTINATIONS/DATES: Write in below the destinations you want to order. Then fill in your arrival and departure dates for each destination.

		Month	Day		Month	Day
(Sample) *LONDON*	From:	6 /	21	To:	6 /	30
1	From:	/		To:	/	
2	From:	/		To:	/	
3	From:	/		To:	/	

You can order up to three destinations per Travel Update. Only destinations listed on the previous page are applicable. Maximum amount of time covered by a Travel Update cannot exceed 30 days.

CHOOSE YOUR INTERESTS: Select up to eight categories from the list of interest categories shown on the previous page and circle the numbers below:

1 2 3 4 5 6 7 8 9 10 11 12 13 14 15 16

CHOOSE HOW YOU WANT YOUR TRAVEL UPDATE DELIVERED (Check one):

❑ Please mail my Travel Update to the address above **OR**

❑ Fax it to me at **Fax #** (_____) _____ - _____

DELIVERY CHARGE (Check one)

	Within U.S. & Canada	Outside U.S. & Canada
First Class Mail	❑ $2.50	❑ $5.00
Fax	❑ $5.00	❑ $10.00
Priority Delivery	❑ $15.00	❑ $27.00

All orders will be sent within 48 hours of receipt of a completed order form.

ADD UP YOUR ORDER HERE. *SPECIAL OFFER FOR FODOR'S PURCHASERS ONLY!*

	Suggested Retail Price	Your Price	This Order
First destination ordered	$13.95	$ 7.95	$ 7.95
Second destination (if applicable)	$ 9.95	$ 4.95	+
Third destination (if applicable)	$ 9.95	$ 4.95	+
Plus delivery charge from above			+
		TOTAL:	$

METHOD OF PAYMENT (Check one): ❑ AmEx ❑ MC ❑ Visa ❑ Discover
❑ Personal Check ❑ Money Order

Make check or money order payable to: Fodor's Worldview Travel Update

Credit Card # _____ **Expiration Date:** _____

Authorized Signature _____

SEND THIS COMPLETED FORM TO:
Fodor's Worldview Travel Update, 114 Sansome Street, Suite 700, San Francisco, CA 94104

OR CALL OR FAX US 24-HOURS A DAY
Telephone **1-800-799-9609** • Fax **1-800-799-9619** (From within the U.S. & Canada)
(Outside the U.S. & Canada: Telephone 415-616-9988 • Fax 415-616-9989)

(Please have this guide in front of you when you call so we can verify purchase.)

Offer valid until 12/31/94.